~~~~~~~~

A Guide to

Making Yourself Heard

~~~~~~~~

The
Power
of Voice

The
Power
of Voice

DENISE WOODS

HarperOne
An Imprint of HarperCollins*Publishers*

HarperCollins books may be purchased for educational, business, or sales promotional use. For information, please email the Special Markets Department at SPsales@harpercollins.com.

FIRST EDITION

Image on page 185: Yoko design/Shutterstock, Inc.

Library of Congress Cataloging-in-Publication Data has been applied for.

ISBN 978-0-06-294103-9

21 22 23 24 25   LSC   10 9 8 7 6 5 4 3 2 1

To the two pillars of my life: my mother, Mary E. Woods, and my aunt Sylvia P. Woods. They shaped me and held me until I was able to find my own authentic voice.

And to Tim Monich, who handed me the voice and speech baton and showed me how to run with it to the finish line. Thank you.

Contents

Foreword

....

BY MAHERSHALA ALI,
ACADEMY AWARD-WINNING ACTOR

When I take on a role, I'm interested in the character's whole spiritual journey. Even if he's an atheist, it's a spiritual journey because it's based on a set of conditions and beliefs that character has about himself, his culture and upbringing, and the world around him. Some of the reasons why people speak a certain way are conscious, while others are unconscious. How they see themselves, or want to see themselves, all leads back to something that impacts mind, body, voice, and speech. It's a lot, which is why, each day before I walk on set, I say a prayer, asking for help to deliver each scene as truthfully as possible. I don't feel I have the capacity to do this without calling on something larger than myself.

I also call on Denise Woods, because getting the voice right is one of the hardest things to do as an actor, and it's one of the most important tools of our profession. It's like tuning in to a frequency that's different from our own, then sustaining it over the course of weeks and months. It takes a certain degree of focus to maintain consistency, matching the voice of the character you've developed while at the same time allowing for a certain fluidity, considering how a voice is going to resonate differently in any given situation, be it tragedy, joy, crisis, or confrontation. There are so many factors that come into play.

Denise understands how multifaceted the human voice is and how much it can convey beyond words. She gets that the voice must resonate with total authenticity and that developing a character takes place in a sacred space that is all about lifting up the story.

I first met Denise during the filming of *Hidden Figures*, in which I played the supporting role of Colonel Jim Johnson, one of the love interests in the story. Denise wasn't there for me, exactly. She was on the set to help two of the movie's top-billed stars—Taraji P. Henson and Janelle Monáe—refine their southern accents. When you're in the lead of a big-budget film, it's not uncommon to have professionals of Denise's caliber on hand to bring out your best and most honest performance.

But while waiting around between takes, when Denise also had some time to kill, I sidled over to her at the craft service table and struck up a conversation. Over the next couple of weeks, we talked about many things: where we were from, war stories about the industry, our experiences on the Broadway stage . . . and we just clicked. She indulged me as I described what I had in mind for my own character's voice, intention, backstory, and many other things besides. Denise immediately picked up on what I was trying to do and shared insights that were exactly the affirmation I needed as I developed my character. Throughout the filming, she'd check in on me and correct me here and there. Each conversation with her gave me a greater sense of confidence, so I made a mental note to work with her as soon as I was in a position to do so.

About two years later, while developing Don Shirley's voice in the movie *Green Book*, I reached out to Denise. Finally, this gracious lady was a luxury I could afford!

Finding the right voice for a role based on a real human being can be especially fraught with challenges. This is where you become acutely aware of how important it is to be honest in your work. It's your job to get rid of anything that feels inauthentic, like litter in your yard. You've got to look for it and pick it up, taking a holistic look into every corner where there might be inaccuracies. The voice of Don Shirley—a gay African American classical and jazz pianist and composer of the sixties—had to be conveyed with subtlety, not flamboyance.

Denise taught me how, by sitting and standing tall, holding my head up just so, my voice naturally went into a higher register while maintaining a demeanor of utmost dignity. Understanding my intention, Denise helped me make all those small but necessary adjustments, stripping away the vocal distractions to enable this unique character to speak his truth.

I was simultaneously cast as the lead in HBO's *True Detective* series. I traveled from the set of *Green Book* in New Orleans to northwestern Arkansas to begin a six-month journey with a vastly different but equally compelling character. Again, Denise was my first call. We spent the next several months together, from March 2018 to the end of the summer, filming.

It was an immersive experience. I knew I'd gotten myself into something particularly challenging. Wayne Hays was a complex character. I had to cultivate the regional dialect of the Ozarks, as spoken by an African American state police detective and Vietnam War veteran living in the seventies, and then looking back as an old man in the present day, battling some form of dementia along with his haunted past. Denise helped me work through all of those layers.

The success or failure of the storytelling hinges on finding that authentic voice for my characters. Voice is the conduit to a deeper connection with the audience. It's what engages people and makes them care.

And that is what this book can do for you as you share your own message with the world. All the voice and speech work I have ever done as an actor has spilled over into my daily life. The awareness it brings, and the empathy as I listen to others, is profound. My vocal work has taught me to truly listen, paying attention to every nuance of tone and inflection. It helps me hear and understand in depth what's going on with my wife, my family, and my intimate circle of friends. It also enables me to respond in ways that accurately reflect what's in my head and my heart, enriching the communication that's foundational for any human relationship.

Knowing I have these vocal tools at my disposal also gives me confidence. Yes, I still get stage fright, and not just in a professional acting context. There are any number of situations that can jangle my nerves, from meetings with the folks who write the checks to delicately negotiating the complexities of work/life balance with my strong, beautiful, beloved wife as we raise our daughter together. But I remind myself that I have the power of voice and speech within me, ready to deliver the right message, at the right time, and in just the right way.

You don't need to be an actor to benefit from finding your unique "voice print," as Denise calls it. When you do the necessary work, clearing your voice of distractions and pairing it with your personal narrative, it can be liberating. There's no more powerful way to unleash your true self onto the world and fully connect with others.

So, if you're going to play the leading role in your own story, why not invest the time to find your authentic voice so you can tell your story the way it deserves to be told?

Between Two Worlds

*Freeing yourself was one thing, claiming
ownership of that freed self was another.*

—TONI MORRISON

I am an African American woman born and raised in Manhattan's Lower East Side housing projects during the sixties and seventies by a single working mother. But the typecasting ends there.

Painfully shy and soft-spoken as a child, I was notably different from the folks in our neighborhood. Our community started out as a wonderful place for families of all ethnicities to live after World War II. It was a hotbed of creativity and home to countless musicians and artists, with jazz clubs, the Third Street Music School, and the Henry Street Settlement. But the Lower East Side deteriorated into a haven for drug abuse, teen pregnancies, and street fighting by the time I'd reached school age. My mother, a strong southern woman, wasn't having any part of it. She kept my sister and me busy with the church and, my saving grace, the arts.

Every spare minute, my mother was involved with Metropolitan Baptist Church in Harlem. When she wasn't going about church business, she was overseeing our schooling, becoming PTA president, and signing us up for every creative outlet she could find. She did her research and got us enrolled in one of the better middle schools in our district, about two miles north of where we lived. Whatever advantage was available to us, our mother would find it. She was determined to keep her daughters off the streets and out of trouble. And she kept us to a high standard. Mom never allowed us to use slang and would chide us if we failed to enunciate. However tough our financial situation might have been, we were to carry ourselves with dignity and pride. We were taught to walk tall with our spines straight and to speak clearly, like the fine, upstanding young ladies she was raising.

Mom worked hard, holding down multiple jobs to give us every advantage in life that she could. We'd lost our father in 1963, when I was just five, but Mom educated herself, earning a higher degree from Pace University and eventually a position on the New York City Board of Education. She was larger-than-life, as was my older sister, and I was always surrounded by an extended family of similarly powerful women. My aunt was Sylvia Woods, the famed "Queen of Soul Food." Every weekend was spent in Harlem at her eponymous restaurant, pitching in by serving customers collard greens, fried chicken, and black-eyed peas alongside my cousins, aunts, and uncles. It was a protective bubble of family and church folks who lived by a code of humility, hard work, and doing the right thing. Whenever I needed to check in with my moral compass, I always knew where to turn.

But my loving family circle couldn't shield me from the world entirely. My awkward shyness made me the target of several older bullies in the neighborhood. That's why, when the New York City Opera came to audition young singers at my junior high school and I made it into their children's company, I kept it hidden from the other kids. They would have crucified me! Those weekend commutes to rehearsals at Lincoln Center raised a few eyebrows from the kids in the neighborhood.

"Niecie, where you goin', gur-rell?" my friends on the bench outside my building would ask. "How come you go out every SAD-a-day mawnin'?"

I'd avoid their gaze and mumble something vague in response. In their eyes, I was different enough. My sister had already been brutally attacked by a few neighboring girls for "thinking she was better" than they were. And although these girls generally meant no harm, why give them ammunition? I felt I couldn't stop and explain how my passion had been ignited by those Sunday school lessons at the Metropolitan Baptist Church, where we learned about legendary Black singers and performers like Paul Robeson, Marian Anderson, and Leontyne Price. At thirteen, I wanted to be the next Leontyne. In hindsight, I wish I had stopped and shared.

At the opera audition I sang my heart out and made it to the callbacks. I can still remember my mother driving me uptown and waiting outside as I descended the stairs to the stage door on Sixty-First, where I was greeted by a sweet lady in the audition room. She was iconic opera singer Beverly Sills. I made it into the company and went on to perform for three straight seasons in the children's roles for *La Boheme, Carmen, Mephistopheles,* and Gian Carlo Menotti's *Help, Help, the Globolinks!* And I relished every moment. I loved the opera and lost myself in the stories and characters. The experience exposed me to a whole other world and sparked big dreams of a career in the performing arts.

From an early age, I navigated multiple worlds. It wasn't easy. I struggled with self-esteem and identity issues. After winning the title of New York's Miss Black Teenage America in the summer of 1972, I was thrust into a fast-living crowd of wealthy Black kids and even went on a couple of dates with Aretha Franklin's son Eddie. While dining in fine restaurants, getting backstage passes to every major band, and being whisked around town in stretch limos, I'd grown ashamed of my life in the projects.

But I slowly discovered the power of my singing and speaking voice, which allowed me to hold my own with folks from a variety of backgrounds, while proudly retaining my identity as an African American woman who was raised in a very nurturing family and, yes, raised in the projects as well. It wasn't necessarily a conscious thing. I didn't deliberately switch gears depending on the company I was keeping—it just happened naturally. The process began during my formative middle school years in the early seventies, when there was a whole movement of self-discovery afoot in African American culture.

My best friend in junior high introduced me to the social and political world of the Black Arts Movement and the powerful poetry of Nikki Giovanni and Sonia Sanchez. Together we discovered Nina Simone, Maya Angelou, Miles, Dizzy, and Bird. It was Kathy, a fellow traveler in this world between worlds from the projects in East Harlem, who first brought the drama department at the High School of Performing Arts into my awareness. I duly auditioned and was accepted into the "Fame" school and finally found my tribe. Kathy, much to my dismay, did not get in.

In high school I was one of many kids of color straddling worlds, never fully accepted by either one. Yet we fit in here, among people from all walks of life, ethnic backgrounds, cultures, and religions. PA, as we called it, was a melting pot. The one thing that we had in common was that we were all talented and perhaps even a little strange! This gave me the freedom to explore who I was beyond the world I was born into. Like the actors I coach today, at PA I played several roles that allowed me to modulate my voice and speech to fit the character, the period, and the genre.

We all do this to some extent. We pick up nuances of speech and communication influenced by the people and environments we find ourselves in. Whether we're among our friends from the neighborhood, on a sales call for work, dealing with our kids' teachers, interacting with the bank teller, or chatting with the local grower at the farmer's market while shopping for some peaches, we are *all* actors playing numerous roles in life. Even at that young age, I knew I was multidimensional.

That's not to say I was being inauthentic. In fact, quite the opposite. The more I explored the dialects of different regions, the more I was able to find my true voice. There is a cadence and lilt to the way I speak that's distinctly all my own. I enunciate crisply and clearly, taking ownership of the broad vocabulary of words I'd learned through my love of theater, poetry, fiction, and opera, pronouncing them with appreciation and precision. However, when you listen carefully, you may also detect a subtle New York regionalism, or the hint of musicality that dates back generations to my West Africa by way of South Carolina tobacco field roots. All of these layers and notes are in my voice. They became a part of me as I grew more culturally and socially conscious and I embraced them all.

This journey of discovering and honing my voice continued at the Juilliard School, where I was accepted at the age of seventeen into their Drama Division. I already had a flair for the dramatic. Singing opera as a child further fueled my rich imagination. Whenever the pit orchestra struck that first chord, I'd get chills. There was something so hauntingly familiar about this music. Then my imagination caught fire as I discovered characters of the stage and screen. Whether it was Julie Andrews's Maria von Trapp in *The Sound of Music* or Ruby Dee's Ruth Younger from *A Raisin in the Sun*, I'd lose myself and *become* those characters. As a teenager, I was single-minded in pursuit of this career, riding my bike along Houston Street to the West Village every Saturday morning for private coaching in method acting.

These were the foundational moments that put me on the path toward becoming the woman I am today. I did go on to act in several Broadway productions, network soap operas like *Guiding Light* and *Loving*, and numerous plays. In 1980, I was the first African American woman asked to join Juilliard's Acting Company, and I toured around the country playing leading roles in Shakespeare's *Twelfth Night* (Olivia) and *A Midsummer Night's Dream* (Titania)—the earliest examples of their kind of "color-blind casting." In 1986, I was nominated for the Drama Desk Award for *The Cradle Will Rock*, directed by John Houseman, which also starred Patti LuPone. My singing and acting abilities got me cast in several musicals, including the Canadian production of the Broadway cabaret hit *And the World Goes 'Round*. I even did what were then called "books on tape" and won that industry's version of an Oscar for my reading of the 1937 novel *Their Eyes Were Watching God* by Zora Neale Hurston, an author who writes in heavy Floridian dialect. Now that was a labor of love!

I enjoyed a busy and robust career as a performer. But then I got bitten by the teaching bug. In 1992, I became the first African American female to join the Drama Division faculty at Juilliard. I was on tour in Toronto when I got the call, and I leaped at the chance. As mother to a four-year-old son, I needed the stability of a regular paycheck, health insurance, and a less itinerant lifestyle. But it was much more than that. As I assumed the role of teacher and mentor to hundreds of voice and speech students from all walks of life, I quickly realized this was my passion. All roads led me here—acting, singing, operatic training . . . All along, I was learning the craft of voice so that I could help others discover *their* voices.

Having been a voice, speech, and dialect coach for more than three decades—on the Voice and Speech faculty at the Juilliard School, at California Institute of the Arts, and in my own studio on Sunset Boulevard—I am now in a position to share some of Hollywood's best-kept voice and speech secrets and the ways those effective techniques can empower you. I've worked with everyone from A-list celebrities like Idris Elba and Maggie Gyllenhaal to broadcast journalists like Norah O'Donnell, Soledad O'Brien, Chris Hansen, and Maria Bartiromo, giving them vocal warm-up exercises and tips for breath control, vocal resonance, and crisp articulation.

Haven't you ever wondered what gives movie stars that certain charismatic quality, or how they are able to turn it on at will? Most actors train for years, developing the skills necessary not just for film but also for press junkets and social settings (in Hollywood, image is, without a doubt, everything). These individuals come to me—even demanding in their contracts to have me on the set with them—because they know that a richly expressive voice and clear, effective speech will help deliver a standout, Oscar-worthy performance. Yet a beautiful speaking voice that is infused with personality can be developed by anyone with the right set of tools.

My celebrity clients are the folks who've learned how to use the voice as their paintbrush. They have a certain mastery that puts them in the stratosphere. They're able to carry themselves, connecting to the breath and utilizing the voice in a way that projects personality and emotion according to the variety of circumstances that their many characters face. But even though some of what they do is specific to the camera or the stage, much of it carries over into everyday life. We *all* face a variety of circumstances in which we would greatly benefit from honing our vocal tools. We can *all* inhabit characters, bringing forth different aspects of our personality through voice and articulation.

Consider these next pages your official invitation to the world of vocal empowerment, whatever your life's calling happens to be. The techniques I have used with film and television's biggest stars will help you develop your own voice, whether it's to help resolve the issues surrounding America's number one most feared task—public speaking—or simply to help improve the experience of your daily interactions.

Voice has been the one constant that has gotten me through

the many dramatic twists and turns in my own life as I left a marriage and raised my young son, fell in love with a music icon who passed away, and found myself facing a devastating health diagnosis. I won the battle with my health only to be dealt another blow when an assault nearly cost my son, Terry, his life. Throughout these dark moments, I quietly turned inward, finding my strength through the breath—an essential element of vocal development. Getting back to the breath connected me to my faith and gave power to my words when I was finally ready to speak. My ability to harness the power of voice and speech was not only the through line of my experience, it was my saving grace.

I will share these stories in more detail with you in the chapters to come. You may not know it yet, but our emotional journeys shape the voice. How we communicate, how we make ourselves heard, is inextricably linked to our battle scars of pain and our badges of triumph. The tragic moments I've lived through have further clarified my life's mission as a vocal coach, giving me the level of empathy necessary to tune in to my clients and understand how their own stories affect the way they express themselves.

During the COVID-19 pandemic, there were many circumstances in which our voices were all we had. It simply wasn't possible to be close enough to someone to feel their energy or fully see their body language. Physically isolated for our own protection and each other's, we communicated via phone or Zoom screen, whether for teaching middle school math, checking in with friends, or bringing comfort to an elderly relative who was feeling anxious and alone in a nursing home.

You, or someone you know, may even have had to say goodbye to a loved one from the other side of a digital screen, unable to sit by the hospital bed and hold that person's hand during their final hours. No one had to tell you what to say or how to say it when there was nothing left to do but express to a parent, partner, sister, brother, or child how you felt. Instinctively, you knew what to do, focusing all the nuances of voice and emotion into your final message for that precious being. Your voice became a bridge that connected you spiritually even when, tragically, you couldn't be there in person.

Now, just imagine your vocal power once those virtual limitations are removed. As human beings, our power to communicate is our greatest gift. You have the ability to convey something much more profound than mere words; you have the ability to convey your essence. Your voice, speech, and gestures are a reflection of who you are, where you come from, and where you'd like to go, and that power is limitless.

Again, I'm an African American woman born and raised in New York City. I have southern roots, values, and traditions that go as far back as my African heritage. However, I'm that and more. I am a well-traveled artist, a mother, and a devoted daughter to an octogenarian mom, and I am a woman of faith with an intuitive spiritual conviction that guides my every move. How do I wrap all of this into a package that authentically represents the multifaceted individual that I am?

I think the character Bynum Walker, in Pulitzer Prize–winning playwright August Wilson's play *Joe Turner's Come and Gone*, says it best:

"It was my song. . . . I was making it up out of myself. And that song helped me on the road."

Thankfully, I have found my song, and it is my joy to help you find yours.

....

~~~~~~~

....

PART I

Relax

Early in my career as an actress, I was often blessed with the opportunity of having a second, third, and sometimes fourth callback for major theater, television, and film roles. At the time, I never saw it as a blessing. It always felt as though I were in some way inadequate and didn't have what it took to land the job. Eventually, as I got closer to these highly coveted gigs, I would in small ways sabotage my opportunities by telling myself that I wasn't worthy.

During this period, my survival job was waiting tables at my aunt Sylvia's restaurant in Harlem. It was actually much more than a "day job," as it was a place to see and be seen. During the eighties and the early nineties, Sylvia's Restaurant was humbly developing the iconic status that it deservedly enjoys today. A large part of its profile in the New York City community has everything to do with my aunt's warmth and welcoming personality.

I remember going to work at the restaurant one afternoon after coming from a fourth callback for a huge network television sitcom. I had just been informed that they had decided to "go in another direction" for the role. Aunt Sylvia met me at the door, eagerly awaiting news, but she could tell from my face that it wasn't at all what she was hoping for. I fell into her arms, sobbing, as most of our family members often did when we were hurting, whereupon she softly said, "Baby, relax and let Time be Time."

In that very moment, I got it! It has become one of my mantras, and I'm honored to share this gem of wisdom with you. Get out of your own way, relax, breathe, and allow life to unfold as it's meant to unfold. This section will explore the fundamentals of relaxation and the effect tension has on your voice. To that end, we will begin gently. Consider this your invitation to begin this journey with me.

1.

An Invitation

....

AS YOU EMBARK ON YOUR VOCAL

JOURNEY, KNOW YOU CAN DO THIS

The human voice is the organ of the soul.

—HENRY WADSWORTH LONGFELLOW

When Lonnie Rashid Lynn Jr. first walked into my Los Angeles studio, I knew he had something special. From somewhere deep within his being, the actor, rapper, and poet known as Common radiated a kind of glow. Not only was he tall and handsome, with a shy smile that could light up a room, but there was something not-of-this-world about him, as if he were the walking embodiment of Spirit. His very presence was a gift.

And then he spoke.

Common's voice was so held and constricted I could barely hear him. It was placed way in the back of his throat, preventing him from fully shaping and articulating sound. To catch all he was trying to say, the listener would almost have to lean forward. While his message was well worth the effort, you had to "get" this fact about him before the conversation even started. Otherwise, the strain of listening often became distracting.

As Common began to garner more cachet as an actor, he was asked to give more comprehensive interviews, and they often fell flat. His team of managers, assistants, publicists, and agents knew this. All Hollywood stars have their people, but Common was intensely loyal, and those around him were folks who had known him most of his life. They, more than anyone, understood that the world wasn't getting the full depth of Common's personality, humor, or humanity, and that's why they reached out to me.

Our appointment was supposed to last one hour, but we talked for two. We each shared deeply personal details about our lives. Common listened to my story with great interest and compassion. He was engaging and funny—a captivating storyteller. The more I got to know him, the more I understood that the way he spoke was a by-product of his profound sense of humility. Taking up the space around him with his voice felt arrogant to him somehow. He preferred to fly under the radar rather than above it, and as a result, his special something was shrouded in a kind of bashfulness and the need to maintain a "cool" persona. But when he was appearing on a late-night talk show or doing press junkets, that natural reflex to hold himself back was doing him a huge disservice.

To be heard fully, so that the whole world could benefit from his wisdom, he needed to place his voice farther forward, allowing the vibration (which is all voice is) to pass through the part of the mouth that shapes and augments sound. As it was, his voice was trapped too far away from most of the *important* articulators—his lips, his teeth, his jaw, the tip of his tongue, and his hard palate. All he needed were a few minor modifications.

"But I don't want to change who I am," Common protested. "I don't want to have a higher pitch."

"That's not what this is," I assured him. "Who you are won't change. You are simply placing your voice farther out front."

I got him to try some exercises. I'll go more deeply into these techniques for vocal placement later, but this was a relatively quick fix. By demonstrating what these simple steps could do to help him physically transform his voice, he realized that this was not a change to his persona so much as an enhancement. Through these subtle adjustments, he could fill the space between himself and his listeners with his positive energy.

Common's phone kept pinging. His people were calling because we'd gone over time and he was running late for a press event. But before he left, I had to give him one last thought.

"You are a gift to the world, and if you don't give us this gift fully, you are robbing us of who you are. You are a generous person, and yet you are being stingy with your personality. Don't chintz on the gift of who you are, Rash. Don't dim your light!"

And what I said to Common I now say to you:

Don't chintz on your gift!

~~~~~~~~~~
~~~~~~~~~~

Press Record

Have you ever played back a voice mail you were about to leave someone and thought, "Oh, nooo! That can't be the way I sound. Or is it?" Many of us get self-conscious the moment we hear our speaking voice on a recording. We are suddenly acutely aware of little vocal tics or habits that we don't like. But that's okay. Sometimes the best way to start on this journey of vocal work is to hear yourself. Try recording yourself reading this passage from "Cicely's Dream" by political activist, lawyer, and novelist Charles W. Chesnutt (1858–1932):

Cicely climbed the low fence between the garden and the cornfield, and started down one of the long rows leading

*directly away from the house. Old Needham was a good
ploughman, and straight as an arrow ran the furrow between the rows of corn, until it vanished in the distant
perspective. The peas were planted beside alternate hills of
corn, the cornstalks serving as supports for the climbing pea-
vines. The vines nearest the house had been picked more or
less clear of the long green pods, and Cicely walked down
the row for a quarter of a mile, to where the peas were more
plentiful. And as she walked, she thought of her dream of
the night before.*

*   She had dreamed a beautiful dream. The fact that it
was a beautiful dream, a delightful dream, her memory
retained very vividly. She was troubled because she could
not remember just what her dream had been about. Of
one other fact she was certain, that in her dream she had
found something, and that her happiness had been bound
up with the thing she had found. As she walked down the
corn-row she ran over in her mind the various things with
which she had always associated happiness. Had she
found a gold ring? No, it was not a gold ring—of that she
felt sure. Was it a soft, curly plume for her hat? She had
seen town people with them, and had indulged in day-
dreams on the subject; but it was not a feather. Was it a
bright-colored silk dress? No; as much as she had always
wanted one, it was not a silk dress. For an instant, in a
dream, she had tasted some great and novel happiness,
and when she awoke it was dashed from her lips, and she
could not even enjoy the memory of it, except in a vague,
indefinite, and tantalizing way.*

Be sure to read this text aloud in its entirety. Next,
play it back to yourself, but without judgment. Just bring
it into your awareness. Jot down a few notes about what

you'd like to adjust, then set it aside. We will come back to it at the end of this book.

Oh Yes, You Can!

The year 2020 left an indelible mark on history—from an unyielding and deadly pandemic to the fervent protests against racial inequities, to the economic catastrophe with millions of unemployed and small business owners struggling to stay afloat. Whether trying to make crucial societal change or trying to bridge a digital divide, never has it been more apparent that using one's voice is a key component to positive change and, ultimately, healing.

Most of us at some point have experienced the frustration and pain of being marginalized, sized up, dismissed, or stereotyped based on gender, sexuality, politics, race, or culture. But how you speak, filling the space with your words and your passion, is the one thing that can cut through all the typecasting, revealing your individuality and compelling your listeners. Let the world *hear* your light! Don't allow your precious words to get lost in the delivery. Learn to speak them clearly so that your message will land where it's supposed to and move your audience of one, or thousands, to understand, appreciate, and remember all the unique ideas and observations you have to share.

Do not for one moment think that any of this is beyond you. It may take some conscious effort. You will have to commit twenty to twenty-five minutes of your day to the exercises I describe in this book. But once you hear and feel your progress, you will want to take this vocal journey as far as it can go. You will be amazed by some of the transformations that I have been privileged to witness as people from all backgrounds and cultures emerge from my studio. You, too, are on the brink of your own transformational shift to vocal empowerment.

As we begin to tackle uncomfortable issues through conversation, listening, and understanding, you will be able to use the true power of your voice, whether behind a computer screen in a Zoom meeting or behind a face covering. I challenge you to train your voice, no matter how big or small, to become the expression of change you want to see in the world.

Breaking Through

One of the most startling transformations I've ever seen was in Martin Sensmeier, a young Native American actor best known for his role as Red Harvest in the movie *The Magnificent Seven* alongside Denzel Washington. Most of my clients have one major area to work on, but Martin had several. His speech combined remote Pacific northwestern idiosyncrasies with the Valley talk of Los Angeles. He couldn't get through a sentence without saying "um" and "like" or "yaknowwhaddimean?" He also mispronounced words because he'd only read them and at the time had never heard them spoken.

But Martin was a quick study, applying himself with diligence to reading assignments like Dylan Thomas and Rumi poems and Eugene O'Neill and August Wilson plays, which are rich in phonetic sounds, alliterations, and evocative, challenging vocabulary. When he didn't know a word, he'd look it up, study the exact pronunciation, and find opportunities to use it in a sentence until it felt natural.

"When you give me homework, I'm going to do it," Martin promised, and I believed him.

The improvements came gradually. We took a multipronged approach to his vocal challenges, using many of the techniques you're going to learn about in the coming chapters. Martin practiced every day, doing vocal warm-ups and paying close attention to his pronunciation and articulation until he was comfortable. They were small, daily steps that got him to where he is today.

Many of our sessions together involved long, in-depth conversations about the many adventures he had before reaching Hollywood. To help me identify the unique vocal and speech gifts to bring forth, I often get my clients to open up about their lives, sharing their experiences in ways that feel most natural and comfortable to them. Martin's narrative could have been a movie. He'd lived a bit of a nomadic life, traveling the country as he worked in fishing camps, oil fields, and construction sites. His breakthrough moment with me occurred when he began sharing vivid stories about his cultural heritage. Speaking from the soul, Martin put power and conviction to his words, bringing these stories to life in rich and evocative detail. I was as proud, well almost as proud, as if I were watching my own son graduate from college.

All that work he'd put in over months had built vocal muscle memory. His mesmerizing descriptions came naturally, effortlessly. These weren't lines he had to memorize for a scene. He was describing a piece of his authentic self, and his voice was rich and resonant, with the passion and reverence coming through unmistakably in the cadence and rhythm of his words. It was as if, after all the vocal work we'd done together, he finally showed up. Like the great orators and storytellers, he knew instinctively when to pause, breathe, and punctuate. He placed the emphasis exactly where it needed to go to drive home his meaning, powering each phrase and thought with breath and the full vocal range of his instrument. Martin was doing precisely what he'd come to Hollywood to do.

"When I speak about my family, my community, and my ancestors, it's as if I am answering to a higher calling," he told me.

Everyman

Hollywood is full of young, talented, and beautiful hopefuls, and I've come across my share of them. But Martin's story is about something much bigger than finding fame and success in the film industry. He couldn't tell his story the way it deserved to be told—he couldn't be fully heard—until he learned to access his true voice. The fact that he did so, in spite of all the challenges he has faced, is proof positive that any one of us can discover and hone our best vocal selves. We just have to be willing to put in the time and effort.

Like many young actors who lack the benefit of families with Hollywood connections, Martin made his way to Los Angeles from his tiny coastal village in Alaska with a strong work ethic. He also possessed a fierce determination to show the world the beauty and richness of his culture.

Although the close-knit community he came from was proud, he grew up amid poverty, drug addiction, alcoholism, and tragedy. Contemporaries died of suicide and overdoses, and boating accidents aren't uncommon. Several friends and relatives were lost on the water.

"When you are around death so much, it can break you," Martin shared. "But for me, that sense of the fragility of my world evolved into deep appreciation of it. It made me want to take myself more seriously and do the work."

Wild Harvest

Born to a mother from the Koyukon-Athabascan tribe in Alaska's northern interior and a father of German American and Tlingit descent (the Tlingit are an indigenous tribe of the Pacific Northwest; the name translates as "the language of the tides"), Martin had little in the way of creature comforts growing up. In fact, the next meal was often whatever could be caught on land or at sea. It's not like they could just walk into a Trader Joe's. Wildlife like moose, caribou, deer, seal, and fish were their main sustenance. At $10 for a gallon of milk, which must be flown in or transported by boat, food insecurity in the region is real.

When the bills went unpaid for too long, his parents would heat their double-wide trailer with the oven and light it with candles. When they did have power, Martin watched the one channel they received, as well as a few VHS movies, on a television with a twenty-inch screen. Of course, there was no cable, so they jerry-rigged an antenna with tinfoil.

"If you closed the door too hard, it would mess up our TV," Martin recalled.

Those shows and movies drew young Martin in. He soaked up whatever culture beyond the wilds of Alaska he could, imagining himself in those worlds. His brother, who is fourteen years older, eventually got a steady job working for the city, saving up enough money to buy himself a flat-screen television, along with a laser disc player and surround system. Martin was in heaven!

He became a fan of Denzel Washington's, memorizing lines in his movies.

"One day I'm going to work with him," he told his brother, with astonishing prescience.

At seventeen, Martin took up a trade and became a welder—a sure way to earn a living and help out his family. But he heard that the real money was to be made on the oil rigs a thousand miles away on Alaska's North Slope. At twenty-one, he obtained one of the prized spots on the Alaska pipeline and paid his dues mopping decks and training to learn all the skills of a rig operator. The days were long, but the nights were longer. One month each winter was shrouded in total darkness as Martin worked two weeks on and two weeks off.

"Sometimes I'd get back to work and feel like I'd never left," Martin told me. "That place was miserable. I hated it."

One day, in the middle of a polar ice storm, he looked out at the swirling snow and had an epiphany: "I could do this forever, or I could follow my dream."

In 2007, Martin packed a small bag with the few possessions he had and moved to Hollywood, for a time commuting between the two starkly contrasting places, picking up part-time gigs to finance his dream and pay for acting classes. With his chiseled features, it wasn't long before he started getting work as a model. That led to movie parts, mostly stunt and extra work where he was almost always cast as a Native American. By 2011 he was earning enough in Hollywood to quit moonlighting altogether. But it would be another three years before he landed his first speaking role in a feature film. Two years later, in 2016, he got his first lead as one of the "seven" in *The Magnificent Seven*. It was shortly after the filming of that blockbuster that we began working together.

Lock-Jawed

With a role like that, many actors might have thought they'd arrived. Not Martin. He knew he had to up his game. Cast alongside greats like Ethan Hawke, Vincent D'Onofrio, and his acting hero, Denzel, he observed them closely, seeking their advice and using every opportunity to learn. When filming began, he asked Vincent who he studied acting with, because he wanted to surround himself with the best teachers. It was my friend Sharon Chatten, one of the best method-acting coaches in the country. And the moment Martin opened his mouth, Sharon referred him to me.

This young man clearly had intelligence, exceptional looks, and acting chops. But what he lacked was a voice, and he spoke so quickly his words were incomprehensible. I kept asking him to repeat himself because I could barely understand a word he said.

It wasn't his fault. Yakutat, a town of 550 people, lies several hundred miles from the nearest city, Anchorage, and is completely inaccessible by road. Martin's vocal habits were partly regional, defined by this insulated community. But local influences weren't all that shaped Martin's speech. Like many talented actors, he had a sharp ear for dialects and accents, soaking up pronunciations and speech patterns from a variety of sources. His father, who was born in Oklahoma and went to high school in Idaho, spoke with a "country boy" twang. Martin left his community in his teens to work jobs all along the West Coast, from New Mexico and Los Angeles to Seattle and Canada, picking up yet more speech idiosyncrasies along the way. During the five years he spent on an oil rig, his coworkers either came from other villages and tribes throughout Alaska or were from other oil-producing states like Texas, Wyoming, and North Dakota.

"I am an amalgamation of all the places I lived, worked, and was raised in," Martin told me. "I think I was an actor before I ever knew I was."

Added to this linguistic hodgepodge was a tendency toward rapid-fire speech.

"Growing up working outside in the cold, your elders yell at you and talk fast because they're usually trying to get a job done so that they can go back inside and get warm," Martin explained. "It can be the difference between catching frostbite, or not."

Those experiences in the cold air may have also contributed to a tight jaw, which constrained Martin's voice, leaving minimal space in the back of the throat. It's not unusual for people who have spent time in colder climates, where the frigid air makes them grit their teeth. Whatever the cause, it was forcing his voice into the head and nasal region. Consequently, the placement of his voice was higher, creating a mismatch between the way he sounded and his physical presence. Although Martin is muscular and tall at six foot two, his voice was small because it lacked a deep chest resonance. He had to learn to breathe in through the mouth, release his jaw, and give his tongue ample space to articulate with the teeth, gum ridge, and hard palate. This technique essentially creates an open space in the mouth, allowing maximum room from the tip of the tongue to the back of the tongue, and from the roof of the mouth to its floor.

Articulation becomes blurred and less succinct when you minimize the space in your mouth. It's what causes speech to sound mumbled or garbled. The teeth, tongue, gum ridge, and hard palate (the articulating organs of speech) need space to come together effortlessly, which can't happen when your teeth are chattering! Martin began a daily regimen to release his jaw with a gentle chewing motion, then gently massaging and stroking open the jaw with his fingers or the palms of his hands. Afterward, he focused on releasing the jaw and uttering the most open-back vowel sound in spoken English, "ahhh." He then preceded that back vowel "ahhh" sound with "m," "n," "l," "th," "v," and "z" to create the sounds "mah," "nah," "lah," "thah," "vah," and "zah." These exercises gave Martin an acute awareness of the need for breath and ample space in his mouth as it relates to efficient vocal production.

I'll go into more technical detail about these speech sounds in a later chapter, where articulation is discussed, and in the Voice and Speech Workout provided at the end of this book. But suffice it to say, Martin became diligent in his daily practice of several of these exercises.

A Single Breath

Here is an exercise you can try. It's one of my favorites because it addresses breath, voice, and articulation simultaneously. Begin the sequence by using one breath per line, then gradually add another line on one single breath, until you are saying the entire sequence on one breath. Feel the placement of your voice on the lips and the tip of your tongue. You can go across in the sequence, or down. Remember, a sustained, relaxed breath in through the mouth and accurate articulation are your goals. Speed will come with practice.

Mah Nah Lah Thah Vah Zah

May Nay Lay Thay Vay Zay

Mee Nee Lee Thee Vee Zee

May Nay Lay Thay Vay Zay

Mah Nah Lah Thah Vah Zah

Maw Naw Law Thaw Vaw Zaw

Moo Noo Loo Thoo Voo Zoo

Maw Naw Law Thaw Vaw Zaw

Mah Nah Lah Thah Vah Zah

A Star Is Born

Martin's career quickly began to change once he started addressing his voice and speech issues. An actor of such depth would never have been content simply relying on his looks, but had he not worked to improve his vocal craft, his career could easily have plateaued.

Opportunities began to flood in. Off the set, he was able to command a room, interacting with producers, impressing casting directors, and doing all the other things a successful actor needs to do to conduct the business of Hollywood. Bit by bit, his confidence grew.

As soon as Martin found his true voice, he got more speaking parts. In 2017 he was cast in the lead role of a biopic called *The Chickasaw Rancher* about Montford Johnson, who built a ranching empire in Texas. He also starred alongside Jeremy Renner in *Wind River*. In the 2018 season of the hit series *Westworld*, he nabbed the recurring role of Wanahton. And Angelina Jolie cast him as the legendary Native American athlete Jim Thorpe in the upcoming feature film *Bright Path: The Jim Thorpe Story*.

Native Americans rarely see themselves accurately depicted on film and television. They are just beginning to tell their own stories from their vantage point. Martin now has the vocal dexterity to play a broad range of roles. But he is one of a handful of Native American actors putting his culture in the spotlight in a way that feels authentic.

"Denise, ever since I started working with you, my life has changed," Martin recently told me. "Now, when I am speaking with people, they believe me."

It's his mission to authentically share his heritage both on and off the big screen. Through his *Magnificent Seven* costar Denzel Washington, who is a national spokesperson for the Boys & Girls Clubs of America, Martin has become a Native Ambassador, speaking on behalf of the ninety-five thousand Native youths who are served by 187 clubs across America. He is also the face of the Native Wellness Institute, promoting healthy living and nutrition among Native American communities afflicted by addiction, diabetes, and obesity. He regularly gives commencement speeches at high school graduations, inspiring young members of tribes across our continent by showing them what global success can look like.

"Learning what my vulnerabilities were and breaking speech habits that didn't serve me have helped me grow in ways I never imagined possible," Martin often tells his transfixed audiences. "Finding my voice has helped me to become the expressive man I am supposed to be."

What's Already There

Martin is no different from any of us. We all have this higher calling. We all have a story to tell that connects us to one another in profound ways. Your voice is a beautiful thing that should be heard, in all its nuance and resonance. Don't let regional quirks, distracting speech habits, bashfulness, fear, past trauma, or anything else hold you back and mask who you truly are.

There's no need to be intimidated by the tools and vocal exercises I'm about to share. Before you embark on this journey with me, I want you to relax and understand that I am merely giving you access to what you already have. As Martin observed, "It's not so much that you're restructuring my voice as uncovering what's already there." Great speech is within you!

Once you've found your true voice, you will be amazed by how your listeners respond. Like it or not, first impressions are everything, and whether we are speaking in front of an audience, getting ready for a job interview, or prepping for a date, most of us obsess over our physical appearance, from getting our hair just right to picking out the perfect outfit. But the last thing we tend to think about is our voice, and that can be a deal breaker.

This vocal work is not just for actors, public speakers, or newscasters. This is for everyone!

Talk Your Way Through It

Having vocal skills can prove empowering on many levels and in multiple situations that the average person might find intimidating. How, for example, do you use your authentic voice on a first date when you're nervous and trying desperately to leave a lasting impression? Or when you're trying to win over a traffic court judge with the sincere plea that you were going fifteen miles per hour over the speed limit because you were late for a funeral? Or when you're trying to strike up a conversation with a stranger at a party, leaving her with the impression that you are relaxed and enjoying yourself, even though your palms are sweating and you're feeling incredibly awkward?

You can even leverage great speech during a heated exchange, for example, when you are trying to return damaged merchandise. Great speech can make your auto mechanic think twice about upselling you some unnecessary and expensive work on your car's transmission, and it can help you persuade your boss to give you a long overdue raise. An empowered voice can also help you articulate your contributions and worth to earn better terms on a contract or gain you fair access to your children in a custody battle.

Not only does putting power and passion behind your words make your life better in a myriad of small ways, but it can also be transformational. Whenever and wherever you need to accurately convey your message and intention, win over your listener, and be truly heard, your voice can be your superpower!

At the very least, your voice should be your calling card, your instrument of self-expression and storytelling, and it deserves the same care and fine-tuning as the rarest Stradivarius violin. As Nina Simone said: "Did you know that the human voice is the only pure instrument? That it has notes no other instrument has? It's like being between the keys of a piano. The notes are there, you can sing them, but they can't be found on any instrument."

Transforming or enhancing how you speak may seem like a daunting task, but you will soon discover that, by peeling back the layers and unlearning the distracting vocal habits of a lifetime, you will come to it naturally. This is a journey back to who you truly are. It starts with the realization that you were born to bring your authentic self into the voice and master the power of speech. Just as a newborn baby knows how to breathe, the knowledge has always been inside you. I'm just helping you remember.

First Impressions

In addition to sharing many stories like Martin's throughout this book, I am going to give you several techniques to help you overcome any vocal issues that may be holding you back from being heard the way you deserve. And there are many such issues, including vocal nasality, vocal fry, a high pitch, a lisp, and regional idiosyncrasies. To that end, I'm going to take you through the same stages of voice and speech work I learned at Juilliard, which I now teach to my clients in Hollywood and all over the world: relaxation, breath, voice, articulation, and communication.

At the end of this book I am also going to give you a Voice and Speech Workout, with detailed descriptions of all the sounds of General American Speech, along with word lists for you to practice. Repeating the exercises layered throughout these chapters, and practicing daily the elements of speech listed in the workout, will yield extraordinary results. Your friends, family, and colleagues may not be able to put their finger on what exactly is happening, but they'll hear the difference. People will respond positively to your clear, crisp, and powerful delivery. You may not even be aware of your vocal distractions, but they get in the way of telling your story because they require the listener to come to your voice instead of your voice reaching the listener with ease. By the end of the book, we are going to flip that script.

Why does it matter?

I believe that how you speak is largely responsible for the way you are perceived. Yes, this belief is based on my experience with a myriad of professionals, my work as a singer in the New York City Opera, and my career as a television, stage, and voice-over actor. But it's my daily interactions with everyday people that sparked my interest in the connection between the voice and social perceptions.

A few years ago, I called an upscale grooming salon for pets. I was a doting dog owner and wanted to pamper my fur baby in his declining years, so I called to see if their services were within my budget. When I brought my pup in the following week, I greeted the receptionist with a simple "hello."

"Hello, Ms. Woods," he replied. "Welcome!"

I was shocked. *How did he know my name? Was he telepathic?*

"Your voice!" he responded. "It's so distinctive, I remembered it from our phone conversation."

That moment was revelatory for me. I was thrilled to be able to make a memorable impression in such a commonplace, perfunctory situation. More often than not, my voice gets me phenomenal customer service and positive attention from those around me, and it has allowed me to communicate my point in even the most difficult circumstances.

Through the advent of social media, many have forgotten this art. We rely too heavily on the text or the tweet for communication, losing vocal expression and color along the way. Truly connecting with others requires more than 280 characters. Your message needs feeling! How many times have you tried to be funny in an email or a text, only to find that your message offended the recipients? They couldn't hear your voice or your inflection, so your words came across as snarky or mean-spirited. Your voice would have given them access to your true intention— a glimpse into your heart and soul.

Voice Prints

Our voices are truly unique, like our fingerprints. We all possess the power to leave an indelible vocal imprint with the simple words of a phrase. Our voices should be used effectively and passionately, without fear of social or racial ridicule. You've heard the adage "The squeaky wheel gets the oil." I challenge you to replace your vocal squeak with a mellifluous and articulately produced voice. How wonderful to be able to navigate your world and be comfortable in any given environment! How powerful to be able to enunciate in a way that enhances the influence you have in all your social dealings!

Of course, I get pushback from some clients. Their agents and managers have sent them to me, and they've been resistant. I can't tell you how many times I've heard, "This is me. Accept me for who I am. Why should I change?"

"No one is trying to change you!" I assure them. "But would you prefer a box of crayons with eight colors or 120?"

I'm offering you seven shades of blue and five shades of orange, so you can define, shade, and color a beautiful canvas with your voice.

Think of it another way. Instead of showing up for meetings or events in one suit or one dress, wouldn't you rather own a complete wardrobe of outfits, each one perfectly expressing your mood and your personality, appropriately and meticulously matched to the occasion?

Take it from me, an African American woman who proudly continues to navigate vastly different worlds: clear and concise speech is an asset no matter where you come from. This is not about changing the essence of *you*—it's about adding so much more to those very things that make you special. You are much more than a particular region, ethnicity, or community. Yours are the notes "between the keys." This is about removing limits and expanding on the possibilities of all that you can be.

Intentionally or unintentionally, we all do things that hide or limit all that we have to offer this world. But now is the time to shine your light. Consider this your opportunity to bring forward your own rich mixture of experiences and influences so that others can benefit from the unique story you have to tell.

This process will be rich in self-discovery. As you explore this work, you may be surprised by some of the additional benefits of these vocal exercises and techniques. Some of my most memorable experiences with clients have uncovered personal trauma that affects the voice. This is not therapy, but finding your voice can sure as heck be therapeutic. The deeper we breathe, for example, the more we connect to our emotions. Oftentimes, voices get closed off because we don't want to go there. But it's well worth it when we push past the reluctance and fear, as you will see. Learning how to breathe from deep within your core can be a profound emotional release. A lot of "stuff" gets unpacked in these sessions, and lives are changed for the better, forever.

That's the power of voice.

Speak It!

As you approach your vocal transformation, understand that we all have a voice that's meant to be shared. Don't allow yourself to be daunted by the work that lies ahead. Instead, imagine all that you can do with the power of voice in every area of your personal, professional, and public life. I want you to embark on the upcoming exercises not only knowing that you can do this but fully believing that you can achieve your desired results.

It begins with building your confidence. Yes, I know, it's easier said than done. As you will learn, even the biggest movie stars get stage fright, but they have tools in their toolbox to overcome it. Let me share a few of the tried-and-true tips that have helped me gain the level of confidence I enjoy today. I have incorporated these principles into my everyday life and rely heavily on them when I feel I'm at my wit's end. These deceptively simple practices may not be altogether new to you. They may even seem obvious. Nevertheless, please humor me. The more intentional you are about these practices, the more you will find that they center you. And being centered, for me, is the ultimate confidence booster.

1. **Find your tribe or village and a mentor.** Connect with those who make you feel safe enough to be your truest self.
2. **Set realistic physical exercise and nutritional goals.** Establish a routine of self-care, and verbally affirm yourself every day, because physical and mental wellness serve your instrument.
3. **Surround yourself with natural beauty.** Then commit to reading engrossing literature, listening to great music, and seeing inspiring artwork. These actions will take you out of your own head. A few of my other tips for banishing self-consciousness include:

    Encouraging someone new each day. *This could be something as simple as giving a stranger in a coffee shop a sincere compliment.*

    Doing for others and being of service in your community. *That could mean something as simple as helping an elderly person get safely across the street or giving things you no longer use or need to your local shelter.*
4. **Embrace the mistakes.** Believe that when you fall it's an education and not a punishment. It's not a setback so much as it is a setup for success.
5. **Be forgiving,** kind, and gentle to the ones you love and, most of all, to yourself.

2.

Tilling the Soil

....

RELAX YOUR BODY IN PREPARATION

Stop a minute, right where you are. Relax
your shoulders, shake your head and spine
like a dog shaking off cold water. Tell that
imperious voice in your head to be still.

—BARBARA KINGSOLVER

My mind would not be still.

I was lying on the classroom floor at Juilliard with nothing but a thin towel between me and the cold linoleum, doing my best to relax. It was 1975: I was eighteen years old, just a week or so into the fall semester, and entering the first phase of the school's legendary voice class. Before we were even allowed to utter a sound, the object was to release the body of all its tension and unleash the imagination. We lay there, day in, day out, working on bringing the muscles and ligaments of our instrument into our awareness, listening to guided visualizations, focusing on the breath, and eventually releasing an occasional monosyllabic sound. The process lasted for weeks. Our mouths would not be permitted to form words, much less full sentences, before Halloween.

This was the classroom of Elizabeth "Liz" Smith, one of the founding members of the Juilliard Drama Division faculty. In those days, there were no limits on the way teachers could address their students. The teaching model then, whether in the arts or for professions like medicine and law, was about breaking you down to build you back up. It was rigorous, intense, and at times infuriating. Unlike today, when teaching professionals must be more culturally sensitive, members of the Juilliard faculty, viewed as gods, could cross racial and sometimes sexual lines without repercussions. It wasn't usually that overt, but a sense of their superiority just hung in the air. You felt it, particularly in the Voice and Speech Department, where Liz staunchly roamed her classroom in stockinged feet like a character from a Dickens novel.

So it was no easy task to relax. Hypersensitized as I was, the ticking of the wall clock, the buzzing of the fluorescent lights, or the light snore of a classmate who had unintentionally drifted off to sleep on the floor next to me seemed unusually loud. The meat-locker temperature also wasn't conducive to letting my mind drift. Every classroom had a Steinway piano, so we weren't allowed to touch the thermostat lest the conditions become anything less than optimal for these precious instruments. (We often joked that the pianos were more valued than the scantily clad actors and dancers.) To make matters worse, our voice class followed our morning movement class, so we often found ourselves damp with sweat that soaked through our tights, creating the added distraction of teeth chattering. Although that wasn't half as distracting as the chattering of my mind!

Once I settled into the Juilliard community, I couldn't help questioning its rigid and oftentimes elitist approach to voice and speech instruction. Numerous times during my freshman year I'd been made to feel less-than, as if I were an interloper. I wasn't just some doe-eyed kid; I was proud of my previous dramatic and classical music training. I was also deeply proud of my South Carolinian Gullah roots, my Lower East Side dialect, and the

other rich cultures that resided within me. The constant insinu-
ation that it was somehow not good enough was unsettling. *I'll
show you*, I said to myself in silence. *I'll prove you all wrong!*

But by my sophomore year, something quite phenomenal happened as I followed Liz's guided visualization floor exercises:

> *Imagine that you are on the side of a beautiful, cool, green
> mountain on a sunny spring day. Imagine the sounds and col-
> ors, a light breeze, and the warmth of the sun. Feel the rays of
> sunlight on each isolated portion of your body, starting from
> your head to the tips of your toes. Feel the wonderful rays of
> heat melt away tension. Feel the solid mass of tension become
> liquid and melt into the ground beneath you. As this heavy
> solid melts into liquid form and flows away, feel a light, airy
> breeze flowing through your body and dissolving any residual
> tension. You are feeling lighter, and you are also becoming
> lighter. Brighter . . .*

Her words seeped into my imagination, helping me release all
the tension that was residing in my jaw, throat, tongue, neck,
shoulders, torso, and spine. At that point, I realized it wasn't the
messenger that mattered. It was the message. I could follow Liz's
visualization technique and make it my own. She couldn't tell me
what my side of the mountain had to look like! I could take this
gift she was giving me to let go of baggage—any baggage—and
ultimately relax with my own imaginings, my own music, and
my own stories.

Feel Fresh and Good

Before you embark on this journey, understand that physical relaxation is key. The voice is not at its best without a good night's rest.
Vocal training tends to produce better results in the morning, when

the cells have renewed after plenty of REM sleep. When you wake up from blissful sleep, you should address the tension that exists in all parts of your body. As Julie Andrews said, "Young Broadway singers and anybody who is an orator of any kind—lawyers who have to speak in court or pastors or anyone who has a lot of stress on their vocal cords: You should do the maintenance. You should do whatever it takes to feel fresh and good."

Now, I am not proposing that you lie on the floor for months. But the old-school method of teaching voice got some things right. You *do* need to till the soil before putting seeds in the ground. On a string instrument, the tighter the string, the higher the pitch. Similarly, when we relax the instrument—our bodies—we sound less tense, more soothing and inviting. Filmmakers know the importance of a music score for eliciting the desired emotional effect on an audience. There is nothing more nail-biting than the sound of high-pitched violins on the soundtrack of a horror movie. Anyone who has ever watched the shower scene in *Psycho* knows the knife slashing is coming. It's an ingenious use of tension. But when it comes to your speaking voice, a high-pitched, tense instrument can have a repelling effect on the listener.

Little Momma Bear

Not only does tension impact the quality of your communication, but it can also do physical damage. Several years ago, I taught voice to a seven-year-old girl, Lauren, who was the daughter of an NBA player. Kids can be cruel. The poor girl was being teased on the school playground because other children thought she sounded like a boy. Normally, I would refer someone with an issue like this to an ear, nose, and throat specialist, but I knew the family well, so I agreed to go over and do a deeper assessment of the situation.

Immediately, I realized that this young lady, the oldest of five children, was taking on the role of "second mother" to her siblings. Her own mom was laid back and soft-spoken, so I guess Lauren felt she had to step in as the disciplinarian, as is the prerogative of big sisters everywhere. She was constantly screaming at the top of her lungs to be heard by her naughty little brothers and sisters, scolding them and telling them what to do.

The family's huge mansion was typical of the Los Angeles nouveau riche, with high ceilings, Italian marble floors, and dozens of rooms. The grown-ups in the house communicated with one another via an intercom in each room, but Lauren wasn't tall enough to reach them. So instead she screeched. That physical stress left her hoarse; if it continued, she'd wind up with nodes on her vocal cords. Her issues were part environmental, part behavioral, and part personality.

But the very young are fast learners. They don't have as many deeply seeded habits to break as we adults do. All that was needed was a little playtime, or so Lauren thought. We assembled all her favorite dolls, and I asked her to make up a few stories about them. Finally, I told her to imagine that they're misbehaving and she's reprimanding them, much like she does her siblings. Each time her voice started escalating into a scream, I gently said, "That's too much. They can hear you. You don't need that much voice."

I instructed Lauren to breathe in and out through her nose and gently massage her face, rotate her head around in easy, relaxed circles, and then squeeze her shoulders up to her earlobes and release them, all while keeping her lips together and jaw released. After three or four of these sequences, I had Lauren breathe in deeply through her mouth instead of her nose and repeat the doll exercise. She quickly figured out how to breathe in through the mouth while releasing her jaw, which created more space for vocal resonance when she spoke. Lauren was, at last, using her "indoor voice" in a relaxed, powerful, and safe way without pushing.

Finally, I added fun, catchy phrases for her to practice while tossing a balloon across the room to me:

My mommy makes milkshakes while I make magic.
Sing a song along with me, someone.
Ninety-nine noodles never need nutmeg.

The balloon toss was an exercise to take her mind off the vocal work and release her vocal power effortlessly on the breath while engaging her body. The specific phrases allowed her to practice nasal resonance—bringing out the fullness of her voice to the front of her entire face, as opposed to just the nasal cavity. (Think Meryl Streep versus Fran Drescher.)

The work we did taught this little momma bear that her strength doesn't come from shouting at the top of her lungs. She could still throw a barrage of words—she just had to relax her body, breathe in through her mouth, and release her jaw first. Lauren learned that her little brothers and sisters could know she meant business without screaming herself hoarse. A well-placed stern look or a pregnant pause could also suffice. And her siblings were in on it. They had permission to calm her down and remind her not to scream. The whole family was on board! Lauren was eventually able to take her relaxed, breath-supported indoor voice onto the playground and command more respect and attention from her taunting peers without causing herself vocal harm.

Bucking Bad Habits

If anything, by shouting you give away your power. It's one of the best ways to not be heard, whether you're a frustrated seven-year-old big sister exercising your bossy prerogative or Howard Philip "Buck" McKeon, a long-serving Republican congressman from California.

I first met Buck in the early 2000s when I was on the faculty of California Institute of the Arts. We were introduced by the school's president, Steven Lavine, who happened to be an old friend of his. Buck had lost his voice. While Buck was paying a visit to the school, Steven asked him what happened. In answer, Buck scribbled on a legal pad that every time he came back from serving on the floor of Congress in Washington, DC, it would take him two days to get his voice back. The distinguished congressman, who went on to become chairman of the House Armed Services Committee, was a screamer.

Now, it probably goes without saying that I am a lifelong Democrat. But that sweet man, with his broad smile, ruddy cheeks, and affable manner, had me at "hello." The former western-style clothing retailer and Mormon missionary had an outsize personality and a passion for his causes that was infectious. But physical tension was sapping his vocal power. And whatever he was doing on the floor of Congress did not match his authentic self.

Buck wasn't hoarse by the time we sat down together. He'd had enough time to recover. But from the way he was speaking, I instantly recognized the root cause of his vocal distress. His jaw and tongue were so tense that he wasn't creating enough space in his mouth for his voice to be released. You can have all the breath you need, but if your jaw is closed and your tongue has cradled up to the roof of your mouth, it creates an obstruction to the open space in the back of your throat. All that breath is for naught. It's like trying to squeeze air through a small funnel.

When people don't have a released jaw and power of the breath, they tend to overcompensate by muscling and pushing down on the larynx, which can potentially cause callus-like nodules on the vocal folds. That's what causes the shrill sound. Fortunately, in Buck's case it hadn't gone that far.

I had him massage his open jaw with his thumb and forefinger. Then we practiced saying "kuh, kuh, kuh" and "guh, guh, guh." These sounds engage the back of the tongue with the hard palate. Releasing them helps gently relax the back of the tongue and create maximum space in the back of the mouth. The "k" and "g" make the articulators come together, while "uh" releases into an open vowel sound. Similarly, a good yawn helps create that open sensation in the back of the mouth, allowing the voice to come out full throttle. Buck caught on to this quickly, rediscovering his vocal power, raising the roof on Capitol Hill, and occasionally giving Congress a run for its money with some good old-fashioned civil discourse before retiring in 2015 at age seventy-seven!

A Smooth Vocal Ride

Both the politician and the little girl ultimately learned that their true vocal power comes from a place of calm. Complete relaxation is that feeling you get just before drifting off to sleep, the sense of peace as you stretch out and breathe on the floor at the end of a yoga class, or that refreshed outlook from a day of pampering at the spa. It's about letting go of distraction and being present in the moment. But relaxed energy in a vocal context is something quite specific, as is the means of getting there.

To obtain a released and freed voice, you must start with deep rib, diaphragmatic breathing. Imagine a low-revving car in its neutral gear—malleable and available for navigation at a moment's notice. If your voice is your tire and breath is the wheel, relaxation is where the rubber meets the road. It's what gives you that nice, smooth ride. But failure to reach that state could land you in a vocal ditch.

The effect of tension on all those parts of your body that are vital to the production of sound is profound. Over three decades of doing this work, I've discovered that one of the most glaring vocal issues is related to jaw tension. I've always said that the jaw is to an actor what knees are to a basketball player. I'm no athlete, but I know how fragile a basketball player's knees can be as a result of the hustle and grind up and down a basketball court.

Our own twenty-first-century daily hustle is having a profound impact on our health, our eating habits, and our sleep.

The number of nightly teeth grinding and jaw paining clients I see in my practice has increased exponentially over the past decade. These stress-related issues can wreak havoc on the voice. When jaw tension, which can potentially lead to chronic pain, minimizes the amount of space in your mouth, the voice becomes trapped, held, or constricted. With nowhere to travel freely, the voice will inevitably creep into the nasal region of the head, resulting in an annoying nasal quality, or it will be trapped in the back of the throat. Listeners will constantly ask you to repeat yourself because you are not being heard.

But you can't fix a tense instrument in isolation. It's a process.

Human Ball of Stress

Let's Begin

- Start with your posture. How are you sitting right now? Are you slouched, with your shoulders rounded?

- Adjust your spine by lengthening your torso. Just imagine you are being pulled by a string from the top of your head. Make sure that your chin is not jutting forward or tucked in.

- Now imagine that you are being pulled by a string from both sides of the point where your upper arms meet your shoulders. This gentle imaginative pull will allow your chest to widen without forcing or protruding it.

You are now creating maximum space in your torso and back for lung expansion. You are also creating space for the voice to resonate in the chest cavity with relative ease.

This spine adjustment can have an additional beneficial effect on your head, neck, shoulders, and jaw—like dominoes. The goal is to create maximum space between each vertebra of the spine, space between the tip of the upper spine and the base of the skull, and finally space in the jaw and the back of the throat. When you compromise this small but precious real estate, the negative vocal impact can be huge. Take, for example, that minute but highly influential space between the tip of your upper spine and the base of your skull.

1. See it in your mind's eye. Place your fingers at the base of your skull, and gently massage that spot. The space I'm referring to is about the distance of your four fingers stacked one on top of the other.

2. Now imagine that you're able to insert a golf ball in that four-finger space. That simple golf ball image will help create a cavernous space in the back of your throat, allowing for an unobstructed release of voice.

3. If you add to that image the simple act of blowing out through the lips, this will raise the soft palate in the back of the throat and naturally create more space without hyperextending. I'm not talking about blowing out through the lips as if you are extinguishing candles on a birthday cake. I mean a more vigorous but relaxed fluttering of the lips; you may also add gentle sound.

The common thread through all the exercises in this chapter is the total release of unnecessary tension. But not everyone is capable of melting into relax mode. In fact, "relax" is a word that, when delivered as an imperative, can have exactly the opposite effect. For anyone who is tense, wound up, frustrated, or in a state of panic, being told to "calm down" puts their teeth on edge. No one wants to be commanded to do something that feels physiologically impossible when they're facing a deadline, dealing with a toddler meltdown, or stuck in rush-hour traffic. You know your rapid heart rate and rising blood pressure aren't good for you, dammit! You'd do something about it if you only could, but relaxation is just one more thing on your overwhelming to-do list!

Take it from me, a woman who has spent hours stuck in LA traffic: learning how to relax your body and mind is a challenge. Letting go of thousands of life's stressors, large and small, that have accumulated in our bodies, tightening our muscles and clenching our jaws as we cycle in and out of fight-or-flight mode, is not like flicking a switch. These days especially, we're expected to be "on" for our employers and clients 24/7, reacting like Pavlov's dog to every instant message ping on our iPhones. We've become so wired, with the stress hormone cortisol flooding through our bodies as we react to so much external and internal stimuli, that we've been fooled into thinking it's just who we are.

I knew from the moment I spoke with Phaidra Knight that she was a human ball of stress. The edge in her voice was unmistakable.

A Hall of Fame rugby player who was named USA Rugby's Player of the Decade in 2010, Phaidra was described as the "most feared" player on the pitch, in addition to the most respected for bringing the sport into this country's consciousness. But beyond being an athletic powerhouse, Phaidra was blessed with a brilliant mind. She had been earning her law degree on a partial scholarship at the University of Wisconsin when she was introduced to rugby. When she finally retired from the sport as both a player and a coach in 2017, it seemed obvious that this thought-ful, poised, and articulate woman was destined for the booth as a sports commentator. There was just one problem: her voice had no oomph, no charisma. That's death in the broadcasting world, where one of the main currencies is likability.

TV journalism had been a lifelong dream of Phaidra's. She'd majored in speech communications and political science as an undergraduate. She'd traveled the world as an athlete and had a curiosity beyond sports, with a unique perspective as an openly gay African American woman.

"Broadcasting is just part of the journey," Phaidra told me. "I want to host something that reaches a massive number of people; I want to utilize media to advance social change and have an impact on all the things that matter to me."

Phaidra rightly saw herself as an example of the diversity that was missing from television. Sports commentating is a male-dominated field, and she didn't want to be that girl in the tight dress interviewing athletes on the sidelines. She had every right to expect to take her place in the booth alongside the many male sportscasters who had fewer accolades and qualifications but were getting regular work with the major networks. Yet no matter how hard she worked, Phaidra was getting only occasional work with NBC Sports, ESPN, and SportsNet New York.

"I am probably the only female rugby player in the US pur-suing this full-time, so I am going up against a bunch of guys," Phaidra told me. "Beyond the struggles of being female in a male-dominated occupation, you can never disregard the fact of being African American and having to be twice as good to get half the opportunities. That's just the reality, so I accept it as normal."

Yet it was not acceptance I heard in her voice as we contin-ued our conversation. It was anger. And who could blame her? Phaidra approached her career the way she did all things in life, by pushing herself. She wanted to forge that path, sitting at the anchor desk with the guys, bantering back and forth, and she deserved her seat at the table. But her time would not come until she could inject some personality and passion into her presentation.

"Phaidra, you have a great knowledge of the sport, but I can't hear your love and passion for it in your voice," I told her bluntly. "If you leave your personality on the sideline, I can easily google the stats."

Grinding It Out

Phaidra had a work ethic that was insane. But as the months went by, I wasn't seeing much progress. Her standards were much higher than most. She was the "smart one." The lawyer. The perfectionist. But when it came to vocal development, those traits all worked against her. You never felt like you were getting to who she was at her core. Phaidra was one tough nut to crack! What was up with this woman?

As is often the case with my clients, it was a question of digging deeper into her past experiences. You wouldn't know it from her dialect, but Phaidra was a small-town girl from Irwinton, Georgia, about two and a half hours southeast of Atlanta. She and her older sister grew up on her family's farm where, from the age of four, she was expected to pitch in and help, picking vegetables in the summer and hoisting pigs into the trucks headed for the slaughterhouse.

It was a strict, religious household headed by a father with a quick temper. Her grandfather was a minister, and her father, a small business owner, was a deacon. Her mother, a teacher, served as secretary in their local church. Sleepovers and dates were not allowed in high school. In addition to her chores, Phaidra was expected to study. Both parents graduated from historically Black colleges, and in her household, education was everything.

"Our childhood was full of work and discipline," Phaidra

shared. "In that way we were a typical African American family in a rural community, and I was privileged to have parents who passed on their solid values and tremendous work ethic."

The rest of her free time was dedicated to athletics. Recognizing her restless energy from an early age, her uncle, a basketball player, installed a basketball hoop in her family's field. She wanted to join little league football, but girls weren't allowed, so she joined the cheerleading squad instead. In high school she lettered in basketball, traveling all over the state with her team. She also played varsity tennis, belonged to a 4-H youth program, and earned high enough grades to be in the National Honor Society.

From an early age, Phaidra felt that her Irwinton southern drawl might hold her back, so she used every opportunity to speak with people from other regions, including a cousin from Maryland who used to spend summers down on the farm with their grandparents. She involved herself in local public speaking engagements to become the best communicator she could.

"I was wired a bit differently because I paid attention to how other people spoke and could switch it up like hats."

Holding Back

Amid all the bustle, Phaidra buried her true self. She didn't even realize she was gay as a child, nor did it matter because she was "too busy just being Phaidra." By the time she did recognize her sexuality, the idea of coming out was unthinkable—*especially* in the strict religious African American household where her father was a deacon.

Gradually, as Phaidra began to trust me more, we talked about how that suppression could have impacted her vocally. There had been a tightness to her voice that happens when you're holding a big piece of yourself back from your audience. Phaidra, now forty-five, came out to her parents when she was in her mid-thirties, and it was messy. Her dad was "fired up," and as her mother looked on passively, the conversation "unraveled all kinds of other issues we had growing up."

Her parents have since reached a state of acceptance, embracing Phaidra's wife and even staying with the couple in their New York apartment, although Phaidra is aware that they still struggle to reconcile her sexuality with their faith. Therapy, patience, and love have healed her relationship to her parents, but Phaidra's voice was still held and constricted in the back of her throat.

True to her character, she worked hard on the breathing and vocal exercises I gave her to help release her voice, practicing relentlessly until the techniques I taught her became second nature. Before long, Phaidra's few vocal tics had much improved. But the heart and soul in her voice—the ability to connect with the listener—had yet to show up. It was completely confounding!

Then, about a year into our work together, Phaidra blew me away. We were chatting about nothing when I suddenly noticed she was completely in the pocket. She showed up! She was joking and laughing. You could hear the energy and joy in her voice. It was as if she was a completely different woman from the tensed up, slightly bitter person who first appeared on my Skype screen. If we had been meeting face-to-face, I'd have given her a high five, because that was the Phaidra we wanted to see at the anchor desk.

"Phaidra! Girl! What happened? What have you done that's different, because vocally this feels like a whole new you, and I'm loving it!"

She finally shared that, since sixth grade, she'd suffered from a hormonal condition called "premenstrual dysphoric disorder," or PMDD. This isn't like PMS, where you feel a bit cranky and crave chocolate a few days before your period. PMDD, which affects from 2 to 10 percent of women of reproductive age, causes severe distress and dysfunction. For two weeks out of the month, her estrogen levels would be cut in half. Phaidra would struggle with terrible mood swings. There would be moments, even on camera, when she felt enraged. That rage would then morph into depression, and all she wanted to do was crawl into a hole and be by herself.

Not enough is known about the condition or how best to treat it. Some researchers believe it can be triggered or exacerbated by trauma. The current wisdom identifies one possible drug treatment using serotonin, the "happy chemical" in our bodies that contributes to a sense of well-being. Other treatments involve lifestyle and nutrition changes, as well as vitamins.

Phaidra had been meditating and doing therapy long before she met me. Her body was her temple, and her eating habits were impeccable. She was doing everything that she was supposed to do. But it wasn't until she started working with a nutritionist specializing in women's health, trying out different diets and supplements, that she had her breakthrough.

It was a combination of many things that allowed Phaidra to bring her whole self into her voice: the supplements, the self-care, the vocal practices . . . all these actions led to this moment. I thought I was going to have to tell her that the networks were not in her future, because all this time I could not hear her. But listening to her now, it felt as though I was finally getting to the core of who she was. We sat there, looking at each other through our digital screens, crying tears of relief. Phaidra's voice had been the warning siren that indicated that something was fundamentally wrong. Her voice had been resonant with the trauma, shame, and fear that robbed her of her personality. But now her voice was restored, and it was almost as if she'd been set free.

The lesson for me was just how profound the body/mind/spirit connection is to voice. No one single thing can heal it. We don't just get fixed with therapy or diet or the vocal exercises themselves. Even that which might seem purely physical, such as a hormonal imbalance, can affect our instrument. So many factors that you might not expect can affect the voice. We must put that into our awareness as we continue our lifelong journey to understand and care for our whole selves, learn to relax, and till the soil.

In 1992, when I became the first African American woman to join the Drama Division faculty of Juilliard, I brought this awareness to a new generation of students in my own voice and speech class. Yes, we still did the floor exercises. Certain foundational tools are time-tested in their effectiveness, and my first teachers certainly knew their business. But everyone's vocal journey is unique and deserves some custom tailoring. I like to think I brought to class a compassion for my students and a desire to know and develop them as individuals. These kids used to come to me and ask, "Why are the other teachers so mean?"

"The day they stop being on your ass is the day you worry," I told them, explaining that the other faculty members were coming from a place of tough love.

My classroom was the safe space where they could be seen and heard as themselves, where they could relax and breathe. I've created the same type of sanctuary in my West Hollywood studio today, and you can create a similar place as you practice your vocal exercises in your car, at home, or with the Starbucks barista.

~~~~~~

Speak It!

Relaxation is the foundation for deep rib, diaphragmatic breathing. To achieve maximum results, commit to doing this exercise first thing every morning. It takes 3–5 minutes to complete. These simple steps will create a more relaxed and available body, from head to toe, on which to build the principles of breath, voice, and articulation:

Lie on the floor, flat on your back, with the back of your head propped easily on a one-and-a-half-inch-thick book and with your legs lifted and resting on the seat of an armless chair.

Make sure that the small of your back is connected to the floor and that the weight of your legs is being completely supported by the chair.

Now adjust your head on the book to ensure maximum distance between your earlobes and shoulders. Feel long through the neck and spine and wide across the chest.

Breathe gently and slowly through the nose. While breathing, bring attention to each part of your body, from the crown of your head to the tips of your toes.

Become aware of where tension is being held in your body. If it's your head, rotate it gently from side to side. Or your shoulders? Wiggle them gently to initiate the release of tension.

With your awareness on each body part, gently rotate, wiggle, or shake free from the stress and tension that is being retained in your muscles and limbs. Be very thorough. There's no rush.

Once you've finished, remain still and quiet, giving yourself permission to just *be*. Feel the weight of gravity connecting your head, jaw, neck, shoulders, arms, torso, back, and hips to the floor. Feel a similar connection of your thighs, knees, calves, ankles, and feet to the chair. Keep breathing deeply and effortlessly. Give yourself permission to do absolutely nothing. This moment of silence is golden.

Gently float your fingers to your head and begin to massage your face, sinuses, jaw, temples, forehead, and scalp.

Breathe as you physically and psychologically let go of the tension.

After a minute or two, release your hands down to both sides, palms facing up, and enjoy the peace and quiet of your mind.

~~~~~~~~

PART II

Breath

Have you ever wondered why your speaking speeds up when you're nervous or when you're excited to share some great news? It's because you're not breathing. Why do you think people ask you to repeat what you've just said when you know that you're not speaking softly? That's also because you're not breathing; you're lacking vocal energy.

Not long ago, I worked with the Ivy League–trained broadcast journalist Rachel Boesing. Rachel is smart, witty, and very articulate, so she was surprised when her NBC boss suggested she study voice with me. As she gave herself permission to slow down and breathe between her thoughts, her voice became more expressive. Her bright and witty delivery became richer, less tense, and more intensely felt. We'll discuss in the next two chapters why breath allows you to connect more deeply and become more confident.

So, if you are dreading that upcoming wedding toast or making an oral presentation to a group of colleagues, this is the section for you. The technique I'll discuss served me well as I faced some of my greatest life challenges, from dealing with my own heartbreak and mortality to the biggest challenge of all: my only child's health and well-being. Whatever situation you are facing, breathing will help calm your nerves as well as buy you a bit of time to collect your thoughts, so that when the time comes to be heard, you can speak your truth with power.

3.

Like the Motor of a Car

....

DEEP BREATHING

POWERS THE VOICE

I took a deep breath and listened to the
old brag of my heart. I am. I am. I am.

—SYLVIA PLATH

Like all great athletes, Greg Louganis understands the power of
the breath. In fact, his breathing technique is so much a part of
his success as a four-time Olympic gold medal winner for diving
that he has mentored subsequent generations of Olympians on
Team USA. At the London and Rio games, he taught them to
time their breaths at the most crucial moments of their dives in
a way that feels rhythmic and natural, so that they could build
a kind of muscle memory for the intake and outtake of oxygen.

"A big inhalation happens as I make my forward approach,"
Greg, one of my best students, recently shared. "Then I expel all
of the air out of my lungs and I press into the hurdle. The biggest
expression of energy comes as I push the board down, then all of
the breath."

The rest happens instinctively. He fully inhales again at the peak of his dive, taking in air as he performs the flips and twists that have made him an icon of the sport.

"Bringing awareness to where the breath goes to support the execution of the dive gets you inches higher and makes it that much easier—it just clicks."

So, what does this have to do with the voice? Everything!

Bringing in all that oxygen through the lungs and distributing it throughout the body creates energy, allowing the mind, muscles, and vocal cords to work together in harmony and strength. Like the motor of a car, it's what makes you go! The word "motor," which is rooted in the Latin word *movere*, meaning "to move," first referred to the propulsive force, and then later to the person or device that initiated the movement. That's the power of breath.

Focusing on the inhalation and exhalation doesn't only enhance your physical performance. Done right, breathing steadies you. When you draw the breath with deliberation, from deep within your diaphragm, and let it carry throughout your entire body, it calms you and allows you to be in the moment. It gives you the focus and power you need to take that leap off the high-dive board, whatever you are trying to accomplish in life.

Greg knew this when he made his historic dive at the 1988 Summer Games in Seoul. Less than half an hour earlier, during a reverse somersault in the preliminaries of the three-meter springboard competition, he'd hit his head hard enough to require five stitches. Shaken and embarrassed because "great divers don't smack their heads," Greg forced himself to climb back up onto the board. In that moment, much was going on in his mind. Besides the fear of hitting his head again, he'd only recently been diagnosed as HIV-positive. If that knowledge had become public, he wouldn't have been allowed to compete in South Korea. You can't catch the virus by sharing a pool with someone, but as he felt the blood trickle down his neck, Greg also felt a great weight of responsibility. And yet here he was, pumped and ready at what would probably be his last Olympic competition. How could he not go all in?

As he heard his name and they announced his dive, his heart was pounding. This next dive would be a "reverse one and a half with a three and a half twist." He heard an audible gasp when he stepped forward. That's when he realized, "Oh my God, people are afraid for me!"

He took in some air through his nose, then patted his chest, feeling his heart go thump, thump, thump. Realizing what he must be feeling, people in the vicinity saw the gesture and chuckled nervously. In that moment, Greg understood how much the crowd was rooting for him, and he laughed at himself. As he drew in another deep breath, so did they, and he felt a visceral connection with the onlookers in the stands. Then he expelled, releasing all that tension before executing the best-scored dive of the day, leading to an eventual gold medal that established him as the greatest male diver ever.

Forgotten Superpower

Years later, as he transitioned to a career as an inspirational speaker, the man who'd mastered his breathing technique to the point where it was his superpower confessed, "I've lost the connection between my breath and my voice."

Referred by his husband, who knew about me through a mutual friend, Greg came to me after delivering a talk on drowning prevention that was lackluster at best. The feedback he'd received on his speaking skills was terrible. He was all over the place, unfocused, losing the crowd as he wandered off on tangents.

"Oftentimes I am much more comfortable showing what I can do through dance, diving, gymnastics," Greg later shared. "It's easier for me to allow my body to express itself; I'm not always comfortable expressing myself in words."

When we met, it was mutual adoration at first sight. I couldn't wait to help this enormously talented man hone his message and its delivery, because there was so much great raw material for me to help shape. Our ultimate goal was to create his backstory and match it to his authentic voice, but much more on that in a later chapter. First, we had to get back to the fundamentals of his breathing. All the elements were there. As a dancer, singer, and athlete, his knowledge of how breath could fuel his performance was impeccable. He'd mastered the power of breath while he was young, and its rhythm was in his bones. But until he became an actor, doing theater and some film parts, he never realized that the breath is as critical to acting and speech as it is to athletic performance.

A few simple exercises soon synced his voice back up with his breath. We began, as always, on the floor, where I had Greg breathe in a few times, slowly, through the nose, then out through the mouth.

"Feel the expansion of the ribs in your back and in front against your thighs," I told him, as he curled into a kowtow position on a yoga mat in my West Hollywood studio. "Now visualize free and relaxed muscles surrounding the rib cage. Breathe in through the nose on a count of three, and gently release an 's' over the tip of the tongue for a steady count of seven."

I made him repeat the exercise five times and sent him home with a daily practice to lay the groundwork for the other work we had yet to do.

Greg wasn't alone in his voice/breath disconnect. Few understand how critical breath is to good voice and speech. Instead, most of us take it completely for granted. After all, if we didn't breathe, we wouldn't be able to sustain life, would we? But there's more to it than simply breathing in and out through the nose. Singers also know that a deep breath (through the mouth) that expands the lungs, reaches all the way below the rib cage and releases the diaphragm, and then slowly works its way through the throat and out of the mouth again can create a richer, fuller sound. The same goes for your voice. A deep breath releases all the tension, opening the throat and giving energy to the vibration of sound.

We've already talked about relaxing the mind and body. It's the beginning and end of all the work that we do in this book. The breath is what gives life and makes things grow from the tilled soil. But that deep diaphragmatic breathing can only happen once you are in a state of deep relaxation. That's when you can blend the breath with sounds to create the vibrations that result in a rich vocal resonance. That's when you can release the emotional life of the voice and sound like your authentic self. An added bonus is that it feels wonderful. I had one student tell me, "I feel so tingly and high right now." Oxygenating the brain with the breath creates a natural sense of euphoria and yes, darling, it's free! All you need to do is figure out how to access it.

Don't Put Clare in a Corner

Learning to breathe properly is not always as easy as you might think. Clare Berman, a fiercely intelligent young woman, had never quite understood the restorative, calming, and energizing gifts of good breathing. Proficient in just about every other area of her life, her voice/breath disconnect was holding her back, and there was no simple fix. Bringing her attention to the breath would cause her to panic, then hyperventilate. The more she tried, the worse it got. For her, taking a deep breath involved throwing her head back and squeezing together her shoulders, breathing into her chest, and creating tension through that whole region of her body—like a woman drowning at sea.

Clare's inability to breathe properly was directly linked to her state of mind. Like so many of my more cerebral students, she lived in her head and tended to overthink, and this was affecting her voice and speech. She would conceive how something should look or sound and get stuck inside that notion, unable to let herself experiment for fear it would fall short of a finished product. She was a perfectionist, and if something didn't match her preconception, she would falter or freeze. That's partly why her voice was so high-pitched and thin. That reedy, breathless sound was coming from the nasal area at the front of her face and couldn't carry more than a couple of feet, much less across a room.

This was a problem for Clare in many situations. Because she sounded like a little girl, people tended to dismiss her or not take her seriously. She was bullied, talked over, and put upon at her job as an assistant in a corporate office. She had opinions about how things should be done, but she was never heard. By the time she arrived at my studio for our first appointment, she was done with allowing herself to be treated that way.

"It's nice to meet you, Denise," Clare said when she walked through my door, her voice quivering. "By the way, I just quit my job, and you're the first person I've told!"

Clare started to sob. For years, she'd sucked it up. She took it all, quietly and stoically, until her boss told her, "Your opinion doesn't matter." She couldn't take it anymore, and the pent-up emotions erupted into a total meltdown.

Putting Others First

Clare's insecurities began when she was a child growing up in a small town just outside Detroit, Michigan, where her mother was a single parent raising four children. Although her extended family was always supportive, Clare was a devoted daughter who put pressure on herself to help raise her siblings.

Seeing how dedicated she was, Clare's aunt and uncle, wealthy business owners, paid for her to study entrepreneurship at Brown University. After college, she jumped from one job to the next to make a living and help her family financially. Instead of pursuing her passion, as most graduates do, she took secure administrative and personal assistant jobs. "Everyone told me I was good at being organized," she explained, "and it would be a good way to guarantee a paycheck."

Clare took supportive positions because it never occurred to her that she could live her own life. While some positions were rewarding, most left her feeling less-than. The decision to leave her recent job was a pivotal moment for Clare, who'd spent most of her life "feeling like I can't take up space in the world." The job she had just left, where she was treated horribly and required to perform tasks way below her abilities and intellect, had been grinding down her self-esteem. The experience, she said, further reinforced her lifelong perception that she "didn't deserve to speak up."

Underestimated No More

The more Clare talked, the more moved I was by her story. Culturally, we were from completely different backgrounds, but in many ways I could see myself in her. People mistook her kindness for weakness, and they would walk all over her. As a woman, particularly a woman of color, I can relate to those subtle and not-so-subtle put-downs in the workplace. Okay, I'll just say it. I've had to put up with a lot of crap. There have been times I've felt almost invisible, dismissed, underestimated, or worse.

Early on in my career as a Hollywood dialect coach, I was invited by the lovely British actress Rachel Weisz to join her on the set. She needed help developing a New York accent. The director of the movie, a young man considered to be one of the industry's up-and-comers, apparently did not know who I was or why I was there, as I happened to be the only person of color on the set. He looked me up and down with an annoyed look on his face, which was my first clue that he'd made a few assumptions about my qualifications to do the job based solely upon my appearance. After the actress's first take, the director looked over at me, his eyebrow raised, and yelled, "Does that sound like a f*#&ing New York accent to you?"

Incensed, I shot back, "Yes, it f*#&ing does, because I am from New York! And I am old enough to be your mother, so don't you ever speak to me like that again!"

Well, if you don't stand for something, you'll fall for anything. Not surprisingly, my agent called the next day to tell me what I already knew—that I'd been fired. I wondered if I'd ever work in this town again. But it wasn't long before I was asked to coach Will Smith for his Oscar-nominated role as Muhammad Ali, and I haven't looked back since.

I shared this story with Clare to express how much I identified with her experience of not being invited to the party. But I fought back, putting energy and righteous indignation into my voice through the breath, and, boy, did it feel good!

"My dear girl!" I told Clare. "You can be whoever you want to be; I've got you. I will help you take back your power through your voice. This first class is on me!"

Fortunately, Clare had recently married a supportive husband with enough financial security that she could afford to take some time for herself, to explore and figure out what she wanted to do with the rest of her life. She started taking acting classes, seeing a therapist, doing yoga, and talking to career counselors. Whether it was going to be acting, film production, or something that would combine her artistry with her entrepreneurial skills, her next move would be about creating her own agency instead of looking to others for direction. This was her opportunity to be reborn.

But we had work to do. Clare's lifelong panic attacks could be triggered by something as simple as the meditative breathing that comes at the end of a yoga class. The breath was her ticket to relaxation, but it was doing the opposite. Instead of trusting her body to naturally breathe through the mouth and complete an idea through the breath, she almost sounded as if she were gasping, rushing through her words in the meekest of tones. When her voice wasn't cracking or quivering, she was suffering the dreaded vocal fry, the sound of a voice that is trapped so far back in the throat it sounds like static on a radio or the sizzle of frying bacon. The more she thought about the breath, the harder it was for her to connect it to her voice.

Get Down!

As someone who constantly felt as if she had to prove herself, Clare had been operating from the chin up. Cerebral people typically (not always) tend to produce sounds in a higher range because their voices are unconsciously being generated from the head region. When they read aloud, their voices are often monotonous, almost treating the passage as a clinical exercise and losing the emotion behind it. I wanted Clare to start thinking from the chin down and speak more from her chest, her heart, and her core. She needed to release her jaw, relax, and feel connection to the text and words in a way that was more visceral than cerebral.

As I had with Greg, I started with Clare on the floor. I wanted her to get grounded. Have you ever noticed how indigenous people, when they are praising or celebrating, tend to dance with movements that are more earthbound? The Native American grass dance, to the steady rhythm of a drum, comes to mind, as does the powerful Zulu warrior dance. In contrast, ballet dancers' movements are more upward reaching. They dance on pointe, extending their arms upward toward the sky. But even a ballerina's feet must touch the floor sometime. Vocally, Clare was like a dancer about to jeté off the stage. She'd lost her center of gravity, and we needed to get her back to it. I told her to think about the ritual dances of indigenous cultures, where the motions are more rhythmic, reflecting a closer connection to Mother Earth and the life-giving properties of the elements of nature.

Another way of visualizing it is to think of the deep, dulcet tones of the cello versus the violin. The higher-pitched violin tucks under the chin. But you embrace the cello with your whole body, cradling the instrument between your open legs. I wanted Clare to think of herself as that cello and feel the origin of sound work its way up to the chest from the pelvic area. I wanted her to feel the energy in the space between the knees. I encouraged her to listen to Yo-Yo Ma and develop an appreciation for those lower notes. Not that the higher tones aren't beautiful, but she needed to develop the lows, and everything in between, for a full range of vocal expression.

Stretching out the back and feeling that gentle pull down to the floor helps bring all the parts of the body involved in the breathing process into your awareness. It facilitates the full-bodied breathing that brings out all those rich cello notes. Thus reclined, I had Clare place one hand on her chest and the other on her diaphragm, relaxing her shoulders to avoid heaving into her chest, which creates more head than chest resonance. This was key, because the goal was to get her lungs and rib cage to expand, tripping a domino effect, naturally releasing the diaphragm and moving the abdomen muscles. Without that expansion, the intercostal muscles surrounding her rib cage would be so tight that she wouldn't be able to feel the movement of breath through her body.

Once I could see that natural rise and fall of deep, relaxed, diaphragmatic breathing, Clare gently breathed in through the mouth and released a long "zzzzzz" sound on the exhale. Through the physical engagement of hand to chest and abdomen, she could feel her chest resonating with the vibration of sound.

When Clare completed the exercise, her voice was instantly richer and fuller. She didn't even sound like the same person.

Feel the Vibration . . .

We will explore vocal vibration in the upcoming chapters; however, I want you to begin to feel the benefits of a relaxed body and the powerful impact breath can have on the voice. Are you seated? If not, seat yourself in an armless chair. Be aware of your posture: hold your torso erect but not tense, shoulders and jaw relaxed, and legs spread shoulder distance apart. Gently shake out your upper body to ensure relaxation. Now float your fingertips to your face and very gently massage it, concentrating on the jaw area. After 30 seconds of massaging, release your arms down by your sides, and take a few cleansing breaths in through the nose and out through the mouth.

With every exhale, imagine tension floating out of your body. Now bend over in the chair, allowing your abdomen to touch your thighs and your head to float freely between your knees. Allow your arms to dangle very easily by your sides. Take a few breaths in again through the nose from this position, and feel the expansion of your rib cage. While still bent over, shake out briskly but remain relaxed.

Now, breathing in through the nose again, release the breath on a sustained "ssssss" sound. Repeat five times. Breathing in through the mouth this time, release on a sustained "zzzzzz" sound. Whenever you utter a sound, you will always breathe in through the mouth. Feel the vibration of the "zzzzzz" sound on the tip of your tongue, in your chest cavity, and, if you're really lucky, in your back. If you're not feeling vibration in your back yet, don't worry; you definitely will by the time you finish the book. Repeat the "zzzzzz" sound five times.

Still seated in the chair, slowly return to an upright position, and gently shake out. Float your fingertips to your face, and gently massage your face again, this time breathing in through the mouth and releasing a sustained "mmmmmm" while massaging. Feel the vibration on your lips, in the front of your face, and in the chest cavity. Breathe in through the mouth, and gently chew with the lips together while releasing the sustained "mmmmmm" sound. Repeat five times. During the sequence, alternate between massaging the face, chewing gently, and cupping the palms of your hands together about two inches away from your mouth to feel vibration in your hands. Is your voice resonating in your mouth, in the front of your face, and throughout your body? If so, congratulations! The work has begun! If the results are minimal, fret not. This book is designed to help you relax while finding your voice at your own pace.

After our first session together, I sent Clare home with an assignment. I wanted her to read aloud, timing her breathing with her phrasing. Since she had to perform the famous Mark Antony passage from Shakespeare's *Julius Caesar* for her new acting class, we started there. When we met again the following week, as she delivered the line "Friends, Romans, countrymen, lend me your ears . . . ," Clare sounded as if she were trying to jog and speak Shakespeare at the same time, speeding through each phrase and gasping for the next breath. Clare knew it, and she was visibly disappointed.

Dare to Suck

Change doesn't always happen with the flick of a switch. You don't muscle it. You practice, letting it come to you, and build on the breath-to-voice connection, gently retraining the mind. A lifetime of panic attacks and rushed, shallow breathing can't be undone in one vocal session. Clare would seemingly master the technique, then lose it the next time she felt her anxiety levels rising.

"Just keep doing the daily exercises, in addition to your yoga and therapy, and you'll get there. I know you will."

Clare needed to give herself permission to stumble.

"My darling, please don't be afraid to suck," I told her. "Allow yourself to be in process. This is how it sounds right now, but by taking this step and the next, you're getting ever closer to your goal."

Part of the work we did together involved releasing her fears about how others were perceiving her. She could read out loud just fine in front of her husband and family, but larger audiences paralyzed her. Clare needed to let go of that fear. When she was standing in front of a group of people to present a story, it didn't matter what she was wearing or whether she was having a bad hair day. The only thing of importance was the story, and the consistent breathing that lends itself to consistent voice in service of that story.

A few weeks into our work together, Clare reported back to me that she had taken another turn at *Julius Caesar*. She read and reread the play, internalizing it and becoming impassioned about its lessons on moral conflict, love of country, ambition, friendship, and jealousy. The story, and its relevance to the times we are living in, captured her imagination, and everything else fell away. She forgot about the fact that she was standing awkwardly in front of her acting class being watched and listened to by a group of people she barely knew. She just delivered the lines with feeling, bringing the words to life exactly as the Bard had intended.

Once Clare was able to connect these dots of breath, voice, speech, and how she saw herself in relation to the rest of the world, she had a breakthrough. Intellectually, she'd always understood that breath had the power to calm her anxiety, but she'd never been able to internalize that knowledge. Her daily practice of deep breathing with vocal exercises pushed her past that mental block. Now it was a tool she could pull out of her toolbox whenever she felt that familiar beast of panic rise within her. The realization made her weep.

"Oh, Denise, when I think about all those years wasted over this damn anxiety issue . . ."

Heart in Mouth

The breath powers your voice and gives you strength. It's something we need to call on even, and especially, when our voice seems to abandon us. Coming back to those deep, full-bodied breaths will always get you through the anxious times we all face.

I've had a few earth-shattering moments in my life when I searched for breath. (Yes, even I have been knocked breathless and speechless.) Like the time I received a phone call no parent wants to receive. On the morning of August 9, 2008, just as I was getting ready to leave for church, my son's best friend, Ohre, called to inform me that my son, Terry, had been in a fight and was in the emergency room of an Orange County hospital. Ohre purposely didn't reveal that Terry had, in fact, been the victim of a brutal assault and was lying in a hospital bed in a medically induced coma. Terry and his college friends had been celebrating the end of summer at the home of one of their buddies, three hours south of where we lived, before heading back to school in San Francisco the following week. Two guys, who no one knew, crashed the party, and my son ended up taking a blow to the head that nearly cost him his life. I jumped in my car and broke every speed limit in the rush to be by his side. As I was driving, I kept praying, breathing, and trying to remain calm. Thank God, I had no idea of the enormity of the situation.

When I got to the hospital, I thought I would be directed to the emergency room to be with my son, but instead I was escorted to the head doctor of the trauma unit. Not knowing the magnitude of my son's condition, I tensely, but optimistically, asked if my son was going to be all right. The doctor was dismissive, as if he was annoyed by the fact that he had to deal with this frightened mother.

"You obviously don't know anything about head injuries. If I were you, ma'am, I'd start getting my house wheelchair-ready," he warned in an acerbic tone.

I was in total shock, and at first the words would not come. The situation hit me like a truck, knocking all the wind out of me. That feeling of not being able to get enough air is a common physiological response to a traumatic or stressful event. It's part of the human body's fight-or-flight reflex, a natural reaction. But you don't have to stay there. You can consciously choose to get back to the breath, drawing in a lungful of oxygen, as I did in that next moment. "Oh, hell no!" I said to myself.

I took a few beats to live in the silence, breathing in and out, in and out. Then I told those doctors and nurses how this was all going to go down.

"This boy is going to walk again," I told them, and myself, gathering all the power and authority I could muster into my voice.

I've never forgotten that feeling of empowerment through the breath. It was life-altering.

You don't need to experience the trauma of nearly losing a child to benefit from connecting your voice to deep, full-bodied breaths. Settling in and fully utilizing your breath can help you get through the many situations in life that would have otherwise left you stifled.

The breath is essential on many levels. Powerful speakers know when to pause for the breath, which creates that space for your audience to download and respond to your message. The breath powers your words and gives you strength, whatever you are going through.

Remembering how to breathe—finding that rhythm—helped to power me through whatever had to happen next as I supported my son in his healing process. It gave me the strength to stand up, face the doctors who had an all-too perfunctory approach to treating my child, and advocate for him. It allowed me to put all the love, warmth, and compassion into my voice as I spoke to my unconscious son during my and his father's days-long bedside vigil, so that he could feel our energy. And yes, I thank God every day, Terry made a full recovery!

After all, what is voice but vibration? It is the vocal manifestation of the spirit that connects us as human beings. It can also heal. They say the cat uses its purr—an example of breath to sound in the animal world—to repair damaged tissue. And medical science is continually discovering new ways to use frequencies to heal body and brain. So perhaps it's not too much of a stretch to say that your vocal vibration contains more positive power than we can possibly know.

Now imagine what being more intentional about connecting your voice to the breath can do, not just for yourself but for the people you interact with each and every day. At a minimum, making this change can transform your relationship to yourself and the rest of the world.

Clare recently shared with me a line from a Mary Oliver poem:

Listen, are you breathing just a little and calling it a life?

She acknowledged that's what she was doing before she made that fateful decision to walk away from her abusive boss. For much of her existence, Clare had been breathing just to get to the next intake of breath, but she was never fully present for herself and all the good things life had to offer her. Today, she's breathing with purpose, connecting voice to the breath in order to show up, be heard, and take control of her own destiny.

"This breathing technique is life-changing," Clare told me. "It's not just about voice; it's about your whole being."

Speak It!

Applying Voice to Breath

The exercises in this book will often seem similar and overlap, but that's okay. Repetition, with subtle shifts in emphasis and sequence, will help you grow and adapt, depending on what you'd like to address at any given time. This exercise works best when it follows the relaxation exercises. I am quite deliberate in the way I have structured these chapters and exercises. However, each exercise can also be done on its own for as little as 5–7 minutes at a time, or with a more in-depth combination of exercises for as long as 20–25 minutes at a time. As with anything, the more time you invest, the greater and more rapid your results will be.

1. **Begin by lying on the floor on your back** with a two-inch-thick book under your head. Once on your back, bend your knees with your feet planted fully on the floor. Make sure that you are lengthening through the spine and widening across the chest. Adjust your head on the book so that you are not jutting your chin forward or tucking it in. Your head should feel as though it's an extension of your spine.

2. **Using the relaxation principles of the previous chapter, begin breathing in through your nose.** Feel your ribs expand as your lungs fill up with air. Make sure that your breath

does not creep into your upper chest cavity, shoulders, or neck, creating tension. Keep your breath low, allowing the gradual expansion of your rib cage like the expansion of the gills of a fish. Feel the back of your rib cage as it connects to the floor. Use the floor as a gauge to feel the expansion in your back. Gently float your hands to the base of your rib cage, and feel the gentle expansion on both sides of your body.

3. **Gently allow your head to release to the right and then slowly to the left.** Now gently speed up the side-to-side motion while remaining completely relaxed. Come back to center, and stretch your body with your arms raised above your head, much like a cat would stretch out after a nap, fully extending your arms and legs; raise the soft palate (at the back of the mouth) into a yawn. Yawning is a wonderfully natural stretch for the jaw, the tongue, and the back of the throat.

4. **Come back to center with your knees up** and your feet flat on the floor. Center yourself by gently breathing in and out through your nose three or four times. Now breathe in through your nose, but this time release an unimpeded, smooth breath on an extended snakelike "ssssss" sound.

5. **Now breathe in through your nose on a slow and steady count of three.** When you've reached capacity, immediately release a thin stream of breath on an "ssssss" sound over the tip of your tongue for an easy count of seven. Repeat five times.

6. **Remain relaxed on the floor.** Center yourself by sending attention to different parts of your body, particularly concentrating on your rib cage and abdomen.

7. **Slowly turn over onto your left side.** Push the book from under your head, and place your left arm under your head as a cushion. Keep your head free and lengthened as if it were an extension of your spine again. Place your right hand on the right side of your rib cage. While breathing in, feel the right side of your rib cage expand into your right hand and the left side press against the floor.

8. **Breathe in through your nose on a count of three**, and gently release a smooth, extended "ssssss" on a count of seven. Repeat five times.

9. **Stretch your body and turn onto your right side, allowing yourself to yawn** by raising the soft palate in the back of your mouth. Remaining relaxed, repeat the sequence on your right.

10. **Turn over onto your stomach, and sit back onto your heels** with your torso touching your thighs. Use both arms and the backs of your hands to cushion your forehead on the floor. Get comfortable in this position, making sure that your spine is lengthened, your chest is wide, and your head, neck, and shoulders are completely relaxed. Your head should still feel like an extension of your spine.

11. **Breathe in a few times through your nose.** Feel the expansion of the ribs in your back and in front against your thighs. Visualize free and relaxed muscles surrounding your rib cage. Breathe in through your nose on a count of three, and gently release on an extended "ssssss" over the tip of your tongue for a steady count of seven. Repeat five times.

12. **Slowly sit up from the floor but remain on your knees.** Easily shake out your upper body, head, torso, and arms for 5–7 seconds. Once completed, rotate your head in a slow and steady circular motion in this position. Then slowly begin to come up into a standing position, allowing the upper body to hang over freely and fluidly as you rise. Imagine you are stacking one vertebra on top of the other through the spine.

13. **Once in a standing position, feel** the space between the vertebrae of your spine, and feel the maximum space between the tip of the spine and the base of your skull without jutting your chin forward or tucking it in. Feeling very wide across the torso, easily shake out your body, head, neck, and shoulders.

4.

Trauma Is a Bitch

The big "Aha" moment is that the
trauma never goes away.

—VIOLA DAVIS

Mary Langford, an aspiring actress who made a living as famed writer/producer Sidney Sheldon's personal assistant, came to me for help at the suggestion of our mutual friend Michele Shay, and I could hear why the moment she opened her mouth. Mary's voice was high-pitched, nasal, and barely audible, almost as if it were imprisoned in the back of her throat, which in a sense it was. You could even say she sounded as if she were being strangled.

Mary was getting plenty of callbacks after she auditioned. A highly intelligent and articulate woman, she had a look that was hard to forget, with wavy auburn hair and striking blue eyes that pierced right through you. But whenever she was asked to read lines in front of a group of people, her voice would give out on her, and she never managed to book the job.

"Put me in a crowded room and my voice disappears," Mary explained. "No one can ever hear me, and it makes me so ashamed."

Something else was going on. I knew there had to be more to this story than a few flubbed auditions. Our first few sessions went nowhere. I was trying to get her to relax her body and breath, but Mary was one of the toughest cases I'd seen. Even after an hour of deep-breathing exercises, her voice still had that thin, tinny quality. I tried my usual visualization techniques, but voice and breath still were not connecting; no fuel was going into the tank. I was at the point of doing something I almost never do—giving up—but I could see how hard Mary was working, so I decided to try something new. I invited her to a session at my house, near the beach.

Close to the Source

There's just something about the ocean. Not a lake, or a river, or a pond. The sea, for me, is the place where I feel the most connected to Spirit, the Source, God—whatever your chosen word for that divine energy that pulses through every living being. Something about its vastness, the breeze, the light smell of the salty water, and the rhythm of the waves cleanses my mind of all life's daily distractions and gets me into a place of deep relaxation. Sitting by the seashore always reminds me that there is something greater than myself, which is comforting. Maybe Mary would feel the same.

We walked the three blocks from my home in Oxnard, California, to the public beach, where families were picnicking in the late-afternoon sun. I threw a blanket onto the sand and instructed Mary to lie down and close her eyes while I knelt beside her and invited her to breathe.

There was no need for imagery in this setting. I often paint a verbal picture to engage the mind in something pleasant so that my students don't overthink. The moment people start doing something with their apparatus, their voice, or their breath, they can veer off and tense up, engaging muscles that do not serve the vocal work. But by the ocean, you don't need to imagine a thing. It's right there before you. You don't have to work as hard. All you need to see, hear, and feel is at your disposal. The water rolling up to the shore, then immediately back out to sea perfectly mirrors the rhythm of breath.

I instructed Mary to open her mouth and breathe in the cool air, creating an open space in the back of her throat, which had been tense and tight for so long she had no idea what a relaxed instrument felt like. When we do this, when we open up the back of our throat, it's like relaxing the strings on a bass. I encouraged her to open wide and give herself over to the power of the Pacific and its pounding waves.

"There's nothing to do or think about," I told her in my most soothing voice. "Relax your tongue on the floor of your mouth. Keep your lips together and relax your jaw. Just take a breath and let this moment wash over you. . . ."

For the next few minutes, Mary lay there, quietly breathing. Suddenly, I heard a primal, guttural sound. It wasn't a scream. It was more like a rich, deep release, as all those years of held, constrained emotions were being carried out on the exhale. And it was coming from Mary, who sat up with tears streaming down her cheeks. When she spoke, her voice had altered dramatically. She was speaking in a lower register, and it was more resonant. And she had a lot to say.

"Denise, I kept this buried deep inside me for years. No one knew all the details of the hell I've lived through."

Choked into Silence

Mary's truth came tumbling forth. While on vacations in Minnesota and Michigan, her uncle had sexually abused her from the time she was eight years old, causing profound physical, physiological, and emotional trauma. At eleven, when their families were visiting together at her uncle's house over Easter, Mary got up the nerve to tell her dad, but he didn't believe her.

"I can't convict a man without a jury trial," he told her. "I need to hear your uncle's side of the story."

Mary's father approached his sister's husband to have a conversation. When he returned, Mary was told she was just a child with a vivid imagination and a need for attention.

"Your uncle said he might have accidentally brushed up against your breast, but that's all there was to it. You're the child, and he's the adult, so I'm just going to have to take his word over yours."

Thus emboldened, her uncle continued the abuse until, at fourteen, Mary fell pregnant. Her parents finally realized that Mary had told the truth about her uncle; her pregnancy was the product of incest. They sent her out of state, by herself, to have an abortion. When she returned, her mother, a devout Catholic, told her, "Forget this ever happened, get on with your life, and for God's sake don't tell anyone."

So Mary kept quiet. She swallowed her emotions time and again, burying the atrocities deep into her subconscious. She experienced symptoms of PTSD for the next thirty years, but she never connected her trauma to what was going on with her voice. As we worked together and she looked back on those pivotal events of her life, Mary realized her voice had indeed changed from the time the abuse began. Before, she was as loud and boisterous as any other child on the playground. She'd whoop and laugh to the point where she had to be reminded to use her indoor voice. She told me that, after the assaults, the pain, the shame, and the grief, "I was constantly clearing my throat; members of my family would even ask if I was getting a cold."

Blown Away

The more we talked about what had happened to her, and the more Mary released those muscles and learned how to breathe, the better she felt. Her voice told a story beyond words. It needed to be heard. Being able to articulate what happened was no substitute for therapy, but it was part of the steps on her journey to heal. Finally, she was free of this deep, dark secret. Giving herself permission to share it so fully with someone else helped her take control and reclaim the voice that God gave her.

"Denise, until I met you, I never understood how much the abuse was impacting my voice," Mary said. "But now it all makes sense to me. When you're a little girl and someone forces himself on you, then you're constantly told that you're wrong, that your experiences are lies and you are not to be heard, of course it's going to damage your voice! Or, in my case, practically extinguish it altogether."

That afternoon, on my neighborhood beach, it was as if the wind were blowing away her previous narrative. The golden late-afternoon sun was shining down on her. The moment was so powerful that we had to sit with it for a while. We stayed there in the sand, watching the sun start to dip below the horizon, with tears of relief and joy in our eyes. To hear Mary's voice transform right there on the spot—and to see how the experience of nature combined with deep inhalations and the release of voice on the breath can shift a traumatic experience—filled me with gratitude.

Sucking It Up

Again, I'm no therapist, but I've always been able to hear trauma in someone's voice. Though you may not realize it, the breath is where we hold our emotions. Babies know how to let it all out with a good, loud, lung-powered wail. But as we get older and more cultured, we are taught how to hold our breath and not cry. You know all those clichés: "Boys don't cry," "I'll give you something to cry about," or "Suck it up!" In modern-day western culture, we're taught to hold our emotions down. As a result, we lose that innate way of breathing, becoming more cerebral and less visceral in how we process our feelings.

This habit of "sucking it up" also affects the voice, which can become higher pitched and more nasal the less we breathe deeply from within. I can't tell you how many times I've taken people through breathing exercises and the tears started flowing. All those years of pent-up, sucked-up emotions were being released. Psychic wounds linger in the body and soul like old scar tissue. Their impact is physiological and profound.

Have you ever noticed how a great massage, releasing all those knots, can sometimes make you want to weep? Those are your old emotional wounds, buried beneath layers of muscle and tissue, being set free at last. In the same way, taking in and releasing the breath, then connecting it to voice, brings cleansing energy to your instrument. Trauma is a bitch, and it greatly affects voice and speech. But never underestimate the healing power of the breath, which can help you get to the root of past trauma and reconnect with your true self.

We all go through traumatic experiences in life. To be human is to experience pain, although thankfully not always at the level endured by Mary. And even what we may consider the smallest of injuries, things we may have long since dismissed or discounted, can have a negative effect on our voices.

Vocal Mismatch

Shah Granville came to me perfectly formed. Or so I thought. I must admit that even I could not detect any trauma in her voice, which sounded clear, resonant, and expressive in casual conversation. This former model and athlete was seeking to improve her acting chops through vocal work. But when she reached out to me early in the summer of 2018, I was busy working with Mahershala Ali on the set of the HBO series *True Detective* and was unavailable for new vocal clients. I suggested she download my *Speak It Clearly* MP3 in preparation for our first meeting that fall. Not only did she do her homework, she practiced the vocal warm-ups, including breathing exercises, daily. (You'll hear more about the importance of practicing consistently in the chapters to come.)

Shah's goal was to free her voice from the constraints she'd been carrying since childhood. She was self-aware enough to realize that her emotions were affecting not only her vocal resonance but the authenticity of her expression. When she felt misunderstood, she noticed her voice would go into the back of her throat and she'd sound small, like a little girl. When she wanted to show passion or enthusiasm about something, her vocals would get too strident. When she was nervous, she tried to mask it with bravado, hoping her loud voice would distract from her shaking hands or clenched fists.

In short, there was a profound mismatch between her voice and her true self. Shah's vocals were inconsistent and would chop and change depending on her mood, although they weren't necessarily reflective of how she was actually feeling. Not only was it negatively affecting her acting, it was hurting her real-life interactions. People couldn't access what was going on in that sweet soul of hers. They found her to be disingenuous, which she most certainly was not.

"I know I make people uncomfortable," Shah told me. "My voice can't catch up with my persona, and they think I am being inauthentic. They don't quite trust me."

It didn't help that, at five foot nine, this poised and stunning African American woman was being judged by her appearance. Yet her looks belied her self-perception. She never thought of herself as beautiful. No one believed she could possibly have any confidence issues, but she sure did.

"I can't tell you how many times I've hidden in the bathroom to avoid meeting people," Shah confided. "Or how many auditions I've walked out of."

Her performances felt disembodied. There wasn't emotional logic to the way she delivered lines. She would scream, cry, or dial up the volume at the wrong moments, as if she were overcompensating. At times she would hear her words and feel as if she had stepped outside of herself. Her other default mode whenever she felt unsure was to make a verbal retreat, staying silent or, when pressed to speak, sounding soft, sweet, and apologetic.

This kind of distortion is typical whenever we have issues that we are cloaking. Vocally, we are either too loud or too soft, which was the case with Shah, or too fast or too slow, which was the case with Clare. The nuanced color of voice, its natural variety, cadence, and rhythm, falls by the wayside in the effort to mask something, hide, or show the world you're not afraid. Everything gets stuck at two speeds.

The disconnect added to the misperception that Shah was either being "fake" or snooty, because people were also mistaking her quiet demeanor and shyness for arrogance. This poor woman just wanted to be accepted for who she was. She knew what was wrong, but she didn't know how to fix it.

"Ms. Denise, why can't I transfer the game to the rhyme?" Shah wondered. "I feel like I'm in a state of conscious incompetence."

The answer soon revealed itself. One of my favorite perks of this job is getting to know people on a much deeper level than the usual client/professional relationship. I get them to talk so that I can listen for vocal tics and habits. But I also want to learn as much as I can about the human being sitting before me. I don't interrogate so much as gently probe, sharing details about myself to establish a level of comfort and trust so that we can go deeper into the archives of their lives, which almost always reveal the root causes of their vocal issues.

Through the natural course of conversation, I learned that the dichotomy between the outside and inside of her life went all the way back to childhood.

Public and Private Personas

Shah, a native of California, came from a prominent family in the track and field sports world. She and her siblings were raised in an extremely competitive environment by a protective father. Both parents were highly accomplished, pillars of the community who were admired and respected. And they expected nothing less from their children, whom they raised to be reflections of their own vaunted public images.

"Our parents were controlling, but they wanted the best for us," Shah recalled.

But *their* best and *Shah's* best didn't necessarily align. Shah was naturally outgoing as a little girl, but her father began to impose restrictions on the way she could express herself as she approached womanhood. One could even say he put a muzzle on her. Despite their public image, her parents' relationship was volatile, and it was not a happy home. They underwent a difficult divorce, but heaven forbid anyone outside the family discover this fact—hence the strict rules and micromanaging.

As a child, Shah wrote plays and loved to act, often appearing in school productions, but her parents put an end to that when she entered middle school because, they told her, that's what "fast girls" do. Shah wasn't permitted to do a monologue for a musical, although she was allowed to play clarinet because it meant she would not have to speak.

But even her musicality was frowned upon. Shah's parents

insisted she concentrate on her academics, particularly science, instead. So she put her head down and studied, presenting her findings on various scientific projects and even winning a 4-H award. She continued to write poetry in secret, once even sneaking out to perform at a poetry slam. But she kept that artistic side hidden from her father while she hit every other achievement milestone, graduating as her high school's valedictorian and with departmental honors from UCLA.

She moved to New York, where she soon got regular bookings as a model. Even though she'd grown up feeling like the "ugly duckling" in her family, Shah was catapulted to the top of her industry and became the face of national and international brands like Clairol, Sean John, and Nike. This brought her financial independence from her father and a chance to carve her own path, although the irony of taking on another "silent role" was not lost on a young woman who lives for language and self-expression.

"In modeling," she told me, "you shut up, you don't eat, and you look pretty. You're encouraged to never grow up or have a full sentence spoken out of your mouth."

But Shah could not have been two-dimensional if she tried. She caught the attention of producers, who urged her to try acting. With the support of her loving fiancé, she started auditioning and nabbed several roles in B movies, television, and theater. The problem was that Shah wasn't tapping her full potential, and she knew it. As much as she wanted to, she wasn't sharing of herself. In the limited parts she got, she was acting out whatever people projected onto her.

"The residual effects of being silent were heavier than I imagined," Shah told me.

Before we met in person, she committed herself to doing the daily exercises on my MP3 recording. With the typical self-discipline of an athlete, Shah dedicated herself to the practice knowing that doing the work would eventually lead to a transformation. But the articulation and vocal warm-up exercises made her self-conscious.

"Even in my solitude, I felt embarrassed," Shah recalled, although she forced herself to practice in the car during those long commutes through LA traffic.

It worked. In general conversation, her voice was resonant and rich. But acting—giving herself over to the lines of a script or a play—was another matter. That's where I felt the cognitive dissonance between her voice and the beautiful soul that was aching to express itself. The trauma caused by years of repressing her creativity froze her. She could not break the pattern of allowing others to dominate or project onto her, as if she were a blank canvas. But the solution, as always, was the breath.

Feel the Warmth

Our work together focused on connecting her voice to the breath. Shah needed to think of breath in an entirely new context. Some athletes are trained to use the tensing of certain muscle groups as a source of power; such was not the case with Shah. As a sprinter, she learned very early that relaxation and sustained breath equal speed. She now needed to approach breath as a tool for her artistry.

I invited her to use her mind's eye.

"Picture yourself in a vat of chocolate, and feel the warmth enveloping you . . ."

That didn't quite work, so we tried something else.

"Imagine yourself on the side of a mountain, and it's gently raining vibrant, energetic drops of light down on you . . ."

Now we were cooking.

"Feel the healing warmth of the sun caressing your rib cage . . ."

Because Shah began working on her voice weeks before we

met, I immediately saw a rhythm of deep, diaphragmatic breaths. So I moved right away into vocalizing and had her breathe in through the mouth and release the gentle fricative sound "z" over the tip of her tongue four times, then breathe in through the mouth again and release the smooth nasal sound "m" on her lips four times. Finally, Shah breathed in through the mouth and released the combined sounds "zm" four times. We continued building on the breath-voice connection by adding a single vowel sound, "ma ma ma ma ma ma." Next came a word, then two words, then whole phrases, and finally thoughts, all fueled by the breath. "We are the music makers . . . and we are the dreamers of dreams . . . wandering by lone sea breakers . . . and sitting by desolate streams . . ."

At first Shah did not feel that this powerful affirmation belonged to her. But with each inhalation she was owning it. I could see the expression of wonder on her face as she began to feel the resonance in her chest and along her rib cage. Those deep, fluid, easy breaths animated her and gave her the energy to use her voice in a mellifluous way. By taking the time and giving herself permission to breathe, she was able to slow down and find the many shades of color that had been in her voice all along. Breath was the key that opened her locked self, allowing her to become the powerful actor, and woman, she was meant to be.

No longer content to be the understudy or stay behind the scenes, she now has the confidence to go for the most challenging lead roles. As I write this, Shah has just been accepted into the summer program at the Royal Academy of Dramatic Art (RADA) in England. She recently wrote to me, excitedly letting me know that she'd auditioned for the prestigious Antaeus Theatre Company and Academy in Los Angeles. She chose to audition with a monologue from the role of Viola in Shakespeare's *Twelfth Night*. Playing the role of someone who disguises herself as a man was quite a leap from the one-line, walk-on parts of the past.

"[Actor] Kitty Swink was blown away, and found my use of

voice, switching between the male and female characters (and the feelings of humor and charm to empathy and remorse), impressive. They found my ideas and interpretation of Viola were fresh. She personally offered me a membership to the Academy. This is a great step on my road to RADA and beyond!"

Learning to breathe and adding breath to voice was the breakthrough for Shah. It helped her recognize what was going on deep within her psyche. She now recognizes that her vocal discord was the result of years of silencing and emotional trauma. She continues to draw on our breath and vocal work to keep her voice authentic. But she also uses these tools to check in with herself emotionally. If she has difficulty drawing out certain vowel sounds (as in the words "myyyyy" or "iiiiii"), she realizes there's someone or something in her life that's making her repress her true self.

The Sucker Punch

Throughout the years, whenever I've experienced trauma, I've been able to use my deep-breathing practice to get me through. I've already shared how it powered me through Terry's close brush with death and gave me the strength to fight for his full recovery. Long before that life-altering event, the breath also gave me the strength to get through the most devastating diagnosis of my life.

Back in the early nineties, my sister and I auditioned for a pop band on a whim. We didn't get the gig, not that I was seriously interested in traveling the world, exhausting my instrument for music I didn't particularly care for. I am a huge jazz enthusiast in addition to opera—pop music is hardly ever found on my playlist unless it's Whitney Houston. But I was recently divorced, raising a preschooler, and was just looking for a chance to dress up, have a day out, and escape from the daily routine. We had a blast in that Manhattan recording studio. After the session, a tall, dark, and handsome music producer with the most stunning pair of black suede shoes I'd ever seen respectfully asked for my phone number. When I declined, he handed me his card.

Six months later, I got up the nerve to call him. What ensued was a beautiful romance. We never married, but for the six years we were together he became my mentor, my best friend, and my lover. He introduced me to an incredible lifestyle, but most of all, he introduced me to the world of business and shared his business acumen with me. Then he died.

Until you've experienced the shock of a sudden loss, you'll never know how it can shift your foundation. It left a gaping hole in my heart and a sense of powerlessness. In addition to losing the man I loved, the world I'd known had been turned upside down. As "just the girlfriend," I was left on the periphery of his funeral arrangements, frozen out of the communal grieving process. All the objects of beauty that I had gifted him over the course of our relationship were divided up among his surviving family members. Even a small memento of our love together might have given me closure. But I got nothing.

Well, no, not quite nothing.

Several months after his death, I decided to get serious about creating some security for myself and my eight-year-old son. I became obsessed with financial planning, and I applied for life insurance in case—God forbid—anything should happen to me, leaving my child without resources or support. Part of this process involved a full physical exam. As the weeks went by and not knowing what they were, I threw away the unopened registered letters in the mail notifying me of the results of my blood work. Then, on a blustery New York winter afternoon, just as I was about to pick up my fourth grader from his corner bus stop, my phone rang.

The young rep on the other end of the call glibly told me that I was HIV-positive and, because it was already Friday afternoon, I should seek medical attention no later than the following

Monday. The news hit me like a sucker punch, squeezing all the breath out of me. Then my mind started racing. I didn't feel sick. I hadn't had so much as a cold in several months. I did have a sinus infection the previous spring. Was that a symptom? How was I going to make it through the weekend without going crazy before I could speak to my doctor? How was I going to keep it together for my son?

In that instant, I understood that my confidant, lover, and best friend for over six years had not in fact died of a heart attack, as "his people" alleged, and that it was AIDS-related pneumonia. I had witnessed his health decline, but I never for a moment assumed that it was the dreaded virus so many of my high school buddies had succumbed to. All at once I was overcome with a sense of betrayal, anger, profound sadness, and fear. The weeks following, I would learn that I was just twenty T cells shy of full-blown AIDS. I was at death's door and hadn't a single indication.

Staying in the Stillness

The shock of learning about my HIV diagnosis rendered me silent. There simply were no words. At first, I found myself a crying, hyperventilating mess on the floor. Then I started to breathe, deeply and intentionally.

This has become my habitual response to a crisis. Instead of relying on the power of my voice, I turn to an inner voice; that place where God lives. It's important to recognize when to simply be quiet, because that's when your inner voice becomes stronger. You've got to honor those pauses and periods, because sometimes not saying anything is as important as saying something. It's the rest in music that gives light and energy to the notes. And the small space of silence between statements is where the breath lives. So I instinctively go into that quiet space, inhaling and exhaling until I've gathered my strength. I don't pick up the phone and call friends or family. I press PAUSE.

Staying in that stillness and focusing on my breathing empowered me to finally reach out to loved ones, communicate my needs, and then find the support I needed to take back control of my health and my life. All I wanted was to live another eight years, until I was fifty, long enough to see Terry off to college. God has given me so much more. I am now in my sixties, healthy, and happy, and my viral load is completely undetectable.

The Retrigger

The thing about trauma is that it stays with us, taking on different shapes depending on where we are and what we're experiencing on our life's journey. Sometimes it doesn't fully manifest until years later, when something happens to retrigger the pain all at once.

That's what happened to Mary Langford. It had been more than a decade since I worked with her, and I assumed she'd gone back to her life as a literary assistant, helping Vidal Sassoon, Sidney Sheldon, and other celebrities with their literary ambitions while occasionally taking bit parts in film or on the stage. We had lost touch until about a year ago, when she shared that she'd only recently recovered from a full-blown psychotic episode.

In 2011, at fifty-three, Mary had lost her beloved mother. Grief-stricken and spiraling emotionally downward, she went back home to seek help. Sadly, the move led to her cycling in and out of psychiatric wards for the next six years. Mary was catatonic, unable to function mentally or physically. Convinced that the FBI was bugging her apartment, she was diagnosed with paranoid schizophrenia.

About two years into her breakdown, Mary returned to Los Angeles with one thing in mind: to take her car and drive herself over a

cliff. She did just that, falling two hundred feet, and somehow survived. But as she recovered physically, trying to make her way back
to some semblance of normalcy, her voice became nonexistent.

"I lost the ability to articulate words; it was all I could do to
moan and groan," Mary told me.

Her voice was missing, but it wasn't gone. On one of her dark-
est days, she thought back to that moment we shared on the
beach together. She remembered how her voice sounded at its
richest and most resonant, and she clung to the hope that it could
be so again.

It would take some time. Mary's road to recovery was a long
one, but eventually a former client of hers reached out and offered her a lifeline. The author, Meryl Hershey Beck, needed help
researching and editing a particularly challenging book project
about parents who'd lost their children, called *Loss, Survive,
Thrive*. It was Mary's job to tease out the tragic yet ultimately
hopeful stories of twenty-eight parents who've lived through the
unimaginable. As she began interviewing these folks and learning their stories, something extraordinary happened: "When it
occurred to me that I had to be the voice for these people and
tell their stories, my own voice finally came back, and it sounded
better than ever!"

The Voice for Others

Mary found her true calling, not as an actress, but as a writer. Before moving to Hollywood, she'd trained as a court stenographer,
taking down peoples' truths word for word. Like Shah, for most
of her life she'd been silenced on so many levels, allowing the
narratives of others to be imposed on her. Finding her voice empowered her to tell her own truth, taking the trauma she endured
and turning it into strength. It made her the perfect advocate not
just for herself, but for others who suffer.

Today she does crisis intervention training with the police, teaching them what's helpful for people in a state of active psychosis. Mary has plenty to say on this subject and does so with forceful eloquence. She also speaks through the National Alliance on Mental Illness for a series appropriately called "In Our Own Voice."

For too long, Mary thought of herself as little more than a note taker. But when she found her voice and the breath to power it, she discovered that she was so much more. She was a storyteller.

~~~~~~

Speak It!

Establishing relaxed breathing, the way the body was meant to breathe in oxygen and release carbon dioxide, is essential to your vocal power. But you may be holding on to something huge, like past traumas, or simply the minor stresses of the day. Whatever it is constricting your body and preventing you from taking full advantage of a deep breath, no matter how large or small, it shows up in the body as tension. And tension is not your friend! So, let's begin with ways to quiet the mind and relax.

Lying on your back on the floor, imagine that you are lying on the warm, crystal-like sands of a Caribbean beach. Notice the sunlight as it sparkles on the turquoise water. Feel the coconut suntan oil glide onto your skin. Hear the waves as they gently lap onto the shore, and smell the jasmine as it hangs in the humid air. Let the flavors of the tropics—the honeyed sweetness of mango and the refreshing tartness of passion fruit dissolve onto your tongue.

Really allow your imagination to go there. Imagine the sounds, the colors, the light breeze, and the warmth of the sun. Feel the beams of sunlight on each isolated portion of your body, from your head to the tips of your toes. Feel the heat from those rays melt away tension. Feel the solid mass of tension become liquid and flow into the ground beneath you.

As this heavy solid melts into liquid form and flows away, feel a light, airy breeze flowing through your body and dissolving any residual tension. You are feeling lighter, and you are also becoming Lighter . . . Brighter . . . Remain here for a few moments, basking in the sunlight. Then slowly roll over onto one side and come up into a sitting position.

Remain sitting for a moment or two, and wiggle your upper body to ensure that you are still relaxed. Begin to come to a standing position by hanging your upper body over from the waist and slowly rolling up as if you were stacking one vertebra on top of the other. Your head should come up last. Once standing, vigorously but gently shake out. Now settle in again . . . Take a deep breath . . . You are on your way . . .

....

~~~~~~~~~

....

PART III

Voice

Who hasn't felt misunderstood? Do you notice that people often misinterpret what you are saying? Well, it may not be what you are saying but how you are saying it.

An expressive voice is commanding and demands respect. Who wouldn't want James Earl Jones's delivery of "This, is CNN!"

There isn't a single Oscar-winning actor for whom voice has not played a huge part in the crafting of their characters. I had the pleasure of working with Jessica Chastain when she was at Juilliard. She was always a passionate young woman with social activism at the core of her art. During her four years of training, she developed a versatile vocal instrument to support her brilliant and varied character work as an actress, and she became a leader for social causes such as gender equality.

So, are you standing on the precipice of being a champion for important causes but find that your voice does not match your passion, knowledge, and determination? Look no further than these next chapters. Find your voice, and the platform will appear.

5

Hear What *They're* Hearing

....

I like hearing myself talk. It is one of my greatest
pleasures. I often have long conversations all by
myself, and I am so clever that I sometimes don't
understand a single word of what I am saying.

—OSCAR WILDE

I was catching up with a childhood friend who was in the habit of loudly clearing his throat every ten seconds, or so it seemed. Since our visits with each other are sporadic, I thought he was just getting over a cold. But I soon realized, no, it wasn't a cold, and it was driving me crazy!

That sound sets my teeth on edge. Each time he did it, punctuating his sentences with a loud, dry hack, the mother in me wanted to say, "Stop that, sweetheart!" But I didn't. This was not a child I was raising. Trying to be nonchalant about it, I offered him cough drops. Once or twice I suggested he drink some water. He never got the hint. Then, with love, I offered some suggestions for clearing that pesky tickle in the back of his throat, including an ENT specialist referral. I was genuinely concerned because that chronic sound could be a matter of health and personal well-being.

"Something of this nature should always be addressed by a medical professional," I told him. "It could be the result of a larger issue and remedied with the right treatment." With all of my suggestions, he never checked into it and I finally gave up.

Contrary to what many might assume, I am not a vocal snob. I am as taken as the next girl with the rich and mellifluous bass tones of James Earl Jones, Morgan Freeman, Don LaFontaine, and Keith David. When I hear Dennis Haysbert in the Allstate commercials asking, "Are you in good hands?" I want to run out and buy car insurance. But the constant "ribbit, ribbit" of a toad in the throat would grate on anyone's nerves and, thankfully, there is a happy medium.

Clear the Path

When you misuse your voice so consistently that people start paying more attention to the quirk rather than to what you are saying—whether it is a high pitch, chronic throat clearing, vocal fry, vocal nasality, or a lisp—it needs to be addressed by a voice and speech professional, a speech pathologist, or a medical doctor. These are vocal distractions that can drive your listeners to distraction. Beyond being annoying, something like California "upspeak," in which the voice goes up in inflection at the end of a sentence, can be perceived as ditzy.

It's unfortunate that women can be so easily judged and dismissed this way. Some might even argue that their voices are being policed and that women should not have to change their voices to suit society, especially as what was once gender- and region-specific Valley Girl speech has now, thanks to social media, become socially and culturally pervasive. That said, your listener's subconscious reaction to these vocal distractions is what it is, so persisting with them can do you a huge disservice.

You may not be aware of these tics. If you are, you may even believe that there is nothing you can do about them. It's just your voice, to be accepted, with all its little idiosyncrasies. Wrong! These habits do *not* define you. Your true voice has nothing to do with the irritating distractions that affect so many. Bad vocal habits and compulsions can be changed with awareness and training. The path of communication between you and your listener can be decluttered so that you won't be dismissed or discounted.

People who clear their throats constantly assume it's phlegm or some sort of debris that got stuck back there and needs to be dislodged. However, when the tickling sensation is not medically related, it occurs when our voices resonate too far in the back of the throat. This vocal misplacement is due to a tight jaw or tension in the back of the tongue trapping the voice in the back of the instrument and causing a tickling sensation. This excess wear and tear can be incredibly damaging to the vocal cords, potentially causing irritation and swelling and creating a vicious cycle.

The solution is to release the jaw, relax the back of the tongue, and get the voice farther forward in the front of the face for greater nasal resonance. Here's how to do it:

- Begin by gently massaging your face with the tips of your fingers, concentrating on the jaw and the nasal region.

- With the heels of both your palms, gently stroke open the jaw. This will begin to release the jaw and activate the facial muscles. As you become aware of the released jaw and relaxed facial muscles, gently bring your lips together but keep your teeth apart. The jaw will be released with your mouth closed. Keep massaging gently.

- Now breathe in through the mouth and release on a sustained "mmmmmm" sound. Make sure that the sound is resonating in the front of your face and in the open space of your mouth even now that the lips are together; in other words, keep your lips together, but teeth apart. Do this several times.

- Add a slow, slightly exaggerated chewing motion to the sound as you maintain a relaxed, upright posture, if standing, or an elongated form, if lying down. Remember to breathe in through the mouth before you utter each "mmmmmm" sound.

- Do this for one to two minutes at a time.

Done properly, this will result in nasal resonance to the voice, not a nasal quality. It merely helps project vibration closer to the front of the instrument, balancing depth and bravado so that the voice can be sustained.

As always, I am going to give you several more exercises to practice at the end of this chapter. These exercises address an assortment of overlapping vocal distractions that go back to the breath, which—as we now know—is a crucial component of the effortless release of voice.

Sizzling Bacon

As much as throat clearing is my Achilles' heel, the vocal fry is a fast-spreading vocal distraction that exasperates me. I have no interest in keeping up with the Kardashians, because I can't bear to listen to that creaky, glottal sound popularized by Kim and her sisters, as well as Zooey Deschanel, Britney Spears, Paris Hilton . . . you get the idea.

Vocal fry occurs when your tone gets trapped in the back of the throat. When you breathe in through the mouth to speak, your vocal cords or vocal folds open naturally as the breath passes in from your upper airway into your trachea and lungs. As the breath is released out through the vocal folds, it produces vibration or sound. The cords or folds should never touch during the vibration process (that is, while speaking or singing). But when you affect a constricted sound, your voice essentially sits in the back of the throat without breath to create the opening and flow of vibration/voice through the vocal cords, resulting in an unpleasant, frying sound, particularly at the end of thoughts. Vocal fry is not just hard on the listener; it can potentially cause vocal nodes or calluses on the vocal folds for the speaker over an extended period of time.

It's almost as if the offenders want us to think they just got out of bed. Enamored of their own husky timbre, they languidly draaaag ooout eeeach vowel sound.

This vocal tic—an affectation once the domain of young women from Southern California—has gone viral thanks in part to its prevalence in entertainment and social media, as well as certain societal pressures and norms. One 2011 study found that two-thirds of American college women were doing it, and now men and women of many different demographics and nationalities seem to be guilty of this oddly pervasive vocal tic. So, again, it's also a guy thing.

Many young girls consciously cultivate that frying sound because it affects a laid-back, "too cool to be bothered" vibe. It's associated with being upwardly mobile and on trend. One of my recent clients, Montana Giacci, a lovely twenty-year-old aspiring actress who hangs out with the Beverly Hills "it" crowd, explained it to me this way: "Vocal fry is a cool, aloof way of showing other girls that you are detached and really above it all."

Candidly, it comes across as vapid. A study by the Public Library of Science (PLOS.org) had seven young adult women and seven young adult men record the sentence, "Thank you for considering me for this opportunity," which is what one might reasonably expect to hear at the end of a job interview. Each made two recordings—one in a normal voice and one in the vocal fry. The nonprofit researcher then surveyed a large sample of American adults, who overwhelmingly interpreted vocal fry negatively, perceiving its users as "less competent, less educated, less trustworthy, less attractive and less hirable." This response was even more pronounced toward the female voices. Of course it was! Women have got so much more to fight against, particularly when we're competing in the workplace.

Are You Sure?

Upspeak, or uptalk, has a similar detracting effect on an individual's perceived intelligence and credibility. When I first moved to California two decades ago, I introduced myself to a young receptionist at the real estate office.

"Hi, I'm Denise Woods," I said.

"I'm Ashley?" she responded.

"I don't know, are you?" I replied, genuinely dumbfounded.

I wasn't trying to be cute, I promise. On New York's Lower East Side, in Harlem and Hell's Kitchen where I had lived, the locals tend to be forthright. We never asked a question unless we really wanted to know the answer. I had never come across this strange vocal habit, and it floored me to discover how pervasive it was in my newly adopted home.

So, what's going on here? It's all in the inflection.

Inflection refers to the modulation of the voice in speaking and singing—a change in pitch or tone. There is a myriad of vocal inflections or tones in the speaking voice, which I will discuss more thoroughly in later chapters, but for the purpose of addressing upspeak, it's necessary to understand the difference between a downward inflection and an upward inflection.

A slight upward inflection occurs when you raise the pitch of your voice on a particular word or phrase to indicate to your listener that you have not completed the thought. A full upward inflection should occur only when asking a question. A downward inflection occurs when you lower the pitch of your voice at the end of a statement, which indicates completion but can also communicate confidence, authority, and certainty. Trading a downward inflection for an upward inflection not only turns a statement into a question; it also corrupts the affirming power of your true voice. You have just traded your strength and authority for questioning and indecisiveness. I find it disheartening to hear a seemingly trivial vocal trait afflict an entire generation of bright young people who are inadvertently coming across as clueless. They deserve better for themselves.

Private School Jungle

Upspeak began with young white women living in affluent neighborhoods of Los Angeles and the neighboring San Fernando Valley, but thanks to the popularity of California-based social media influencers, it now pervades swathes of the US population, which includes people of diverse genders and different socioeconomic and cultural backgrounds. Of course, we can't entirely blame the Golden State. This inflection pattern also plagues Canadians, the British, and Australians in varying degrees. As we become more global, so does our speech. Either way, the net effect is a perceived confusion or lack of conviction.

But that is far from being the case, according to Montana, the budding Gen Z actress: "I went to a highly competitive, cutthroat, all-girls boarding school. To be in that world, pressured to conform, fit in, or have a strong point of view, left you feeling constantly insecure. We talked fast and with an uplift, because if you slowed down or indicated that you were finished speaking by going down in your voice, you would never find your way back into a conversation."

In an odd way, these girls are trying desperately to establish dominance.

"We would do whatever it took to be heard," Montana explained to me. "Whoever talked loudest, fastest, or highest won the day. In that setting I rarely got to finish a sentence. And God forbid you should ever pause to take a breath!"

Perhaps in Montana's rarefied private school jungle, upspeak was a tool for survival so that the "mean" girls didn't eat you alive. But I promise you, it will backfire in the boardroom. Imagine if you were an entrepreneur seeking funding for your product. After all the time and effort spent building your business, you would be leaving potential investors with the impression that you were somehow unsure of yourself and the vision you have for your new company. That question mark embedded in your words would almost certainly affect their perception of you and make them question your confidence. It's what continually happened to Clare, whom we met in chapter 3, who has been battling both upspeak *and* vocal fry.

The Waterfall

There's a solution for upspeak, as there is for all vocal issues. I told Montana, and countless other young people I've worked with, to begin by thinking of a waterfall: Have your words start high, at the top of the falls, then cascade down into the river below. Since the vocal upswing occurs on the last word of a statement, let's focus on that. If it's a multisyllabic word like "transportation," the upspeaker typically lowers the second-to-last syllable of the word, "tay," before raising the pitch on the final syllable, "tion." If it's a monosyllabic word like "car," the upspeaker starts low, then raises the pitch on the final vowel or diphthong sound.

Now remember Newton's third law of motion? For every action, there is an equal and opposite reaction. What goes up, must come down! So, reverse upspeak to downspeak by raising the pitch of each syllable that precedes the final syllable, then lower the pitch on the final syllable.

Rest assured, you'll get there. Montana did. In fact, hers was one of my fastest and most dramatic turnarounds to date. I saw a profound difference after just one session. Having lived around the world, including Australia and Europe, with a Polish mother and an Italian father, she thought her inconsistent dialect and occasional mispronunciations were her main vocal issues until I pointed out the fry and upspeaking. In fact, the exposure to different languages and cultures, along with her musical training as a singer and pianist, worked to her advantage. Just as quickly as Montana absorbed the Valley Girl vocal tics of her private school, she unlearned them. In addition to a few of these exercises, all I had to do was help her hear herself to give her back her true voice.

"I never really liked the way those girls around me talked anyway," Montana told me during our second session together. "I much prefer my own style of expression."

I've come across a number of driven and intelligent young women who have unconsciously absorbed these ways of speaking because it was what they picked up from their peers. When they really heard themselves on a recording or voice mail, they were devastated. That's when they came to me.

Although it can be hard on the ego, I strongly recommend that you follow my instructions in chapter 1 and record yourself reading a literary excerpt at the beginning of this journey, and again after a fourteen-day daily regimen of the exercises outlined in this book. You will be pleasantly surprised. Bringing these vocal habits into your awareness is a huge step toward breaking them, and that's where recording yourself can be useful. Quite often, what starts out as intentional becomes pathological. We get stuck in a vocal groove we neither desired nor realized. But we can always find our way back to our best voice, full of range and resonance. We are *always* in control.

Again, many of these vocal distractions can be resolved with the relaxation and breathing techniques I gave you at the end of chapters 2 and 3. These exercises will help you de-stress your instrument and establish a rhythmic flow of breath in and voice out. Once your breath capacity increases, you can concentrate on developing head and chest resonance, because that's what enables the voice to come forth without strain. The resulting vocal resonance gives the voice a fuller, warmer, and more amplified sound. It essentially becomes your inner microphone. The goal is to balance the two types of resonance—head/nasal resonance and chest resonance—so that your vocal quality is unobstructed, dulcet, and smooth.

A voice that is trapped in the back of the throat does not lend itself to compelling storytelling because of the inherent tension and the inability to shape the sounds of speech articulately and effectively. Yet the area in and around the back of the throat, where the epiglottis, larynx, vocal folds, and trachea exist, should not be associated with vocal production because the brain controls those functions. We often think of the back of the throat as integral to voice, and to some degree it is. But it's not as if you can reach back there and massage your vocal cords! The brain controls the breath that travels through the voice box, causing the vocal folds to vibrate, essentially turning breath into sound.

However, there is a simple fix, in addition to relaxing and effortlessly releasing the breath, that will help bring your voice farther forward. It starts with sending your attention to that often-overlooked part of vocal production: the front of your face.

Bring It Forward

Stop concerning yourself with the vocal organs located in the back of the throat, and focus instead on the origin of voice, which is breath. The breathing apparatus—your ribs and diaphragm—we will refer to as Point A. Now turn your attention toward the front of your face: the lips, the nasal and sinus cavity, even the forehead and temples. We will refer to this as Point B.

Start by gently massaging the nasal cavity right above the nostrils, as well as your cheeks, the sides of the nose, your lips, forehead, and temples. Use gentle, circular motions. This will bring awareness to that part of the face, releasing the tension and activating the resonance that can exist in that area. Now breathe in through the mouth (the origin of this process is Point A). Release a warm "mmmmmm" sound, feeling vibration on the lips, nose, and cheeks (Point B). You should feel absolutely nothing between Point A and Point B.

As you release the "mmmmmm" sound, gently massage and activate the muscles in the face, feeling the voice reverberating farther forward in your face and on your lips. Now gently chew with your lips together for a few seconds. Finally, circle the tip of your tongue inside your mouth between your lips and teeth. You can even visualize your voice inside a comic strip bubble in the space in front of you. Drawing a mental image outside of yourself will also help eliminate vocal fry, because you are effectively thinking past those organs in the back of the throat. You are now moving easily from Point A (breath) to point B (facial resonance).

Taking the Reins

It's not often that friends and family will tell you what they're hearing. They may not even be able to articulate what's wrong, especially when the root cause of the vocal distraction is not as simple as the examples I just described. However, public figures like actors and broadcasters have the advantage of directors and producers whose job it is to point out what needs to be fixed.

Early on in Soledad O'Brien's national network career, it became clear to her producers that her voice wasn't matching her talent. Back then, in 1997, I was still living in New York, teaching on the faculty of Juilliard, and doing quite a bit of work for *NBC Nightly News* with on-air talent whom they deemed to have the potential to be among the nation's top broadcasters—folks like Norah O'Donnell and Chris Hansen. Soledad, a Harvard graduate who'd just moved from MSNBC, where she covered Silicon Valley, to begin anchoring on *Weekend Today*, was one of these television journalists. Whip-smart and intrepid, she did her research and knew how to respond in the moment and follow up with probing questions and insightful commentary. But, at times, her voice did not reflect her skill level.

Speaking in too high a vocal register is one of the most common vocal distractions. Her pitch would rise as she rushed out a tsunami of words. This happens to some of the most intelligent people, particularly more cerebral individuals who have a lot they want to communicate. But much of the emotion and significance of what Soledad was saying was getting lost as her information-packed sentences tumbled out and the listener struggled to keep up.

Soledad, an avid equestrian, likened it to horseback riding. She'd break into a gallop when she needed to maintain a trot, because she wasn't in control of the animal. It was most obvious when Soledad was speaking during a live shot versus when she was in a studio, tracking her stories. She sounded like two completely different people. In the live shot, caught up in the emotion of what she was seeing and hearing, it was like "a long ramble down a hill." In the studio, reading from her script, she had more control, but the pacing was off. She sounded a little flat and lacked the knowledge of operative word stress. That, combined with a slight Long Island twang, was holding her back from the big leagues.

Soledad knew exactly where she wanted to go. She recognized that broadcasters like Keith Morrison on *Dateline* had mastered a perfect cadence to their storytelling. They matched the emotion to the important or operative words and phrases, and they made it all seem effortless, like an Olympic rider on the back of a show horse, leaping over the fence while loosely hanging on to the reins, and then coming to a perfect, controlled stop. You never sense that expert broadcasters are white-knuckling it or thinking too hard about a word. They have a subtle command over voice that allows them to hit all the notes, bringing people along by milking each syllable, or not, as they inject the perfect pregnant pause.

"Denise, I know that, at this level, every inch matters," Soledad confided. "I want to bring nuance to my storytelling. I want to be able to work anywhere."

Soledad wanted to go far beyond the generic newsreader's voice to something much more compelling. She wanted to engage her listeners, bringing them along on the journey with her, whether she was speaking about ice fishing in Minnesota, prom dress fashion, or serious breaking news. She wanted her viewers to feel her emotional connection to the story, whether she was viewing a teleprompter, reporting live on camera, or reading from her script back in the studio. She wanted to sound as if she were picking up the phone and describing an important event in her life to one of her beloved parents.

"I need to figure out how to connect to the stories that are in my head and do them justice," Soledad explained when she came to my office at Juilliard. "I want to be authoritative without sounding strident, flailing, overly aggressive, halting, or messy. I need to sync up my mouth with my brain and moderate my voice so that it can be a tool of control."

"I get it, Soledad," I assured her. "You want to be your true self on camera."

Broadcasters are not actors, but they can equally benefit from the imagination. Soledad needed to give herself permission to become more childlike and visceral in her approach to storytelling, especially when she was working inside a studio without the benefit of sensory cues. In fact, her producers contacted me about a story she reported on a burning building. When they played back the live footage, they could feel the sense of urgency and drama in her voice, but it flattened out so much when she supplemented her reporting with studio tracks that it sounded like it belonged to a completely different person. The simple fix was visualization. When she talked about the fire, she had to *see* the fire. She had to imagine herself still standing in front of that inferno, with the fire engines blaring and the rescue workers risking their lives to deliver the occupants of the blazing building to safety.

"If you see it, your viewers will see it," I told her. "The images will color your voice in a completely authentic way."

When Soledad harnessed her imagination, most of the vocal distractions began to fall away. Connecting more viscerally to the images of the story allowed Soledad to slow down, breathe more deeply, have a more mellifluous vocal tone, and instinctively know just the right degree of dramatic emphasis. Even during thoughtful live interviews, where there is a tendency to use words like "um" as placeholders as the speech center of the brain connects to the right words, Soledad's imagination put her in control, allowing her to moderate her voice to put real power into the points she was making.

"Denise, you did it!" Soledad told me at the end of our sessions together. "You got my mouth to slow down; now I'm not blindly hanging on to the reins of a runaway horse!"

Soledad did the work, not me. Again, these transformations don't occur without dedication, practice, and rigor.

All these years later, Soledad still uses visualization techniques and other exercises I gave her, with her own twist. Before she goes on camera, she eats a Snickers bar and takes two shots of espresso before she "wakes up" her mouth with the facial and resonance exercises described in this chapter. Soledad can still be rapid-fire in her delivery—that's just who she is—but it's clear, concise, and on point. Today, she has a signature voice that's recognizable wherever she goes. Soledad was recently boarding a flight at the end of a Caribbean vacation with her young children in tow, no makeup, and her hair up in a scrunchie when the flight attendant exclaimed for all to hear, "I know that voice. You're Soledad O'Brien!"

"It's a blessing and a curse," Soledad later joked.

It's also a career maker.

Deep Dive

In Greg Louganis's case, his voice was a career *re*-maker.

As I mentioned in chapter 3, Greg first came to me following a public speaking disaster, after which his agent decided he needed help. Following the publication of his powerful memoir, he was attempting to launch a corporate and public speaking career, leveraging his experiences as an Olympic gold medalist and pioneering HIV and LGBTQ activist. He had gained much wisdom that would benefit multiple audiences. But Greg had overshared in his talk, wandering down too many paths, going on unfiltered tangents, and leaving precious little to the imagination. He'd gotten too much into his own head and lost his vocal power as a result. It was as if this high-diving icon had found himself splashing around in the shallow end. Meandering without projecting, he was lacking the strong emotional connection to his subject that focus can bring, and the audience felt it. They simply couldn't lock onto what he was trying to say.

I would even go as far as to say that Greg had also lost his voice, but it wasn't due to any physical injury. The root cause was psychological. Beyond the lack of focus, Greg also had a lack of conviction stemming from years of trauma and highs and lows in his life. There was a kind of fatigue at a soul level, as if life had beaten him down. Of course, he wanted to share his truth with the world, and had already done so on the printed page, but vocalizing it in front of a live audience, a room full of strangers, felt daunting.

When we first met, Greg barely spoke above a whisper. But I was instantly drawn to his warmth and vulnerability. Besides our shared love of the theater, we had one important thing in common: we had both been diagnosed HIV-positive back when it was considered a death sentence. We wept as we shared our experiences and discussed how our diagnoses had been transformed from a source of fear and shame to a badge of strength and survival. I was moved by his desire to use his platform to raise awareness and remove the stigma. Our connection was as deep as it was instant, and we talked for hours like two old friends.

I quickly learned that Greg needed a true advocate. His agent had instructed him to seek out a vocal coach, but the first few did not work out. They were trying to make Greg speak with more machismo, so as not to "offend" anyone in the high-paying corporate audiences he would be addressing. When I spoke with his agent on the phone, she asked, "Can you make him sound less gay?" Appalled, I abruptly ended the phone call and told my new BFF, "You need to fire this woman!" He was only too happy to oblige.

Never think you should sound like anyone other than who you are. Greg's natural vocal rhythms and patterns did not have that stereotypical male bravado, but that's not a vocal distraction. You should allow your true self and personality to come out in your voice, however you identify. Yes, clean up issues like nasality and vocal fry to avoid making your listeners uncomfortable. Clear the communication pathway. But if your listeners are uneasy with who you are at your core, it's *their* problem, not yours! Greg's sexual identity was in no way the obstacle to his becoming a powerful speaker. A few people in his professional life, like the agent, were eroding his confidence, making him feel as if he had to pretend to be something he wasn't. That was one of his biggest vocal issues.

The Rule of Threes

Another issue was that Greg has ADHD. His vocal distraction was being caused in part by distraction itself. As someone with a different way of learning, his workaround had always been to use visualization techniques. Greg already understood how to use his imagination to color his voice. As a musical theater performer, he'd learned how to associate an image with a verse from a song. Indeed, he'd even used a system of mental color coding to remember lines from his one-man play. But for some reason, these techniques had not carried over to his public speaking.

Our work together involved building a structure around his story, with a beginning, middle, and end. I taught Greg the "rule of threes." In speaking, as well as in writing, it's best to stick to three examples so that the point doesn't get lost in a list of details.

He also needed to zero in on three key themes or messages, because generally an audience doesn't have the listening capacity to process more. Good, distraction-free speaking is not unlike good writing. To make his talks more memorable, he had to land his three points with power, saving all the color and detail to support his main points and drive them home. This careful edit would allow him to take a much deeper dive into his subject matter, engaging his mind in a way that would animate his speaking voice and rivet the attention of his listeners.

Gradually, we developed his story with the three main takeaways that would serve as a framework that could be adapted or tweaked to any given audience. Greg would not and should not have to repeat the same stories the exact same way over and over again. Doing so would not allow his authentic voice to come through. But having a solid structure would give him the facility to switch up anecdotes, tailoring each joke, analogy, or description to the occasion. As a man with many passions, he needed to be free to extemporize, although being able to feel the structure anchored him and gave him the confidence to focus on what was truly important to get across in any given moment.

Of course, we did other work together: breathing, relaxation, and articulation exercises, and all the other steps necessary to relax and strengthen his instrument. But knowing he had a clear road map gave him that confidence he'd been missing. Then, able to fully match his voice to his story, putting color in every utterance, Greg started booking speaking engagements more regularly.

On the Pulse

One of Greg's most memorable speeches took place in June 2016, a few days after the mass shooting at Pulse, the gay nightclub in Orlando, Florida. Greg was invited to speak in front of hundreds of managers and executives at the banking giant HSBC. He had a beautiful speech written, linking his experiences as an athlete to the workplace, talking about leadership development, team building, and the important elements of a productive corporate environment. But this time he set it aside. It was there in his back pocket, just in case, but Greg would not pass up the opportunity to honor those slain young LGBTQ men and women.

"Denise, I couldn't ignore this," he told me afterward. "I talked about the challenges I faced growing up as an LGBTQ youth, the pain of not being accepted for who I was, and how relevant those experiences remain today."

The audience was moved to tears. Greg had found his authentic voice through the empathy he felt for the victims and their families. He took his listeners on that journey with him. At the end of that speech, the Pulse shooting was no longer just another news event to these executives. They *felt* what Greg felt, to their core.

Greg went on to help raise more than $10 million for the families of the forty-nine people killed and those who were injured. In recognition of this, he was honored the following year with the Voice for Equality award by Equality Florida.

It was a full-circle moment. Like so many great gay athletes of his generation, Greg spent much of his career living in silence, unable to share who he truly was with the world for fear of what it would do to his career. When, in an act of great courage, he revealed his sexuality publicly in 1994, he lost out on many lucrative endorsements. Despite his unbroken diving record, the earlier rumors that he was gay had kept him off the Wheaties box until 2016, more than three decades after his first gold medal. And now Greg is one of the most powerful voices for so many young people who've suffered from discrimination and violence for being out and proud. No longer encumbered with self-doubt, he can unleash the full power of his imagination into his speech, coloring each word with just the right shades of sadness, outrage, compassion, humor, love . . .

What ultimately set his voice free and cleared it of obstacles was self-acceptance. He needed to hear he was more than good enough, to feel completely comfortable with how he identified in that moment, and to allow himself to dial in to a frequency all his own.

"Denise, you heard me for who I was and allowed me to be real," Greg shared with me a few years later. "You unlocked my voice, giving me permission to find that joy and trust in my heart and my soul."

~~~~~~

Speak It!—Part I

With the exception of upspeaking, which is covered in the bonus section that follows, all the vocal issues that I have discussed in this chapter can be easily improved with the same series of exercises because they are similar in nature. Addressing them sooner rather than later can potentially prevent the need for medical solutions. Vocal fry and the persistent clearing of the throat are a result of the voice lingering in the back of the throat, sometimes causing a tickle. Due to a lack of breath and a lack of nasal resonance, the voice will either settle back or escape into the nasal region. Hence, the clearing of the throat, vocal fry, and nasalization.

Breath (as discussed in the previous chapter) is a crucial component of the effortless release of voice. However, if you lack awareness of nasal resonance or a sense of vibration in the front of your face, you will resort to regional or cultural habits like those we are discussing. The following exercises will help resolve these issues. First, follow these steps:

1. **Breathe in through the mouth and blow out through the lips, causing them to flutter.** Blowing out through the lips gives you a visceral and visual sense of the voice resonating

there as opposed to the back of the throat. It also raises the soft palate in the upper back of the mouth, creating more space for the voice to be released.

2. **Do not add voice just yet. Simply release the breath with fluttering lips for the duration of that breath.** If you're finding it difficult for your lips to flutter, it is solely related to the amount of tension in the lips. Gently continue to try until they become more relaxed and you're able to sustain the lip flutter over a continuous blowing out of the breath.

3. **Breathe in through the mouth and add voice to the lip flutter**, easily going up and down your vocal register. Avoid going too high into a falsetto voice or too low, which potentially pulls the voice back into the throat. Be very gentle.

4. **Now breathe in through the mouth and gently release the voice on a vibrant, continuous "mmmmmm" sound.** Make sure that your jaw is released and that the entire body of your tongue is relaxed on the floor of your mouth.

5. **Place your fingers onto your mouth and feel the tickling on your lips.** Move your fingers to your nasal passages and sinuses; gently massage while feeling the vibration there. Do this five to seven times.

Okay, let's take it up a notch. The poetic passage that follows was chosen because of its vast imaginative and emotional landscape. We've discussed breath; we've warmed up the voice with an awareness of vocal placement and resonance. Now let's add the imagination. The impact of the written word on your voice lies in your ability to imagine the poet's thoughts and emotions. All great poets use the phonetic sounds of language to convey deep meaning. These euphonious verses, coupled with the power of imagery, have a profound effect on the voice. Read them aloud. Allow the beautiful sounds of speech and the rich images to ignite deep diaphragmatic breathing and the effortless release of an easy, open, and expressive voice.

The Sea

Barry Cornwall (1787–1874)

The sea! The sea! The open sea!
The blue, the fresh, the ever free!
Without a mark, without a bound,
It runneth the earth's wide regions round;
It plays with the clouds; it mocks the skies;
Or like a cradled creature lies.

I'm on the sea! I'm on the sea!
I am where I would ever be;
With the blue above, and the blue below,
And silence wheresoe'er I go;
If a storm should come and awake the deep,
What matter? I shall ride and sleep.

I love, O, how I love to ride
On the fierce, foaming, bursting tide,
When every mad wave drowns the moon
Or whistles aloft his tempest tune,
And tells how goeth the world below,
And why the southwest blasts do blow.

Other poems to read aloud include "Hymn Before Sunrise, in the Vale of Chamouni" by Samuel Taylor Coleridge (1772–1834); "Sympathy" by Paul Laurence Dunbar (1872–1906); and "Caged Bird" by Maya Angelou (1928–2014).

Speak It!—Part II

Now that we've addressed the physiological challenges that can lead to vocal distractions, let's talk about the intellectual and emotional impediments to clear speech that Greg Louganis and Soledad O'Brien faced. They'd gotten too much into their heads about the story, going off on a tangent as Greg did, or habitually rushing their words as Soledad did. But again, these vocal distractions can be overcome when you use your imagination to make the story the star. These three suggestions will help.

> **Free yourself to take a more visceral approach to the images of the story.** When you come across the word "blue," what do you see? The sky? The ocean? A blue crayon? Simply seeing the word "blue" spelled out won't cut it. You need an image to create an emotional connection and draw your attention out of your head and into the imaginative heart of the story. Color your narrative.
>
> **Take that speech, presentation, or piece of reportage and map out the images beforehand.** Go through the written text and assign visuals to the most important verbs, nouns, and adjectives. Think about these images and how they make you feel. Develop a visceral connection to the story as you practice your speech in front of the mirror, in the shower, or in the car—wherever you feel most comfortable speaking out loud.
>
> **As always, remember to slow down and breathe!** Take your time, using an entire breath for each thought, and a new deep breath will naturally emerge for every new thought.

When you get out of your head and take this more visceral approach to the story, enabling yourself to see the story, you will naturally connect to your authentic voice. When you have the visceral connection through imagery, along with the breath, all those other pesky vocal distractions will simply fall away.

~~~~~~~~~
 ~~~~~~~~~

What Goes Up Must Come Down:
Correcting Upspeak

To correct a vocal upswing on the last word of a statement, think of a waterfall starting high at the top of a cliff, then cascading down into the river below. In multisyllabic words, the upspeaker lowers the pitch of the syllable that precedes the final syllable and raises the pitch of the final syllable:

>   *tion*
> *trans-por-*
>   *ta-*

In a monosyllabic word, the upspeaker starts low and raises the pitch on the vowel or diphthong sound:

>   *r*
>
> *ca-*

Let's reverse upspeak to downspeak! Raise the pitch of the syllable that precedes the final syllable, then lower the pitch of the final syllable:

>   *ta-*
> *trans-por-*
>   *tion*

In monosyllabic words, start slightly higher in pitch and lower the pitch on the vowel or diphthong sound:

ca-

    r

In phrases and sentences, raise the pitch of the word that precedes the final word, then lower the pitch of the final word:

torch

    song

....

                            audience

The singer's torch song made the

                            cry.

Practice Words

Remember to think of a waterfall cascading downward. Avoid making these single-syllable words two syllables.

As you do this practice material, let your hand become a gesture for the voice. Allow your hand to start high and come down as your voice does. An easy physical gesture is an extremely useful visual tool during practice. However, don't allow it to become habitual; excessive gestures can be distracting.

Feet . . . Fit . . . Fed . . . Fact . . . From . . . First . . . Fun . . . Food . . . Foot . . . Fault . . . Fond . . .

Practice Phrases

Start slightly higher in pitch on the first word, then lower the pitch on the final word.

Use upward and downward hand gestures to help see the vocal journey.

Three
    feet

. . . .

   quick
A
     fix

. . . .

   in a
Fed
    shed

. . . .

   a
That's
    fact

. . . .

   to there
From here
    together

. . . .

   and
Thirty-Third
    Third

. . . .

   in the
Fun
    sun

. . . .

   Food
The
    Dude

. . . .

   good
On the
    foot

Paul's
    fault

Fond of
    songs

Practice Sentences

Note that the final monosyllabic word in the statement or the final syllable of a multisyllabic word in the statement go downward.

    the
Please keep three feet from
      street.

    poc
It's my Fitbit that slipped out of my
      ket.

    cal
Ted fed the med tech girls instead of the medi
      head.

    on
Ask the cabbie if he has cash
      hand.

    ge
We went from here to there to
      ther.

    and
Earl met his girlfriend on Thirty-Third
      Third.

had
My mother and brother had fun in the sun and I
none.

....

men
The Food Dude includes stew on his
u.

....

one
The cook shook a good book while dancing on
foot.

....

law
It was Paul's fault that all his daughters were
yers.

....

to
I'm fond of songs that are calming
Tom.

〰〰〰〰〰〰〰
〰〰〰〰〰

Beyond Words

·········

*Words mean more than what is set down
on paper. It takes the human voice to
infuse them with deeper meaning.*

—MAYA ANGELOU

Her Russian accent was so heavy that Nadia, a chemical engineer, could hardly be understood by her colleagues at U.S. Borax,
the California mining and manufacturing company. This wasn't
a problem in the lab, where she felt most comfortable and spent
months testing minerals and developing compounds. Her work
was critical to generating profits for the corporate giant. But when
it came time to present her findings in the boardroom, no one
could understand what she was saying, so her boss sent her to me.

Nadia was a highly intelligent and capable young woman, but
her Slavic accent was holding her back in her career and her social life, or so she thought. In this country, many people dismiss
those who don't sound like them. Have you ever noticed how

some folks not only dumb down their language when speaking to someone from another country, but they tend to shout, as if the person has a hearing disability? That's what was happening to Nadia, and the experience was starting to chip away at her self-esteem. It wasn't that she lacked the vocabulary. She understood her American colleagues perfectly well. This woman had a PhD, and yet people were speaking to her as if she were a five-year-old!

Whenever I meet a new voice student, I start by asking them to tell me a story about themselves. I could sense that Nadia felt frustrated and trapped by her accent. She was desperate to be understood, so I listened to her story intently.

She described how, when she was seven and still living in Moscow, she had a near-fatal accident that almost paralyzed her. Her parents were distraught as their only child struggled through the pain of recovery, and they feared that she might never be able to walk again until a physiotherapist suggested she take up swimming.

Nadia dedicated herself to swimming so wholeheartedly that she eventually made the Olympic team. The rigor and discipline of the sport saved her, not only leading to a full recovery but also making her into a world-class athlete. But at that level, the sport of swimming became so cutthroat that it no longer gave her the same joy. That's when she decided to quit and become a scientist instead.

I learned a lot about who Nadia was from listening to her. I cried when she cried, completely caught up in the emotion of her journey. But here's the thing. She was speaking in her native language, and I don't understand a word of Russian. That's right. Somehow Nadia's vocal nuances and inflections, coupled with her body language, connected her emotions to the story, and I understood it on a visceral level, or at least the gist of it. Clearly, if she had shared a simple story of walking to the grocery store to purchase a loaf of bread, I'm sure I would not have understood a word. But her emotional attachment to this particular story, combined with her intentional, convicted delivery, made her story transcend language, much like music does.

Certainly, I could have guessed a few things if she had told me her story in one of the romance languages like French, Spanish, or Italian. After all, I sang opera for years. But Slavic is so foreign to me that I never would have understood the story based on her words alone.

Nadia was stunned by the accuracy of my playback to her, as was I. I got a few details wrong, substituting gymnastics for swimming, for example, and mixing up gender pronouns. But I understood enough of it to make her wonder for a moment if I spoke Russian.

Thinking it could be a fluke, I started doing this with other voice students for whom English was their second language. A young woman from Istanbul, Turkey, told me a deeply personal story about a romantic relationship. She felt bold enough to share it with me because she figured I'd never understand the intimate details she described in Turkish. When she finished, I asked:

"Did you ever get back together with him?"

"No," she answered, floored. "But you must know my language because that is a good question!"

I did not. Turkish is as foreign to me as Cantonese.

Imbued with Meaning

What this proves beyond a shadow of a doubt is that your voice has power to communicate beyond words. Perhaps my musical training makes my ears a little more sensitive than most. In opera, every syllable is imbued with a musical note that evokes emotions at their most heightened. But clearly your vocal power can surpass language when you are truly invested in what you are saying. The power of the imagination is what gives voice intonation, inflection, and color. It's what moves your listener and helps them truly understand the essence of you.

Being heard that way restored some of Nadia's confidence. It was the first of many breakthroughs and a reminder for her that she had great stories to tell. But for me, it was a profound "aha" moment. The story is the star, as a teacher once told me, but the voice, powered by passion, is what puts it in the firmament.

This discovery meant that I had a new teaching tool. Now, when someone wants a better knowledge of the American dialect because English is their second, third, or even fourth language, I use personal narrative storytelling in their mother tongue for an initial exercise. This has helped free my international clients from the self-consciousness of trying to be understood. We must all start where we are. We must feel comfortable enough in our skin to tap into a compelling narrative, getting out of our own way and allowing it to unfold. What better way to do so than by inviting someone to share, in their native language, a little about her life back home?

I am grateful that my coaching experiences have given me a deeper sense of empathy for the kinds of bias anyone who looks or sounds different must endure. Regardless of race, nationality, region, sexual orientation, ability, or socioeconomic background, everyone deserves to be heard with open-mindedness and respect.

More Than a Pretty Face

Anastasia, a model from Russia, has always been so much more than a pretty face. In fact, she is an artist with a burning desire to express herself. Stunningly gamine, with a pixie bob hairdo and penetrating eyes, she already had a flourishing career in Europe, where she was regularly featured in print ads and editorials for global beauty brands. When the former ballerina was introduced by a mutual friend to a director who was making a feature film about the fashion industry, she was immediately hired to give advice about photo shoots, to lend some authenticity to the production. But the director fell hard for Anastasia's beauty and, finding something compelling behind her eyes, ended up giving her a part in his movie. It was as if this role had been written especially for her—a deaf-mute model who expresses all her feelings nonverbally.

She ended up falling in love with the director as well as filmmaking, and the two were soon married. Her husband, a Russian American citizen who'd been commuting between Los Angeles and Moscow, proposed that they relocate to the West Coast and go all in on her burgeoning acting career. Anastasia, who had already decided to take acting seriously and get training, enthusiastically agreed. She enrolled in one of LA's top acting schools, but her accent was preventing her from fully expressing her characters. Although she had studied English throughout school and university and spoke it regularly from the age of sixteen, when she first entered the modeling business, like many for whom English is a second or third language, her book learning did not always translate well into everyday usage. As a result, Anastasia grew increasingly shy around strangers and acquaintances.

"I was always introverted, the type of person who would rather stay home and watch a movie than star in one," she told me. "Even though it was my dream, it was hard to make that transition from silence to speaking in front of the camera, and this reality check of not being understood because of my accent made me even less confident."

That was an understatement. The more we talked, the more I realized that the stigma of an accent was having a much bigger impact on her self-esteem than she was initially willing to admit, as was the case with Nadia. Unfortunately, Russian women in this part of the world tend to get stereotyped as a subservient nanny or a paid escort, for example. Attractive women struggle enough with the perceptions that a male-dominated society sometimes puts on them. Now imagine how it must feel to have everyone assume you are a calculating gold digger from the moment you open your mouth?

Anastasia was well educated and at the top of her game in her home country. But by the time she met me, she felt less-than. It's not as if she would always get the opportunity to say to someone she just met, "I am Anastasia from Russia, and here is the list of all my accomplishments . . ." People make their judgments within seconds of first meeting someone. Anastasia was viewed as a flawless Russian doll, and she didn't have the vocal skills to show who she really was.

Holding Humanity

To get a better sense of where she was struggling most, I had Anastasia read aloud a passage from Carrie Fisher's book *Wishful Drinking*. The language and syntax of that brilliant, funny, cynical, and self-deprecating book perfectly reflect the natural speech rhythm of an intelligent and educated woman of Southern California, which was how Anastasia ultimately hoped to sound. I often give my clients for whom English is a second or third language passages to read aloud that not only sound American but have an American personality, with colloquialisms and idioms built in and lending themselves to being read with an American sensibility, beyond straight phonetics and grammar.

Many of Anastasia's vocal issues were typical of those who learned English from books and not everyday conversation. Her rhythms were off. But before we could address this, I wanted her to reconnect with the musicality in her voice that was already there. As with Nadia, I asked Anastasia to tell me a story that was full of deep personal meaning. But this time, I added a twist and had her tell it in English first.

She started describing a ballet she'd recently seen, starring Misty Copeland. She'd always wanted to see this great American dancer live, and the experience had moved her deeply. She talked about the grace of Misty's movements, her otherworldly extensions, her impeccable musicality, athleticism, and flawless technique—all heightened by a sense of artistry that completely transported the audience.

"Denise, I had never experienced anything like it. I felt like a seven-year-old girl when I was watching her. The depth of Misty's expression didn't just make me want to be a better dancer; it made me want to be a better person. It was as if she held all of humanity within her body."

It was a powerful description of a ballet told through a dancer's eyes. Still, I didn't quite connect to the story. Something in her vocal delivery was missing.

Next, I had her tell me the same story in her native Russian. Not having to muscle her way through spoken English, she spoke as if someone had taken the harness off her. The story flowed with passion and ease. There was a natural cadence and rhythm to her voice when she spoke in her original language. I could feel the swirl of emotions that Anastasia experienced the moment she realized the difference, allowing the breath to release her voice and emotions into the sounds of Russian speech.

Immediately after her Russian version of the story, I asked Anastasia to repeat it for a third time, again in English. With a rapid switch from Russian back to English, the memory of her emotional connection to the words in her original language was still fresh. Anastasia found an organic way to use her connection to the story in Russian and transfer it to the story once she delivered it in English. It went far beyond the basic phonetic interpretation of words. She discovered a superb articulatory muscularity in her speech that made excellent use of rhythm, vocal placement, and inflection. The challenge, then, was for her to maintain those elements when she spoke English.

When English is not someone's first language, the rules of the original tongue are usually inadvertently placed on the new language. Additionally, there will always be several English sounds that don't exist in the speaker's first language, so the speaker will lack muscle memory for reference, resulting in the limited dexterity to effectively express these new sounds. This muscle memory and dexterity can and must be developed if the speaker wishes to be fully heard and understood. Anastasia knew she had the power within her to move her American listeners; it was just a matter of slowing down and allowing her cadence and rhythm to change in order to appreciate the new rules of communication, much like a classical musician who is suddenly asked to play jazz.

To be perfectly clear, I am in no way saying that Anastasia's Russian accent is a bad thing or that she must fully sound American, assimilate into American culture, and live happily ever after. However, when you attempt anything new in life, be it a language, a sport, or a hobby, you need to learn all the rules so that you're in full command to break those rules if you so choose. In fact, the *only* way to break them is to know them first.

Jazz Spin

America's classical music, jazz, is a perfect example of conscious rule breaking, resulting in musical ideas that reflect a culture of African polyrhythms, oppression, and making a way out of no way—or, in a word, improvisation. There's musicality to any language. The first step to learning General American Speech is discovering its beautiful rhythm. It's the basis for holding the attention of your listeners so that they aren't taken too far out of the story. Without a doubt, rhythms of speech can be difficult to hear unless you are trained to listen for them like musicians and dancers. American speech rhythms are vowel-driven by nature. We express ourselves through uninterrupted, unimpeded vowel sounds as opposed to consonant sounds. This gives our rhythm of speech a more legato, smooth, and flowing manner with an occasional syncopation—much like jazz. I encourage all those who study with me to learn the phonetic rules of speech so that they can choose to put their own jazz spin on the rules and make them their own.

As with any musical genre, you must start with a single tone or, in the case of speech, a sound. In the case of General American Speech, there are twelve vowel sounds, ten diphthong sounds, and twenty-five consonant sounds. I will delve into these elements of speech in much more detail in the Voice and Speech Workout at the end of this book. For our current purposes, just know that these sounds of speech form syllables, which then form words. Groups of words form phrases, and the connected phases create a thought. Are you following me so far? I'm essentially reducing speech to its most basic elements. To "speak the speech" effectively, you must start with sounds that are accurate. The slightest augmentation of a single sound can potentially change the entire word.

Vowel, Diphthong, and Consonant Sounds

The following is a quick snapshot of the sounds of General American Speech. There are three categories of vowel sounds—front, mid, and back—starting with more closed sounds and moving toward more open ones.

The four front vowel sounds are represented in the words "deed," "did," "dead," and "dad." The vowel sounds become more open as the jaw releases for each word.

The three mid vowel sounds are represented in the words "fur," "sofa," and "fun." The vowel sounds become more open as the jaw opens for each word.

The five back vowel sounds are represented in the words "pool," "pull," "poetic," "Paul," and "palm." The vowel sounds become more open as the jaw releases for each word.

In addition to these vowel sounds, we have ten diphthong sounds.

Five diphthong sounds are represented in the words "bay," "buy," "boy," "bone," and "Bowzer."

Five always short diphthongs of "r" are represented by the words "pier," "pair," "poor," "pour," and "par."

Finally, we have the consonant sounds.

The twenty-five consonant sounds are grouped in six categories represented here by these sounds (not letters):

Stop plosives—"p," "b," "t," "d," "k," "g"
Affricates—"ch," "j"
Nasals—"m," "n," "ng"
Lateral—"l"
Fricatives—"f," "v," "s," "z," "sh," "zh," "th" (voiced), "th" (voiceless), "r," "h" (voiced), "h" (voiceless)
Glides—"w," "y"

I will dive into these categories in more detail at the end of this book.

You can hear the need for open vowel sounds in songs. Whitney Houston was masterful at expressing emotion in every note she sang. In the song "I Will Always Love You," you can hear the beautifully elongated diphthong and vowel sounds—"Iiiiiiii" and "yoooouuuu." She is powerfully belting out these pronouns to drive the point of the song. Whitney's artistry shows how vocal expression is more than just a clinical, technical exercise. Vocal expression is where relaxation, breath, voice, speech, and emotion converge.

Once you find a rhythmic connection to the sounds of speech, you will instinctively know when to hang on to or elongate a vowel sound for emotional effect. Of course, there are rules for the lengths of vowel, diphthong, and consonant sounds. I strongly believe that these rules were derived from our innate relationship to the emotional connection to the sounds of speech. Great writers are also aware of this connection. A reader can generally tell the emotional state of a character by the length of the vowel sounds the writer has used.

It was that connection between emotion and sound that Anastasia most desired to make when she spoke English. Her goals were to adjust the accuracy of her phonetic sounds, learn syllable and word stress, and use idiomatic phrases in casual conversation. She was determined to become just as expressive in English as she was in her mother tongue.

Due Diligence

Anastasia and I began by recording all her subsequent sessions. She developed the confidence to listen to herself without judgment, and she was beginning to acquire the tools to make the necessary adjustments on her own. She made a comprehensive list of practice words with the sounds she found most difficult, so that when she came upon the sound in daily conversation she would be able to modify it on the spot.

It was a long list. Her habitual vowel sound in the word "did" became "deed," "dead" became "dad," "pull" became "pool," and "stop" became "stoop." She had no concept of a diphthong sound being the combination of two vowel sounds, and because the consonant sounds "th" and "w" do not exist in Russian, her closest approximation for the sounds were the consonants "t" and "v." Not only was Anastasia's journal handy for jotting down words in the appropriate sound category, but she was able to reference it as she diligently listened to our sessions two to three times a day. This level of dedication gave her the confidence to engage more with the people around her. It also gave her the freedom to concentrate on her acting craft without the burden of wondering how she sounded.

Previously, Anastasia was more inclined to observe quietly. Like so many people who are well traveled, slipping in and out of different cultures, she never really felt as though she belonged. It was as if she were on the outside looking in. Today, she is able to express her point of view more succinctly, building authentic relationships not just with other people, but with herself.

"It's allowed me to dig deep and find my true home within," she told me recently. "Knowing how I felt but not being able to express it was such a bummer. It was like I had a bottleneck of words trapped inside of me. But now it feels as if I've set myself free."

Anastasia still practices voice and speech daily. After more than a year of training, she remains one of my most diligent clients. The work must never stop, the same way that it never stops for a musician or a dancer. At the core of this work is muscle memory. You are essentially replacing old habits with new ones and developing the muscularity to support these new habits with ease. As with any muscle group, if you don't use the muscles involved in speech production, they will atrophy from lack of use.

Building consistent speech habits requires a long-term approach to the work. The overall results and time frame largely depend on the speaker's ear and the amount of daily work they do. You will find all the exercises needed to begin building a solid daily practice in the Voice and Speech Workout section at the end of this book.

A Dialect, Not a Distraction

Let me say unequivocally that a dialect or an accent does not have to be a distraction. An accent occurs when English is not spoken as a first language. Speech patterns are transferred from the original language onto the new language. A dialect, on the other hand, occurs when English is spoken as a first language but regional and cultural influences impact and shift the phonetic sounds and rhythms. But none of these differences need to impede clear communication.

Perhaps you speak with an Italian accent. When you make yourself clearly understood with your accent, it does not deter from effective, powerful, or inspiring communication. "Oh, you're not from here," listeners may be thinking, but they still hear and process your words.

It's often not necessary to completely eliminate all traces of a foreign accent or regional dialect; that option should be left to the individual and not to society to determine. As long as you "play the music" with phonetic and grammatical accuracy, your cultural and linguistic nuances should be used at your own discretion. I use the term "accuracy" quite loosely here. There are often several phonetic ways to pronounce a single word. So, what's right? What's "right" is what feels right for you and, more important, what feels right for your narrative. Years ago, I worked with Australian-born actress Portia de Rossi. Her chance to work with a fellow Australian filmmaker and longtime friend was almost derailed because he felt that she sounded too American for the Australian role.

Portia had been living in America for quite some time and was playing the role of American attorney Nelle Porter on the hit television series *Ally McBeal*. When we started working together, I plied her with dialect samples of both her native Australian region and the character's, then I had her tell me a very personal story. This time the story had to be something meaningful from her early childhood, to help her reconnect to her vocal roots. We drilled the vowel, rhythm, and vocal placement differences between the American and Australian dialects, and in one session she was vocally back where she started in Geelong, Australia.

It was never Portia's intention to completely lose her Australian dialect. It happened as a result of her deep commitment to her role on the television series. After several seasons of portraying the character's vocal rhythms and nuances, it became difficult for her to hear her own. Rediscovering her original vocal imprint gave her the ability to navigate two worlds. It obviously helped her reconnect to her roots, but it also gave her the option to step in and out of it with truth and authenticity. And, of course, she got the part!

Using varying degrees of your accent or dialect can work to your advantage, whether you're an actor going up for a role or an everyday person with an interesting story to tell. A voice print is as individual and unique as a fingerprint. It has the potential to make you more memorable in a myriad of social and business settings. We all have an innate gauge that tells us the right amount of voice and speech nuance for every situation. But it is also possible to consciously modulate your dialect or accent.

If you feel you have gotten away from your vocal roots, like Portia, you can record yourself recounting a personal childhood story to reconnect to a specific place, time, and voice of your earlier life. Once you have your original dialect back in your vocal repertoire, you can switch back and forth by becoming more intentional about it. But before you adjust your rhythm and vocal placement, slow it down. There's a tendency to arbitrarily speed up your tempo in an anxious desire to fit in or mirror whoever you are communicating with. But when you are more deliberate about making that conscious shift, you must give yourself the time to breathe and to visualize what your articulators are doing as you form the desired phonetic sounds of words. This simple technique can take place in a matter of seconds, without disrupting the flow of your speech.

In between professional and social situations, do take the time to practice. I experiment with dialects all the time because it helps develop my ear in preparation for working with actors who are playing dialect-specific roles. During the course of a day, I might go to Starbucks and order my chai latte with a British accent, then chat it up with the checkout associate at Trader Joe's sounding like a Texan. These are safe places to play because I don't know these people and I'll likely never see them again. It can also be a heck of a lot of fun!

I instruct my clients for whom English is a second or third language to practice the American accent in these types of settings for an hour a day during our first week of training, then for two hours a day during our second, to help them build up their new articulation muscles. The more they practice, going back and forth between their original way of speaking English and the newly adopted American dialect, the more they will be able to fine-tune it. This daily practice gives anyone who desires to switch it up the courage to just jump in.

A daily practice or regimen also helps develop fluency. Just as a chef eventually knows which spices to use to make her signature dish without using the recipe, you will have the same capacity (with the tools I'm sharing) to choose vocal colors, inflections, and a vocabulary that will ultimately become your "secret sauce."

Brunch in Brentwood

When I first met James Michael Marshall at a Hollywood party in Brentwood, his accent seemed to define him. He had neither clarity nor dexterity in his speech, which in no way reflected the multitalented man he was or the highly accomplished gentleman he would soon become.

It was hard not to notice him when I first walked through the gated compound, past the lush flowering gardenias, roses, and bougainvillea, and into a palatial estate with a pool, tennis courts, and a basketball court. Tall and handsome, with the most elegant mannerisms, James was the long-term partner of a fabulously wealthy member of the Hollywood elite. It was immediately evident that James was "the host with the most" as he worked the party, offering drinks and exchanging witticisms with an array of artists and politicians and the who's who of Hollywood.

There was a lot of money and influence at that lavish garden party, but it was not the standard, elitist, "I've got more money than you do" crowd that you often get in this industry town. The other party guests seemed open and passionate about the arts, and they were all clearly fond of the affable and welcoming man of the house.

But when I overheard James's voice, my brain made the screeching sound of a turntable needle sliding off a record. This sophisticated bon vivant had a voice, speech, and cadence that just didn't fit, like a man wearing an impeccably tailored suit with basketball shoes (although I realize that is the fashion these days). James's voice had a distinct nasal quality, and his tendency to hang on to vowel sounds slightly longer than usual made it even more apparent. He spoke with what some call a "Kentucky twang." His voice did not match the urbane way in which he carried himself. In fact, it was a distraction. Sounding one way and looking another can be quite interesting until your listeners become less engaged with what you're saying and more intrigued by how you're saying it.

As gracious, accepting, and inclusive as these folks clearly were, I was all too aware that Hollywood can be a tough town where people get sized up in a heartbeat. Hearing James brought me back to my own sense of trepidation when a friend invited me to Elton John's legendary Oscar party. Searching for just the right outfit can sometimes be a daunting task for an introvert who would much rather spend a Sunday evening in workout clothes watching a good Netflix movie. While I'm not one to splash out on fancy designer outfits, I decided that this one time I would splurge on a classy jewel-speckled sheer black silk scarf from Saks Fifth Avenue. I arrived alone on the red carpet. I knew virtually no one at one of Hollywood's most celebrated events, but in less than an hour, I had latched on to a group of men and women with varied backgrounds and fascinating stories to tell. At one point I found myself at the center of the conversation and really enjoyed it. Later, as I summed up the evening's events, I concluded that my voice and my gift of storytelling were my most valuable accessories. The pricey Saks scarf didn't even come close.

That's why I felt so compelled to offer James my services. Choosing your best voice for the situation is like picking out just the right piece of clothing. James had already dressed himself impeccably, and he deserved the same choices when it came to his voice and speech. But how could I broach this without causing offense? Clearly a man of means, he didn't need my charity, but I knew that even the most accomplished among us can't resist a bargain. I approached him by the pool bar, took him to the side, and introduced myself.

"My dear friend, I've heard you speak all afternoon, and your voice really doesn't match who you are," I told him, handing him my card. "I would love for you to work with me, and I'll train you for free."

James looked at my card for a few beats, then at me, beaming. "Yes, ma'am!" he said brightly. "Imma take you up on that."

The next day he called me. I happened to have an opening, so I invited him to my studio that afternoon. Much later in our friendship, James revealed to me that the night of our meeting he'd wept in gratitude. No one had ever offered to help him like that, no strings attached. He'd been thinking about ways he could improve his communication skills. He knew he needed to be better heard and understood. Just as he was wondering how, I came along. My offer helped him solidify his sense that he could be more. It was that little extra push that we all need at certain points in our lives.

During those first couple of hours together we became friends. We had a long chat about where he was from and the many lives he'd led. Although I was raised in New York, my family came from South Carolina, so we shared deep southern roots. James grew up in Shelbyville, Kentucky, a sleepy town just outside Louisville, in a powerful Black family that valued his education and personal development above anything. He'd always been an inquisitive and determined kid. When James was nine, he became an ordained minister on a whim. In a high school of thirty-five hundred kids, he was one of the few athletes to letter in four varsity sports: baseball, basketball, football, and track.

James went on to study behavioral science and play basketball at the University of Kansas before being drafted by the Denver Nuggets. Becoming a professional basketball player exposed him to whole new worlds, and it was eye-opening. He went on to play in Belgium and the Netherlands, "where people don't segregate," he told me. "You're not Black, white, or Asian—you're just Dutch."

Following his playing career, James became a special assistant to Hall of Fame basketball coach Larry Brown at the University of Kansas, where he learned from some of the greatest minds in the history of the game. This was where the top echelons of basketball and the entertainment industry intersected for James. "Rappers want to be basketball players, and basketball players want to be rappers," explained James. "Being a professional athlete can be a passport into some exclusive clubs."

In this setting, he could overhear the most powerful and infamous people, from celebrities to politicians to business tycoons, speak off the record. It was all fodder for material to create plot lines and characters for his real love: the movies.

James excelled as a coach. With his skills, he could have become a general manager. That's what people told him he should aspire to. But he yearned to express himself. He did plays in school but had always been told that the dramatic arts were for "sissies." He always knew that was homophobic bull, and with more resources and contacts at his disposal, he decided to go for it. He began writing screenplays and studying with some of the best acting coaches in the business, but it was only getting him so far.

"I want to be able to walk into a room, command attention, and go to the next level," James told me.

The Workarounds

James and I worked on balancing his nasal quality with more chest resonance, speech, articulation, and tongue-twister exercises for tongue strength and agility, so that James could easily navigate his Kentucky dialect as he chose, depending on the situation. But there was more going on with James beyond his deeply rich southern lilt. Although he knew how to express himself passionately to a small church crowd as a minister, in conversation he often hesitated between his words, either pausing a beat too long or buying time with "ums" and "uhs." As I dug deeper into his history, my suspicion was confirmed. Like Greg Louganis, James's brain was wired a little differently from the average person's.

He had been diagnosed with a form of Asperger's, a condition that subtly interfered with his ability to process language. James essentially memorized words by rote. He also imagined, crafted, and honed personas to match various social settings and called on these tools to give himself a certain comfort level—a workaround, if you will. From the time he was a child, he had employed this technique, which had become effortless and almost completely imperceptible. But there were times when he searched for the right word, and as someone who listens for a living, I knew that this slight hesitation was connected to a much larger issue. The man is a genius and reads incessantly, so it was not that he lacked the vocabulary. But neurologically, James had a split-second lapse in speech. "Sometimes there's a little stutter, almost like I am gagging on a word, because I am looking for the word," James told me.

We see with the eyes, register with our brains, then speak; we call it the eye-brain-mouth (EBM) connection. But James wasn't linking his imagination with verbal expression. He was filled with emotion, but it wasn't flowing naturally to his voice and speech, making him sound almost clinical in tone. So he attacked the problem with the same rigor and discipline any world-class athlete would, and he crafted well-rehearsed social personas. Unfortunately, the technique was only taking James so far, and it created a certain rigidity in his communication. Knowing his mind worked differently was also chipping away at James's self-esteem. I had the sense he was hiding his true self. But there was a solution. He needed to deepen his connection to the words and his imagination.

Great literature lends itself beautifully to linking words with imagery. We sat together and read aloud Edmund's monologue from Eugene O'Neill's play *Long Day's Journey into Night*. You can't help but be moved by the character's poignant, vivid, and evocative images as he describes the feeling of dissolving into the sea.

Instead of seeing words on a page, James began seeing pictures. The beauty of the language was made more vivid when he could see detailed images in his mind's eye and connect these to his voice. Prior to James's discovery of imagery as it relates to the voice, when he spoke or read the word "blue," for instance, he saw in his mind's eye the letters "b," "l," "u," "e." Now, he not only sees a vibrant shade of the color blue, but a morning sky, a vast ocean, or even the forlorn look on the face of a loved one. The specificity of language was the missing element in the methodology he'd crafted around the lifelong challenge he was facing. Visualizing nouns, verbs, and adjectives gave him the fluidity and vocal dexterity he needed to truly own any room he walked into.

In addition to the speech, articulation, and imagery work, I gave James exercises to help free his voice and create more nasal resonance as opposed to his regional nasal quality. They included the methodical repetition of sentences fraught with the three nasal consonants "m," "n," and "ng." These nasal sounds, coupled with a breath in through the mouth, bring a tactile sensation to voice. Putting our hands on the front of the face enables us to feel the voiced sounds of speech as well as hear them, resulting in a more visceral awareness of voice.

Finally, I gave him a series of phrases to repeat, with the following instructions: "Remember to breathe in through the mouth before you speak, then feel an awareness of the warm nasal sounds on your lips as well as the tip and back of the tongue. If you find it difficult to recite an entire phrase on one breath, simply take a catch breath in the middle to ensure maximum support for the end of the phrase. You should be feeling a warm and gentle vocal release on each phrase."

Many moaning men making money in the month of May in Montana.
Nothing, something, and everything.
We were dancing, singing, and skipping along.
The moans and groans of the nanny goats were menacing.
Hanging around with a gang of lean mean fiends.

The madman is making noises at the moon.
What's done is done and cannot be undone.
I'm alone again; alone, alone, all, all alone.
My mother, Mary, and I make muffins on Monday.
It's spring! It's spring! Let's sing!

Today, James's voice not only matches his personality, but he has a variety of vocal nuances that he can draw upon depending on the situation. His ability to comfortably shift between the James of Kentucky and the James of Brentwood without losing a sense of himself is astounding. Just as James the athlete maintains a daily physical regimen, James the artist is now dedicated to a daily vocal regimen. When we spoke on the phone recently, I could hear the hard work he'd been putting into his voice.

"Denise, you have to stay ready so that you don't have to get ready!" he told me.

Standing in My Story

I can deeply relate to James's experience. The desire to travel authentically and effortlessly between worlds is the common bond that underpins the close friendship we have developed since we first started working together. I've already shared how, growing up, I was able to use my voice and speech to adapt comfortably to my circumstances, whether that was fitting in with the other kids on the Lower East Side or interacting with the art patrons, music directors, and singers at the New York City Opera. But it wasn't until a few months into Liz Smith's voice class at Juilliard that I made that visceral vocal connection.

Earlier that year, in the summer of 1975, as a high school graduation gift from my mom, I took a trip to South Carolina with my uncle Herbert and aunt Sylvia to visit my extended family on my father's side. As we left New York, driving south on Interstate 95 and crossing the Mason-Dixon Line that separates the northern states from the South, it was apparent that I was going to be given a life-changing history lesson.

As a child, I had spent most summers with my maternal family in Richmond, Virginia. But traveling deeper into these endless fields of cotton and tobacco felt different. Aunt Sylvia and Uncle Herbert, proud owners of Harlem's iconic Sylvia's Restaurant, had regaled me with tales of their love story in the bean fields of South Carolina as well as the notorious lynching of our family patriarch in the early twentieth century. But as the songs of Miles Davis, Charlie Parker, and Lady Day played on the car stereo, I saw the beauty and ugliness of the landscape with fresh eyes.

Small-town streets lined with majestic oak trees and hanging moss pulled at my heart as we veered off the interstate and traveled routes with no traffic lights. I could feel in my bones that this was the land of my people—rich in traditions and full of bounty. But the reminders of slavery and Jim Crow atrocities were everywhere. Even then, over a century after the end of slavery, you could see Black sharecroppers—men, women, and children—hunched over the dirt rows under the beating sun as they picked those fluffy white bulbs of cotton. The dilapidated homes, with barefoot children playing by the roadside, made the hardships our family had left behind in the South that much more real.

The twelve-hour journey "home" was filled with joy and pain. My aunt and uncle did not spare any details about what had happened to our scattered extended family. When Black folks headed north during the "Great Migration" following World War II, most wanted to leave the South and its horrific memories far behind. By the mid-seventies, the Woods family was heading into the upper middle class. But the need to go back home and remember from where we came had become our annual Labor Day tradition. Food, drink, laughter, and tears colored these tales, giving them a rich patina that sparked my imagination in a way that would ultimately define my work at Juilliard.

Ancestral Heroes

It took a while for the full impact of this experience to manifest in my voice work. The "aha" moment occurred soon after I met one of the few other African American students in the Juilliard Drama Division. Pamela White, who was two years behind me, shared that she was going to change her last name to Tucker-White to reflect her mother's maiden name. She proudly regaled me with the story of her great-grandfather, who decided one day to walk away from all that he'd known in Virginia. Without so much as a few pennies to his name, he made his way northwest to Peoria, Illinois, on foot, leaving behind the hardships of racial oppression and extreme poverty, as well as all connections to his painful past, including his family.

I couldn't believe my ears.

"Did you say your mother's maiden name is Tucker? So is mine!" I told her.

I have a great-great-uncle who is a Tucker and legendary in my family. My great-aunts and -uncles speak of their papa's brother, who just picked up and left Powhatan, Virginia, on foot, claiming that he was heading to Chicago. He was never seen or heard from again. When we realized the connection, Pamela and I stared at each other in awe. We found strength in this fragmented tale, which echoed its way into the halls of Juilliard. We later called our mothers to get more information, but—as is common in so many African American families—they knew few details of our post-slavery history.

At that time, I was finding my footing as an actor. I was in my third year at Juilliard, playing princesses and queens in Shakespeare's comedy and history plays. At first, I was struggling to find the voice of these characters. They seemed so far removed from the life of a Black girl from the projects. But that encounter with my newfound Peoria cousin was a timely reminder that my family's story was just as rich as any Elizabethan play.

Our histories may not be glorified in the same way; they may be forgotten in the annals of time, oppression, displacement, and poverty, but they are still worthy of being heard. My grandparents, aunts, and uncles had a dignity, complexity, and gravitas equal to any European king or queen. Just like Shakespeare's characters, they suffered, they fought, they endured, and they made heroic sacrifices for the betterment of their families.

So as I lay on my towel in Liz Smith's voice class, taking a breath in and allowing my imagination to roam, I went home to my Virginia and South Carolina Gullah roots. For the first time in my life, I fully connected to my story, spiritually, viscerally, and vocally. When I lifted myself up off that floor, I felt empowered.

Upon graduation, I was invited to join Juilliard's professional touring company, the Acting Company. When I was cast as Olivia in their production of Shakespeare's *Twelfth Night*, it was evident that the play's director didn't want me in the role. My character was a princess, she was royalty, so how could a girl of color possibly be the right fit? I knew that's what he was thinking. At one point when we were rehearsing a scene, he screamed, "Deneeez, *please*! She's not walking to the kitchen!" Everyone in the theater froze, murmuring "Uh-oh" beneath their breath. I also froze, then waited for a rehearsal break to give him a few choice Lower East Side words.

I wasn't going to let that man's prejudice make me feel less-than or limit my range as an actress. I was deeply proud of all the stories and voices within me: the girl from the projects, the daughter of the South, the beauty queen, and the child opera singer who took the stage at the New York City Opera. I finally understood that my voice possessed a multitude of layers that could connect to a character who transcends time, with the power that moves audiences across cultures and beyond words.

As an actress, that knowledge was my secret sauce. I played Queen Margaret in *Richard III* and Emilia in *Othello* while I was a student at Juilliard, and my performances of Olivia in *Twelfth Night* and Titania in *A Midsummer Night's Dream* were the first played by an African American female in the Acting Company's history. By embracing every facet of who I was, I had found my vocal power.

That director later became head of the Juilliard Drama Division—not a good period in the history of the school. It wasn't until the legendary Michael Kahn took the helm in 1992 that dancer/actor Darryl Quinton and I were invited to join as the first two full-time African American faculty members in that division.

I vividly remember traveling from Toronto, Canada, where I was starring in the Canadian production of a Broadway musical, for the meeting. As I was sitting in Michael's office, where he informed me that he wanted me to join the Voice and Speech faculty, I was overwhelmed by the full-circle moment. I recalled sitting in that office with the same bright yellow carpet from the seventies as a seventeen-year-old with the Drama Division founder, John Houseman. That encounter changed the trajectory of my life. Now Michael Kahn was opening the door to the conversation of race and inclusion—a conversation that continues to this day.

Of course, there is more work to be done. But I feel good about the direction we are heading. And I know in my soul that my ancestors would be proud.

Speak It!

I have some amazing life stories, as do you. When we tell them, we typically don't have to be told to breathe, phrase, or stress the right words. We just do. However, when the setting is less spontaneous or we must speak truth to someone else's words, the task becomes a bit more challenging. You must now remind yourself to breathe, to phrase, and to stress important words so that your delivery sounds authentic and extemporaneous. Your imagination is your secret weapon, as we discovered with Anastasia and James.

1. Find a monologue from a play that resonates with you. It can be a classical or contemporary piece. Visit the Monologuer at Backstage.com for suggestions.
2. Whatever passage you choose, be aware of the operative or important words of the story, such as verbs, nouns, and adjectives. They have the most value and should be appropriately stressed. Verbs and nouns typically require primary stress, and adjectives require secondary stress, depending on your interpretation.
3. Pay attention to how the story's action is revealed in the verbs. Its characters, objects, and location are shared in the nouns. Adjectives describe the nouns.
4. Allow yourself to fully visualize these elements of language so that they become more than just words on a page.
5. Remember, the spoken word is vastly different from the written word. We write letters, words, and sentences, but we speak phonetic sounds, visual images, and thoughts.

PART IV

Articulation

Mumbling, marbles in your mouth, swallowed words, and dropped syllables . . .

These speech habits can have a similar impact on listeners as voice tics. But they don't have to! You may be wondering about the difference between voice and speech. And you may even think that the habits of all the people highlighted in the voice and articulation chapters are very similar. Let me start by defining the two terms for you. Voice is the production of sound/vibration. Speech/articulation is how the sound is shaped or impeded to create vowels, diphthongs, consonants, and ultimately words. My clients may seem to have similar issues, but my approach to them is very different. It's for this reason that I tailor my private practice for individual study. What seems to be an inherent issue just may be the result of something else. A speech issue may be the result of a constrained or held voice, a voice issue may be the result of a lack of breath, and a breath issue may be the result of a tension. They are all related! The key is identifying the origin of the issue, and as you've seen, that can differ for everyone.

Do you remember how your abs felt after three weeks of working out in the gym? Once the initial aches and pain subsided, the benefit of strengthening that muscle group had a profound impact on other parts of your body. The same holds true for this work. I've crafted a Voice and Speech Workout to be done 20–30 minutes every day; you'll find it at the end of this book. If you follow this regimen, the impact on other aspects of your life will be profound.

7

Trippingly on the Tongue

....

*Speak the speech, I pray you, as I pronounced
it to you trippingly on the tongue.*

—SHAKESPEARE

When Brian O'Hara's acting coach suggested he see me to tone down his "New Yawk" dialect, he was puzzled.

"What do you mean? I don't have a dialect!" he protested.

But knowing enough to trust her feedback and realizing that it behooved him to work on his craft in a town full of other tall, handsome young men competing for the same roles in film and television, Brian duly made an appointment to see me.

It was true, he did not have much of an accent. At least not in casual conversation. Brian was born into a middle-class family on Manhattan's Upper West Side, raised in Westchester, then schooled in Rockland County and at Boston College. I could tell he was from the New York area, but he certainly did not sound like someone born and raised in Brooklyn or Staten Island. However, that perception changed when I asked him to read some lines of Shakespeare's *Hamlet*, and he sounded like he was deliberately layering on a New York dialect.

Brian was making a mistake common to actors who want to be "truthful" in their performance. I put the word in quotes because it's a misnomer. Actors often confuse an honest performance with their go-to speech comfort zone, even doubling down on their cultural *isms* with defiance, as if to say, "This is *my* truth." No, it's just another distraction. That's not a judgment on where you are from. As I will explore in the next chapter, there is no one culture that has the upper hand when it comes to good speech, and all regionalisms and life experiences add to the nuances of speech and voice. The fact is, you can have it both ways, delivering an authentic vocal performance with crisp articulation. But first you must do the work.

As soon as I pointed out what was happening, and why, Brian understood that he needed to change his approach. Self-awareness is everything.

"I thought I was just being authentic in the scene, but now that I think about it, I was just playing a caricature of myself," he observed, soon after we started working together.

It wasn't necessarily intentional, but when Brian was caught up in the emotion of his character, he resorted to the accent and style of speech he would have used when conversing with the family and friends he grew up with, slipping into their vocal habits because they felt familiar. (This happens to all of us. We are speech chameleons.) In typical northeastern dialect, he would swallow consonants, drop "t"s off certain words, and lean into certain vowel sounds: "tawwk" [talk], "cawffee" [coffee], "Lawnguyland" [Long Island], "mawning" [morning], "tomawrow" [tomorrow]. Brian's desire to fill every acting moment with authenticity was also causing his voice to drop into the back of the throat, taking energy away from his articulators, and limiting his range of vocal expression. Since the majority of Brian's characters were not going to hail from the Northeast, and he had already done so much in shaping his daily speaking voice, I was confident that his acting voice could be developed to a much deeper degree.

Shaped by Tragedy

Unlike many young actors who walk into my studio, Brian had lived through a lot by the tender age of thirty-two, and there was much that he could tap into as an actor. He was an incessant reader and deeply analytical—a brooder. One of our earliest conversations was about human behavior in response to real-life tragedy. It's not necessarily what you think it might be. We don't always switch into fight-or-flight mode. Sometimes we cope by doing the mundane, channeling the shock and grief into everyday actions.

Brian shared how, when he was twelve, he and his twin brother had stayed home while his mother, father, and younger sister took a trip to Paris. When a relative informed the boys that the rest of their family had been killed in a plane crash, his immediate response was to go outside and shoot hoops over and over again, as if he were on autopilot.

The tragic heartbreak has shaped and shaded Brian's life and voice ever since. I could hear a tightness in the way he spoke. I knew that if I could help him feel free to use his own vulnerable vocal nuances to inform a character's journey, he'd be able to convey his truth with a more agile voice and a deeper command of speech. He possesses a wellspring of emotional creativity and a self-awareness from years of therapy to process those emotions. All that substance, combined with his ability to channel it into his work, could allow him to become a performer of profound significance, far beyond the surface level of his physical appearance.

Brian already enjoyed a career in media, having worked in ad sales at ABC in New York. He finally decided to take the leap to the front of the camera and move to Los Angeles in his late twenties—a little later than most actors. By the time we met, he'd just signed with an agent and was starting to go out for auditions. To prepare him, we began with tongue twisters, which are, to the speaker, what scales are to the musician.

When working with tongue twisters, address them very slowly and methodically at first. The goal is accuracy and dexterity, not speed. With practice, you'll achieve smooth and effortless articulation at a conversational pace. You never want to do any of these exercises at lightning speed.

> *What a to-do to die today, at a minute or two to two;*
> *a thing distinctly hard to say, but harder still to do.*
> *We'll beat a tattoo, at twenty to two*
> *A rat-tat-tat-tat tat-tat-tat tat-tattoo.*
> *And the dragon will come when he hears the drum*
> *At a minute or two to two today, at a minute or two to two . . .*

Here's another:

> *Peter Piper, the pickled pepper picker, picked a peck of pickled peppers.*
> *A peck of pickled peppers did Peter Piper, the pickled pepper picker, pick.*
> *Now if Peter Piper, the pickled pepper picker, picked a peck of pickled peppers,*
> *Where is the peck of pickled peppers that Peter Piper, the pickled pepper picker, picked? . . .*

Muscle Memory

When I worked with Brian, the point was to repeat the same sounds consistently. If, for example, a vowel sounded different when preceded by a particular consonant sound, we would stop in the middle of the tongue twister and correct the pronunciation, bringing that tendency to slip on those words into his awareness. For the alveolar sounds—"t," "d," "n," and "l"—these were the perfect exercises to address accuracy in curling the tip of the tongue back and up onto the gum ridge, the bumpy part of the upper gums just behind the teeth.

Brian nailed most of these exercises on the first try. But he understood that mastery would take sustained diligence, like a musician practicing scales every day. The more he repeated the tongue twister, the more fluency he had, easily going up and down in tempo. With effort, it became effortless.

"I realize I need rigor," Brian acknowledged. "A lot of actors think they can just show up and be fabulous. But I know I need something concrete to prepare me, so that when the right role comes, I can deliver."

The repetition also helped Brian build up the muscle memory of his articulators, creating a greater sense of ease and confidence. Prior to our work together, Brian noticed that he was feeling tension in the back of his tongue. As a child, he also tended to mumble, to the point where he had to see a speech therapist. He no longer mumbled, but the memory was probably just enough to subtly inhibit his articulation.

Articulating while experiencing a wealth of emotions can be challenging not just for actors, but for anyone, whether speaking publicly or privately. It's like trying to rub your stomach and pat your head at the same time. After consistent and prolonged practice, the brain will effectively process difficult physical actions, and they will become easier regardless of the speaker's emotional or other obstacle.

"Sometimes I find the work constricting," Brian shared with me. "Articulation can take you away from the emotion, and you can get so worried about saying a word properly that you lose the emotional component. I want to be able to get to the point where I don't even have to think about vowels, diphthongs, and consonants."

"You will, Brian," I assured him. "Keep doing what you are doing, and you will be able to maintain the emotional subtext underneath while easily articulating a writer's words."

Brian's dream role is Iago, the villain from Shakespeare's *Othello*. "I find him so intriguing," he told me, although, like most actors, he's intimidated by the Bard's heightened language.

Brian will get there much sooner than he thinks because he is already awakened to the fact that he must do exactly what Shakespeare asked of his own players centuries ago.

"Speak the speech, I pray you . . ."

Owning the Words

Not surprisingly, I love this line from *Hamlet*. It sums up so perfectly exactly what I do with my clients every day. Hamlet is directing a play and pleading with his actors to breathe life and authenticity into their words. Clearly, Hamlet's need for clarity of text is of life-or-death proportion. But what Shakespeare wrote could just as easily have been a request made by a modern-day playwright or screenwriter. Please, *please* do justice to these words I've crafted and toiled over!

Imagine attempting to do justice to some of Aaron Sorkin's fast-paced political monologues, for example, or August Wilson's poetic, jazzlike monologues. Try memorizing and saying lines with confidence when your dialogue consists of medical terminology that you've never heard before, like "epithelial tissue" or "iridoplegia." Imagine delivering a two-page theatrical monologue with the cadence and complexity of a Miles Davis trumpet solo. Not a month goes by when I don't work with a seasoned actor who gets handed pages of script and gasps in fear.

"Denise, how am I ever going to own all of these words?" they ask me.

This intimidation, this deep-seated fear that we'll trip over a word and look stupid, affects us all, whether we are giving a speech, going to court, or simply trying to hold our own at a dinner party. The concern is not about just mangling the pronunciation of a word. Even the fear of not getting a syllable, vowel, or consonant just right can wreak havoc with our self-confidence and prevent us from being our most eloquent selves.

Now imagine if you had dyslexia—a learning challenge that affects as many as 43.5 million Americans. Or if you were also dealing with regional pronunciations. It doesn't matter if you're a wealthy New York prep school kid or your people spent generations speaking Creole along the shores of the Mississippi River. Most Americans, as well as non-American English speakers, struggle occasionally with articulation. As a nation composed of cultural and linguistic diversity, how could we not?

We are primarily taught English grammar, but very little emphasis is placed on a phonetic approach to the language. We were taught the vowels "a," "e," "i," "o," "u," and sometimes "y," right? Well, only the letter "e" is a pure vowel sound. As I mentioned in chapter 6, the rest are diphthongs and a glide consonant/vowel combination. I was shocked when I first discovered this. When you first learn the difference between a single vowel sound and the combination of two different ones, you're prone to being more deliberate with the execution of the sound.

Many Americans have what some consider to be "lazy speech." I don't use that term because it implies judgment. Rather, I would describe our condition as having "under-energized articulators."

We tend to slip into a comfort zone where our speech turns slushy and our words tend to get mushed together. However, no matter our cultural or socioeconomic background, consonant sounds could be crisper, and our vowel sounds could be clearer. Now that you've honed your instrument—your voice—it's time to fine-tune it, making sure it's played perfectly, so that the listener doesn't get distracted by a wrong note.

In effect, if you think of the totality of voice and speech as a piano, voice is the bass clef, which you play consistently and constantly with your left hand to support the rhythm of the song. The voice, as you learned in the previous chapters, carries the emotion. Speech, however, is the treble clef, or the right hand that plays the melody. In a word, articulation is the melody. Now that your voice has caught the listener's attention, articulation helps you to elucidate, telling the finer points of the story.

From Mumbai with Love

Ashish Joshi, an immigrant from Mumbai, India, had already mastered the bass clef of his voice. Having grown up in a former British colony, he learned English alongside his native tongue. In fact, English has almost become the first language of India, spoken at home interchangeably with local languages like Hindi and Marathi. Ashish did not face the same challenges as Anastasia or Nadia. In Slavic countries, American television is dubbed and exposure to spoken English is almost nonexistent, but this is not the case in India. Ashish already had an emotional connection to the language, thanks in part to the BBC and a handful of American-produced television shows that he grew up watching.

Indeed, he managed just fine when he first came to this country as a software engineer nearly two decades ago. Many of his colleagues in Silicon Valley were also South Asian. They comfortably eased between English and Hindi when communicating with one another, and used a slightly Americanized British English when interacting with others.

"I never felt the need to attend a class to reduce my accent," Ashish told me. "In the big, cosmopolitan cities where I traveled, people were used to having people around them who sounded different."

But Ashish had always yearned for something beyond engineering. A successful stage actor in amateur theater back home, where he learned classical Indian music and sang for ten years, Ashish ached to do this work full-time. But like many immigrants, he knew the importance of financial stability for his family, so he became the "good son" and pursued engineering, the career most respected and desired by his parents, putting his personal ambitions and desires aside.

Once he became well established in his tech career, earning enough to send money back to his family in Mumbai, Ashish ventured into local theater in the Bay Area. The experience reignited his love for performing, so he decided to get formal training at the American Conservatory Theater in San Francisco. An extremely handsome gentleman in his early thirties, Ashish soon started getting small parts in plays, ads, film, and television, as well as voice-over work. Much of it was for the Indian market, but not all of it. South Asian culture was finally beginning to seep into the consciousness of mainstream audiences with the success of movies like *Lion* and *Slumdog Millionaire*. Ashish had the talent and presence to break through to the US market.

Ashish was getting ready to move to New York and pursue the stage full-time. Then he got the call from home that every adult child dreads: his aging parents had a medical emergency. So he set aside his own life, packing up his home and his dog and returning to India to take care of them. Ashish reached out to me after both parents had passed peacefully. He was still in Mumbai, waiting for his aging and ailing pooch to also make the transition, when we had our first Skype session together. Although he'd been doing some acting in local Indian theater, Ashish was concerned that he was reverting back to his native accent. Directors in Mumbai told him he sounded too American, and he feared the opposite would be true when he finally returned stateside. He was caught between two worlds, and the result was that he felt as though he somehow fell short.

"Denise, how do I get rid of this thing?" Ashish asked me.

"Why ever would you want to lose that beautiful accent?" I countered.

What I wanted to say was, "You are enough!" I identified so deeply with this beautiful man of color halfway around the world. I understood that, with twice the amount of talent, he had to work harder than anyone just to reach the starting line. Then he tabled everything to care for the ones he loved. So much about his life, intellect, and character resonated with me that I wanted him to be able to hear himself through my own admiring ears.

I loved the lilt of his British and Indian hybrid accent. Accent neutralization was the last thing I would have recommended. Rather, I wanted him to focus on the hybrid. He could do British Indian or American Indian, depending on the opportunity, because he was embarking on his career at a time when cultural differences were beginning to break the glass ceiling in Hollywood. Why would he want to sound like everybody else?

The fact was, he couldn't if he'd tried because full accent neutralization is almost impossible if it doesn't happen during the formative years. There is nothing like the pressure kids feel to assimilate in grade school and middle school to cause them to lose an accent. Youngsters will do just about anything to fit in. But Ashish came to America, and to acting, later in life. So, even though he hired me for the very purpose of accent reduction, I had to be blunt with him:

"Ashish, this really isn't going to happen the way you see it, but that's a good thing. Instead of trying to change, tell people who you are. Put your mark on this industry, and celebrate the fact that you are part of the changing paradigm of what a twenty-first-century American actor looks and sounds like."

We are finally coming to a point where we understand that it's not imperative for all Americans to look and sound alike. Great storytelling comes in all shapes, sizes, and cultures. It's just as American to wear a burka or a sari as it is to wear your favorite team's jersey. Good speech is color-blind. To return to the music analogy, it's the difference between a reed instrument like a clarinet and a brass instrument like a trumpet. One is not necessarily better than the other. In fact, their differences are what creates that rich tapestry of sound in an orchestra. You can inform the sound with your background and personality. But you still need to get the notes right—the way the composer wrote them. That's where articulation comes in.

Ashish just required a few simple adjustments to make his pronunciations crisp and clear. The accent was not the distraction, but the occasional false note, or phonetic sound, was. As was typical for many native speakers of South Asian languages, Ashish would sometimes interchange a "w" sound with a "v" sound, as in "Denise Voods." Equally, his British English was at times preventing him from saying the vowel and diphthong sounds of "r" in words like "here," "there," "poor," "pour," "car," "far," "third," "mother," and "flower."

We repeated some pronunciations so that his articulators could get used to the difference between a single pure vowel sound and the two vowel sounds of a diphthong. For example, the word "car" is not one sound ("cah") but two ("ca-r"). It's a fine line, but anything that could cause the listener to pause and move their attention away from the story must be corrected.

We worked on passages from classic American plays, such as Tennessee Williams's *The Milk Train Doesn't Stop Here Anymore* and *The Glass Menagerie*. This rich dialogue, steeped in the rhythms and syntax of the South, requires anyone who speaks it to be more conscious of how the words are colored and shaped. But I would also have him switch it up midstream from British to American, and back. Ashish needed to build a fluency, so that he could pick up and drop his British-American-Indian speech at will. How much of his British/Hindi accent to add or drop should be his decision, something that he can navigate seamlessly depending on his audience or the character he is trying to portray.

Ashish was diligent, practicing daily. It was the one small thing he could do for himself as he handled his family's affairs, with the goal of eventually setting up in New York to do more theater. He recorded our Skype sessions and noticed progress each time. By paying closer attention to these subtle distinctions in pronunciation, Ashish also became a better actor.

"Denise, I always knew I needed some fine-tuning but was never able to pinpoint exactly where and how," he told me. "Actors need to be able to hear themselves and others. It's part of our training. You made me a better listener of my own self."

Beyond acting, Ashish is feeling a deeper connection with others, which he had lacked in the past, when he'd always felt like somewhat of an outsider.

"The fact that I can stand in front of someone born and raised in the US and they understand me as clearly and easily as someone who grew up next door to them makes me feel closer to people," he recently shared. "It's as if we have more in common and we can relate better. It's liberating."

The work I do with all my clients is resolutely about maintaining a sense of who they are. I don't want to replace their individual voice prints; I want to enhance them by cleaning up what's already there and adding more range. I want to empower people with what they already have.

Code Switching

Empowering her is essentially what I was doing when I was working with Tanasha N. Stinson, one of dozens of bright young students from New York City whom I had the privilege of teaching in the late nineties.

Tanasha, who grew up in West Harlem and Brooklyn, had gone through a nonprofit enrichment program called the Harlem Educational Activities Fund (HEAF). New York real estate developer and philanthropist Daniel Rose had founded the organization to debunk the "Bell Curve" theory and prove that *all* children, given equal sets of circumstances, can thrive. And thrive they did. These brilliant teens in the program graduated with an average 4.2 GPA and went on to study at Harvard, Yale, and Trinity College.

During a HEAF awards dinner, Daniel and his wife, Joanna, noticed that when the students went up to give their acceptance speeches, they had difficulty expressing themselves. Their intelligence was obscured by their inability to enunciate. When other opportunities arose for the students to give speeches, they were hesitant because they had heard each other at the dinner.

The Roses could see that the children felt mortified in that room full of movers and shakers. Joanna suggested acting classes, and that's when Dan decided to call Juilliard for help. His brother happened to be a board member at Juilliard at the time. In fact, the Juilliard dorms are housed in the Rose Building at Lincoln Center. It was the former president of Juilliard, Dr. Joseph Polisi, who suggested that the students study with me. We all agreed that these acutely intelligent and accomplished youngsters should maintain a sense of self.

With the Rose family's support, I founded Express Yourself! in 1996, taking these and many other mostly African American and Latinx teens through the same vocal training and discipline that I taught Juilliard's top acting students. It was never my goal to make these kids over like some inner-city version of *Pygmalion*. Rather, I wanted to give them the tools that would allow them to translate themselves into the mainstream while remaining authentic. Again, I wanted them to have a fluency between worlds, or what we in the African American community call "code switching"—adjusting our speech according to our audience. I've already shared how, as a child, I would do this instinctively. I would go to my predominately Black Baptist church on Sunday in Harlem, but on Saturday I'd be in Lincoln Center singing opera with the children's chorus. I'd go back to my neighborhood and jump double Dutch with my girlfriends, then find myself in a predominantly white junior high school the following Monday.

To be clear, I was in no way advocating that they mimic a distinct group of people (I'll talk more about embracing your regional roots in the next chapter), or implying that their culture wasn't good enough. That's not what this was about. Rather, I wanted these kids to empower themselves with fully expressive voices so that they could be seen, heard, and understood for the true stars they were. I wanted to give them tools to confidently navigate life in ways that reflected their acute intelligence and ambitions as well as their culture, region, and personality.

These young women and men went on to do great things. They are doctors, engineers, scientists, and journalists. One of my students became a pediatrician, using his tools of expression to calm his young patients and educate families in underserved communities about their health and self-care. He also travels extensively, speaking on public health issues to his fellow physicians. Another student is at an investment bank, earning the respect of clients with vastly different backgrounds from her own. And another former student, Yasmin Moya-Guitierrez, is now a teacher at one of the most prestigious private schools in Manhattan.

Express Yourself! is the proudest achievement of my long career. I learned as much from these bright students as they learned from me—lessons about authenticity and identity that I would carry with me and apply to the work I do with diverse global clients from all walks of life.

"The point is not to change anybody here," I assured them on their first day on my classroom floor at Juilliard. "It is not about changing. It's about broadening—about allowing your true selves to emerge. If you have a Spanish accent because English is your second language, I'm not asking you to give that up, because it is a part of who you are. I just want you to speak well within that framework."

Tanasha took these lessons to heart. She went on to get her degree at Temple Law School and has since served all over the world as an attorney for the U.S. Army and a member of the Judge Advocate General's Corps (JAG Corps).

The notion that speaking well was not tied to "sounding white" was a new and compelling idea for Tanasha. As a shy little girl from New York City, she used to listen closely to young white kids on the subway, then try to emulate them.

"Why are you trying to sound like a white girl?" her family would ask her.

"No, she doesn't sound white," her mother would tell her family members. "She sounds intelligent."

Or, rather, intelligible. How one speaks should not be a judgment on one's intelligence; it's one's ability to be fully understood. Tanasha and her mother hadn't yet grasped that speaking clearly was simply a matter of expressing all of her unique qualities with precision.

Back then, Tanasha "didn't understand the importance of authenticity," she told me when we reconnected years later. "But you helped me to understand that I could be who I am while also using my voice effectively. You gave me permission to be a better version of myself."

We worked on several issues, from slouching posture to muffled speech. We also worked on developing a more welcoming sound. In most of our neighborhoods, to keep yourself safe, you had to convey the attitude that you were poised and ready to fight at the least provocation, which can result in a harshness of sound. It's a self-protective stance, but it's not inviting aesthetically. To counter this tendency, I would have the students repeat phrases like "My mind is my own," to bring the voice forward in the mouth for a warmer sound.

Other adjustments included the articulation of diphthong sounds, which had become pure vowel sounds thanks to many of the kids with southern roots—"your" became "yo." Several other kids grew up in non-English-speaking households that did not use the "th" sound, so many were not aware that there was a distinction between "mumfs" and "months."

Tanasha, like most of the young men and women in the Express Yourself! class, also dropped final consonant sounds—"taste" became "tase," "wrist" became "wris," and "giggle" became "giggo." We did exercises to bring the tip of her tongue to the gum ridge to form a crisp, more precise "t" sound and a firm, smooth lateral "l" sound—articulation exercises that she wrote down in her notebook and kept to this day.

Hearing the sounds of speech pronounced with precision was a revelation to Tanasha, as well as to her fellow HEAF students. They grew up in an environment where you don't reveal too much and make yourself vulnerable. You can't sit up straight, relax your jaw, and maintain a receptive and open posture, because that would be perceived as weakness. These kids needed to understand that allowing others to fully hear and understand them was a strength.

"Invite people from another world into *your* world," I would constantly tell Tanasha and her classmates. "Lay out the vocal welcome mat, and let them see how wonderful it is."

Tanasha credits these articulation tools with helping propel her into a life far beyond anything her family could have dreamed for

her. No one in her home had ever been to college, much less graduate school, but Tanasha got herself a full ride through the military. While an undergraduate, Tanasha gave a presentation on the
Reserve Officers' Training Corps. She impressed a retired military
officer, who also sat on HEAF's board of directors, so much that he
became her mentor, guiding her through her entire military career.

It was her impeccable diction that always gave her the edge. It
often made her first pick at trial team auditions.

"I remember seeing the looks on the faces of judges when I first
walked into the room. Unimpressed. I had a stack of note cards
in my hand. Clocking this, one judge rolled his eyes and said,
'I'm going to need you to not read from those.' I put them down,
stood up straight, and started speaking. As I did, I watched the
faces on the panel, and I could see I'd gotten their attention.
They put their pens down and started to smile. Miss Denise, I
wouldn't have had that level of confidence if it hadn't been for
your lessons years before."

Today, Tanasha is a lieutenant colonel and second-in-charge
of a large office of attorneys and paralegals at a military base in
Missouri, where she resides with her husband and two young
daughters. She has adapted so seamlessly to the many different
environments in which she's operated that when she tells her sol-
diers where she is from, they are shocked.

It wasn't sounding like she was from New York City that would
have held her back. Those who were unable to make themselves
understood, regardless of background or region, found themselves at a disadvantage in the U.S. Army. Early on in her military career, Tanasha encountered a woman with a deep colloquial
southern drawl. It stood out so much that she wasn't being taken
seriously. This woman's commanding officer took her aside and
told her to fix her speech or she would never succeed in the army.

"She was being discounted because the audience was distracted
by how she was speaking. What she had to say didn't even matter," Tanasha sadly shared with me. "That's what inspired me to

keep up everything you taught me. You gave me the tools to go beyond my circumstances and helped break me out of the cycle of poverty."

Flooded Out

Often, when individuals step outside their immediate environment, they really begin to hear themselves.

When I first met football cornerback Marcus Cromartie, he told me, "Hurricane Katrina was the best thing that ever happened to me!"

"Really?!"

"Yes, ma'am!"

His family lost everything when their home in New Orleans' West Bank Algiers was flooded out, and his parents lost their jobs. They spent the next five months living out of a small hotel room in Texas while Marcus, a tenth grader at the time, adjusted to life in a new state and school. That's where he first realized that his dialect was so heavy that teachers thought he needed to enroll in English as a second language (ESL) classes. His teachers, classmates, and coaches had no idea where he was from, because "Nawlins" has such a unique gumbo of dialects, from Creole and Cajun influences, to the squads of Brooklyn nuns who descended on the city in the fifties to teach in the local schools. Never having traveled far beyond his four corners, in many ways, he faced a greater challenge than Ashish, despite the fact that he was born in the US. He essentially had to relearn English, phonetically.

Being forced out of his community not only expanded Marcus's linguistic vocabulary; he became more focused on his sports and studies. As a middle schooler, he cycled in and out of mischief, letting his grades slide and taking his natural athletic gifts for granted.

"New Orleans can be a rough town," Marcus explained to me. But his new school and home spurred a kind of rebirth.

By the time I had the pleasure of meeting him he was the whole package, an athlete who had played on various NFL teams and then joined the Canadian Football League's Montreal Alouettes. Even back then, he was thinking of his future after football.

"'NFL' stands for 'not for long,'" he told me. "It's not what you think. You only hear about the top hundred players who are millionaires and superstars, not the fifteen hundred other men who are at the back of the roster, grinding it out season after season for a paycheck. It's scary that we spend our whole lives on football, and by the time we finish in our thirties most of us will have no work experience, not even a job in a restaurant. And for all that, we get painted as entitled, spoiled brats, not men who earn an honest living by putting their lives on the line!"

Marcus wanted to be a voice for all the other players like him: hard workers, fathers, and husbands who live exemplary lives and give back to their communities. Like rugby star Phaidra Knight, he wanted to share his views not just on the sport itself but on the social and political issues that concern us all. To that end, he hoped to parlay his professional career into broadcasting, which was why he came to me.

The problem was that, despite the earlier efforts of his Texas schoolteachers, he still had a southern drawl so deep it could be hard to understand him. Marcus found it difficult to wrap his tongue around certain words, and the slow tempo of his regional speech didn't quite fit in with the fast-talking broadcasters of the East and West Coasts.

"The people who hire from LA or New York have a specific idea of how someone in the media should sound," observed Marcus. "I know my drawl comes off as slow."

But spend a few minutes talking to him, and his quick wit comes through. He reminded me of so many clients who are profoundly book smart but lack the verbal dexterity to match. The dialects and vernacular of the neighborhoods they grew up in may have a completely different connotation and meaning to people outside of their communities. Hence the need for a larger verbal tool kit from which to draw.

Sharp and extremely well informed, Marcus already possessed the material for great voice and speech. It was just a matter of fine-tuning; he had the humility and wisdom to know that it was incumbent upon him to meet these potential employers where they were.

"If someone tells you they don't like the way you sound, it's not something you want to hear, but so be it," he told me. "I viewed it as a challenge. Besides, I am an athlete, and I'm used to trying to improve myself."

We worked on several things, including phrasing, which I will share more about in the final chapter. We also eliminated the "ums" and "uhs" that slowed down his delivery and didn't match his quick wit. Marcus found that using his breath and his imagination allowed him to seamlessly connect images and thoughts instead of individual words, eliminating the need for vocal placeholders such as "um" and "uh."

Marcus hasn't retired from the sport yet. But his newly refined voice and speech skills, which he continues to exercise, will be there for him when he's ready to make that transition. His speech has already transformed into the clear, rapid-fire delivery typical of a professional broadcaster, but flavored with his own Creole spice.

The Articulators

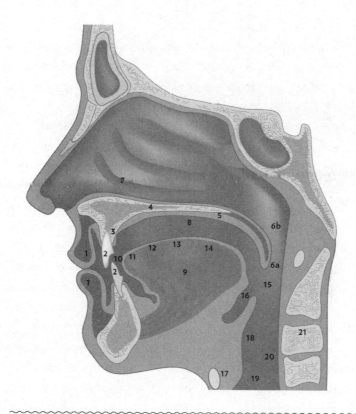

1	LIPS	11	BLADE OF THE TONGUE
2	TEETH	12	FRONT OF THE TONGUE
3	GUM RIDGE	13	MIDDLE OF THE TONGUE
4	HARD PALATE	14	BACK OF THE TONGUE
5	SOFT PALATE	15	THROAT
6	UVULA	16	EPIGLOTTIS
a	RELAXED	17	VOICE BOX (LARYNX)
b	RAISED	18	VOCAL FOLDS
7	NASAL PASSAGE	19	WINDPIPE (TRACHEA)
8	MOUTH	20	FOOD PASSAGE (ESOPHAGUS)
9	TONGUE	21	SPINE
10	TIP OF THE TONGUE		

Speak It!

Just as a pianist practices musical scales in preparation for playing "the music," these articulation tongue twisters will improve the accuracy and dexterity of your speech. As you articulate these fun exercises, go very slowly at first and be aware of the following:

1. The stop plosive sounds "p" and "b" and the nasal consonant sound "m" are formed with the lips coming together (#1 in the diagram on page 185).
2. The stop plosive sounds "t" and "d," the nasal consonant sound "n," and the lateral consonant sound "l" are formed with the tip of the tongue lifted onto the gum ridge (#10 lifted to #3).
3. The stop plosive sounds "k" and "g" and the nasal consonant sound "ng," as in "sing," are formed with the back of the tongue lifted to the hard palate (#13 lifted to #4).

NOTE: Stop plosive sounds "p," "b," "t," "d," "k," and "g" start with the lips coming together, the tip of the tongue connecting to the gum ridge or the back of the tongue connecting to the hard palate, and then are released with a gentle explosive breath for the voiceless sounds and voice for the voiced sounds. The sound of nasal consonants "m," "n," and "ng" is released through the nose. The lateral sound "l" is formed with the tip of the tongue on the gum ridge, and the sound is released on both sides of the body of the tongue.

Now repeat the following:

A tutor who tooted the flute
Tried to tutor two tooters to toot
Said the two to the tutor
"Is it tougher to toot
Or to tutor two tooters to toot?"

Betty Botter bought a bit of butter;
"But," she said, "this butter's bitter!
If I put it in my batter
It will make my batter bitter.
But a bit o' better butter
Will make my batter better."
Then she bought a bit o' butter
Better than the bitter butter,
Made her bitter batter better.
So 'twas better Betty Botter
Bought a bit o' better butter.

Delilah de Dardy was fat,
Delilah de Dardy was old,
(No doubt in the world about that)
But Delilah de Dardy had gold.
Lorenzo de Lardy was tall,
The flower of maidenly pets,
Young ladies would love at his call,
But Lorenzo de Lardy had debts.

Give me the gift of a grip-top sock,
A clip drape shipshape tip-top sock—
Not your spin slick slapstick slipshod stock,
But a plastic, elastic grip-top sock.
None of your fantastic slack swap slop
From a slapdash flash cash haberdash shop;
Not a knickknack knitlock knock-kneed knickerbocker sock
With a mock-shot blob-mottled trick-ticker top clock;
Not a rucked up, puckered up, flop top sock,
Nor a super-sheer seersucker rucksack sock;
Not a spot-speckled frog-freckled cheap sheik's sock
Off a hodgepodge moss-blotched scotch-botched block;
Nothing slipshod, drip drop, flip flop, or glip glop;
Tip me to a tip-top grip-top sock.

8.

Embrace Your *Isms*

....

RECOGNIZE REGIONAL SPEECH
AS GOOD SPEECH

The whole is greater than the sum of its parts.

—ARISTOTLE

With his sandy blond hair, high cheekbones, and sculpted body, actor Kellan Lutz was the physical embodiment of Hercules, the coveted movie role he was destined to play. He'd spent months in the gym working on his appearance to get an edge in a highly competitive industry.

His dedication paid off, and the movie's producers booked him for the part. The former Calvin Klein underwear model had prepared well, and he looked like he was born to wield a sword and ride a horse. But Kellan and the producers soon realized that he sounded nothing like the mythological Roman hero, son of gods, famed for his strength and sense of adventure.

Kellan's speaking voice was trapped in the nasal region of his head and lacked the strength and vocal gravitas of a mythological figure. It was far from Herculean. In fact, it was far from who

Kellan truly was, both physically and in terms of his personality, which was humble, thoughtful, strong, and self-aware. He knew he had his work cut out for him as we worked together tirelessly on deepening and enriching his voice. There was much at stake. The film had already been shot, and it was at this point that the producers realized that Kellan needed to go back into post-production and make his voice match his performance. This was his biggest Hollywood role yet—a chance to break past his previous role in the *Twilight* series and make a name for himself as a blockbuster action hero who could carry a film. The pressure was on, and he *had* to get it right.

Like most athletes, Kellan had self-discipline. Whatever exercises I gave him to do—from breathing from his diaphragm to visualizing the placement of his voice—he did them and practiced with diligence. His work ethic was impeccable. He practiced nonstop, doing all the foundational work I described to you in the previous chapters. I especially enjoy working with gym enthusiasts, athletes, and dancers because they have a built-in discipline. They also have faith that if they stick to a daily physical regimen, they will see results over time. Their bodies are their instruments, and they believe in the process, so much so that I sometimes need to pull them back from working too hard. And yet they're almost bashful as students of the voice, apologizing for coming to the craft so late.

Kellan was no different. I appreciated the fact that he didn't have an entitled bone in his body and approached his vocal training with such respect. He'd made tremendous progress in the time we'd been working together. But something was still missing. We'd worked through some of his most distracting vocal habits, but he sounded nothing like a demigod. Instead, he sounded like a young man from a farm in Arizona by way of North Dakota, the two states where he grew up as one of eight children in a devout Christian household. We needed to bring out the depth in his voice to match his physicality and replace the southwestern and northern plains twang with a sound that would make him more believable in a mythical role of no real time or place. The voice of his character had to be at once commanding and relatable—a blend that suggested both his godlike powers and his human vulnerability.

My choice to use a mid-Atlantic dialect was to give the character an American sensibility while at the same time suggesting a historical context. We achieved this change in the quality of Kellan's delivery through specific vowel, diphthong, and consonant modifications as well as using voice and speech rhythms that land between the British and American dialects.

Choose a Vocal Superhero

Thank God for YouTube! I often tell my clients to choose someone whose voice they admire, then go online to listen to them speak from as many different platforms, and within as many different contexts, as possible. Watch how your voice heroes tell stories. Pay attention to their diction and how they use language.

One of my all-time favorite role models was Peter Jennings, the ABC news anchor who died of lung cancer in 2005. I could listen to him all day. He was Canadian and had a deep, rich, resonant voice that could have come from anywhere in North America. It was neutral but also warm and relatable. He was the voice of our nation: strong, confident, and trustworthy. Another example is my former client Soledad O'Brien, anchor and producer of the syndicated news show *Matter of Fact with Soledad O'Brien*. Her delivery is probing, smart, and thorough, while allowing her witty and delightful personality to shine through.

The more Kellan and I got to know each other, the more I realized that he was still holding back. By all accounts, he was no longer supposed to be the bashful "Aw, shucks" guy from Arizona. He was a golden boy of Hollywood and needed to give himself permission to release his most compelling voice onto the world. Kellan had to add more speech options to his daily speech in order to give himself more choices for character development, ultimately allowing him to become the actor he was always meant to be.

Once we got past his shy personality, once Kellan realized that his origins weren't the only definition of who he was, and that he could reach beyond the sum of his parts, he nailed it! In fact, during a press junket interview after the movie premiered, talk show host Wendy Williams asked him what country he was from. She just couldn't place his accent.

"What's your accent? What do I hear? That's not Jersey. . . . Are you from this country?" she asked Kellan, as she cozied up to him on the couch. "Maybe from Scotland?"

Success!

He was so excited by his breakthrough that he even joked, "Now Denise, can you teach me some Shakespeare?"

You, Only Better

Where you come from does not have to be a source of embarrassment, and a regional accent is not something to be erased. Your *isms* and the rhythm of your speech are a part of what makes you *you*. Kellan and I worked on a dialect for a role that required a certain type of speech, but our goal was not to remove all the regional flavor from his everyday speaking voice. The intention was to free his authentic voice from any distractions, to celebrate who he was and expand on it. It was all good. We just wanted to enhance what was already there.

I write this chapter mindful of the fact that regionalisms have become a hot button. It's at the forefront of people's minds because of the divisiveness of our political climate. We have become so focused on our differences that it's almost tribal. But you *can* embrace and celebrate who you are while still being inclusive. You don't have to isolate yourself or pick a side. And how you speak doesn't have to pigeonhole you. We all make assumptions when it comes to speech, and it's oh so humbling when we realize how wrong we were.

In the winter of 1999, I was on a career roll. I was on the faculty at Juilliard and was working as a consultant at *NBC Nightly News*. I had just settled into my newly purchased condo in Westchester County, a suburb just outside of Manhattan, and had enrolled my son into a private school.

"Okay," I thought. "Now I'm good."

But for weeks a woman from California kept calling me. Fran Bennett, the head of acting in the School of Theater at California Institute of the Arts, was persistent, I'll give her that. She gave me a sales pitch about CalArts and told me how much I'd love it in Los Angeles.

"Fran, I am flattered, truly," I told her. "But my family is here, I'm happy at Juilliard, and my son just started at a new school. My ties to New York are just too deep."

I gave her the names of some other experts in speech whom she might want to reach out to. Christmas and New Year's came and went. Fran called me back again.

"None of them have what I'm looking for," she told me. "Are you sure I can't tempt you?"

"No, I'm sorry. I simply can't leave."

I hung up the phone and took my dog out for a walk. There was an Arctic chill that January afternoon. It was so cold my nostrils were sticking together. Just as I was finishing my loop around the block, a woman came out of her driveway and yelled:

"Why is it that every time you walk your dog, it's on my side of the street?"

"Ma'am, I always pick up after my dog," I told her.

"But he does number one . . ."

"Listen, I'm too cold to stand out here and discuss this with you. Why don't you take it up with the condo board?"

I continued on my way. But as I thought about it, I decided I wasn't being friendly, so I turned around, took my glove off, and extended my hand.

"Hi, I'm Denise, and I'm your new neighbor. I'm sorry we got off on the wrong foot."

She refused to take my proffered hand, looking at it instead with contempt.

"No way. I'm taking the matter up with the board as you suggested," she huffed.

"You know, I feel sorry for you," I replied. "It must be really hard when you get old and crotchety."

"I am not old, you Black bitch!"

"Madam, it's obvious to me who the bitch is here."

I went home and immediately called Fran.

"It's a windchill factor of 16 below, and some woman just called me a Black bitch! I want to know, is that offer still on the table?"

Fran chuckled.

"Well, darling, it's 75 degrees here, I'm reading the *New York Times*, and no one has called *me* a Black bitch today."

"You're Black?"

"Yes, of course I am! Now would you like to come and join me?"

"I'd love to!"

Fran had a mid-Atlantic, old Hollywood way of speaking that made me assume she was an expatriate British voice teacher. She'd spoken that way her entire life, but she'd grown up in the Deep South in a large Black church family. She'd been drawn to literature and had a love of language from the time she could first read and speak. Apart from her family, no one around Fran spoke that way. But it was an authentic reflection of who she was, and no one tried to change her. Everyone accepted this remarkable and erudite little girl who stood in front of the congregation and read from the Bible each Sunday as a gift.

It's only human to make snap judgments about people based on their skin color, the way they dress, and their speech. Putting people in an easily identifiable box gives us comfort because we believe we are dealing with something that's known and familiar. But life is so much more interesting when people can surprise you.

We need to stop sitting with the same group at the lunch table. We need to evolve into a more inclusive mindset. When we embrace our regional and cultural differences, they can serve as conversation starters, helping us learn more about each other. Prejudice is born of ignorance. How lovely to be able to ask people where they are from and get to know them better! We don't live in a homogenous society, so we shouldn't expect one another to sound that way. Why can't we all just accept one another for who we are instead of trying to conform to one model that no longer serves us?

The *Un*-standard

Back in the day, people in the public eye were groomed to sound a certain way. If you've ever watched some of those classic old movies, you may have noticed that actors all tended to sound vaguely British. Think Katharine Hepburn as Tracy Lord in *The*

Philadelphia Story—all lock-jawed and drawling out her sylla-bles, like a New England blue blood whose ancestors came over on the Mayflower. That was the standard, much like the English class system that had for generations excluded those who did not speak with an accent denoting a certain social status or Oxford/Cambridge (Oxbridge) educational background. There was some unspoken rule that *isms* were not okay and that revealing your cultural and regional individuality was tantamount to letting your slip show.

I can still recall listening to conversations, as a child, of how people initially reacted to the way John F. Kennedy spoke. When he first broke onto the political scene, his Catholicism and Bostonian accent were almost scandalous. How he sounded was so antithetical to what Americans were used to hearing in the White House. Then there was Italian American Geraldine Ferraro, the first female vice-presidential candidate, from Queens, no less. Her accent and Italian origin were the subjects of much discussion during her campaign. There were snide remarks about how she and her husband might be connected to the mob and how she didn't have the right political pedigree.

Race, culture, and background have always been a huge issue in this country. Although we still have a long way to go, we are slowly beginning to see a shift in the paradigm. People have more choices in who represents them, who they identify with, and how they present themselves to the world. Diversity and regional-ism have moved to the forefront of the American conversation, and the way we speak does not have to pigeonhole us. Standard American English is a thing of the past.

I don't even use the term "standard" in my practice. Whose standard are we talking about anyway? The regionalism that was once frowned upon is the very thing that makes us memo-rable and unique. As long as you speak to be understood, gram-matically and phonetically, you are communicating *your* truth well.

Word Play

The Welsh poet and playwright Dylan Thomas was the king of onomatopoeia, which is the phonetic imitation of the sound that a word describes (like "cuckoo," "sizzle," and "booing"). He chose evocative words that express the emotion within the word, in a juxtaposition that's fun, rhythmic, alliterative, and foreign to the American ear. Most people are attached to their regional speech habits but they usually find it fun and comfortable to play with language in nontraditional ways. The advantage of reading Thomas's work for my students is twofold: they have no prior attachment to the text, and his language is so out of this world that they can get out of their heads and project just about anything onto it. That's why one of my favorite exercises, which was introduced to me when I was a student at Juilliard, is reading aloud from *Under Milk Wood: A Play for Voices*. Thomas's language is filled with visual images that give you a visceral desire to utter the phonetic sounds that will loosen your tongue and potentially free it, in order to break old speech habits and acquire new ones. "Oh, the Spring whinny and morning moo from the clog dancing farms, the gulls' gab and rabble on the boat-bobbing river and sea and the cockles bubbling in the sand, scamper of sanderlings, curlew cry, crow caw, pigeon coo, clock strike, bull bellow."

My immediate family lives in Los Angeles, but when my son, Terry, was a young boy, he rocked a Yankees cap in Dodger Stadium because we are proud New Yorkers. I doubt that he could do that today as a grown man and make it home safely. We are not Lakers fans; we are Knicks fans, and always will be. New York is such a part of who we are, but not *only* who we are.

Embrace regionalism; maintain that sense of who you are and where you come from. But also realize that the ability to navigate between worlds with fluency is a strength. Iron out those kinks that might be an obstruction to your listeners. Make it easier for them to come to you, so that they can better understand your world. Take the following three steps to become more welcoming in your speech:

1. Elide or gently blend the final consonant sound of a word with the sound that begins with the next word. Don't just omit it—something we as Americans tend to do in our regional speech. This full pronunciation of the word gives a clear delineation of thought. Vowel sounds are where emotion is expressed, but consonant sounds are where the actual thought is expressed. If the consonant sounds are lost, so is the thought as the word trails off.

2. Simply breathing in and releasing your voice from a more forward and open space in front of your mouth, as opposed to the back of your throat, allows you to shape and articulate sounds with the organs of speech such as the lips, teeth, tongue, gum ridge, and hard palate. Listeners who are not in your immediate circle and who are less familiar with your habitual way of speaking will grasp what you are saying more easily.

3. Allow your thoughts to land by definitively going downward in the vocal inflection at the end of every thought that is not in the form of a question. This gives you a sense of certainty and power, leaving an indelible impression on your listener.

Of course, it is your prerogative to go back and forth between these speech characteristics, depending on the situation. Have fun with your newfound speech dexterity. It's something I like to play with, often cracking up my dinner companions as I slip from my "Juilliard" voice to New Yawkese to land a point. Having it both ways does not make you a sellout. It's empowering!

Generally, by the time clients come to me, they are well aware that their communication skills need improvement, be it voice, speech, or delivery. However, there are some clients who approach the work with trepidation. They've usually been sent by their agents or managers and with arms folded across their chest and a look of defiance on their faces, they sit across from me saying, "Okay! Show me what you've got!"

"I don't know what I'm doing here," said a young artist with over a million followers on social media. "The way I talk is the way I talk. If other people don't like it, it's their problem!"

"But if they can't understand you, my friend, you'll lose a whole new audience. So, it *is* your problem," I replied. "This work is about giving yourself more options."

Conversely, I have also had Juilliard students approach me a few years after graduating from the Drama Division to ask for help finding their authentic voices after four years of classical vocal training. The primary colors in their box of crayons had become dull. These gifted, well-trained actors were finding it difficult to transition from classical theater training to film and television. Unfortunately, they had lost their *isms*—the wonderful nuances and rhythms of speech that made them sound unique.

Think of it in terms of the experience of a mixed-race person who says, "I am both. Why do I have to denounce one in order to be the other?" There is a brand-new generation just now coming of age that talks about being part of a "third culture"—with a parentage and ancestry consisting of two, three, or more races. They are proud of being a blend that's as unique as a fingerprint, and they revel in their individuality. *This* is a choice. The fact that this generation has the freedom to embrace their multiple *isms* and create their own unique voices, a freedom that was not afforded previous generations, is a long overdue gift.

As long as people can understand you and are not distracted by your regionalism, by all means exercise your personal choice about how you want to be perceived in the world. Take the good, bad, right, or wrong stigma off speech altogether. Think about the way you want to be identified based on sexuality, race, or preferred gender pronoun. It's all good.

Love Where You're From

Finding freedom in your speech starts with embracing your origins—your *isms*—and by that, I mean the regionalisms, cultures, and individual distinctions that make you *you*. I want people to be able to trumpet from the mountaintop who they are and where they're from. Since my days as a student at Juilliard, I've learned that I have a hodgepodge of cultural influences that layer the way I speak—it's wonderful! I have roots that go way back to the traditions of the Gullah—a distinctive group of African Americans living in small farming and fishing communities in the Low Country of South Carolina, Georgia, and the nearby islands along that stretch of coastline. This community has survived slavery, the Civil War, and modernization relatively untouched, and they have a rich, Geechee language closer to the dialect spoken in Africa's Sierra Leone than anything heard in North America. And yet this rich piece of our country's cultural tapestry, which is chock-full of our history and legacy, is in danger of fading out.

Over the generations, we've been brainwashed into thinking that this vivid dialect—a combination of West African linguistics blended into southern English vernacular—is somehow substandard. I don't want it to die off. I want to be a torchbearer for this and the many other cultures that make up my unique heritage. I want everyone I know, whether they are African American, Native American, or Irish American, to be proud of their identity and not feel the need to give up their unique vocal rhythm. These *isms* are as beautiful as cultural diversity is a strength. Just like a fine vintage wine is complex, with many delicious notes of berry and cherry and oak, so is your native speech.

Rich Soil

Like wine, your vocal flavor comes from the very soil, or soils, in which you were raised. How we speak is not about race. Whether we are of the African diaspora, Europe, Asia, North or South America, we can't help but be products of our culture and region. How one communicates is also influenced by where you live and the people who live around you. I happen to live in a part of the country (California) where few people release their jaw or fully engage parts of the mouth, such as the tip and back of the tongue, the gum ridge, and the hard palate, in order to speak clearly. It must be the weather!

The reason a person speaks a certain way goes deep. Take the Carolinas, for example. Tobacco country! People who chew tobacco in those states (both Black and white) hold it tightly in the side of the mouth, keeping it, and the saliva, from spewing everywhere. Granddaddy does this, then his kids who don't chew tobacco begin to speak that way, passing it on to their kids, and so on. Suddenly a whole community talks a certain way because of one man.

Not pronouncing the "th" sound (as we discovered in Tanasha's story) is another regionalism that sticks. That sound doesn't exist in many languages. Doing what's required to make the sound—placing the tip of the tongue outside of the mouth between the teeth—is considered rude in many cultures. This articulation point can be difficult for many and has persisted through the generations for many African Americans. When African slaves were brought to the shores of the Americas, they were not allowed to speak their native languages nor read or write the language that was forced on them. They had no point of reference for the "th" sound, among many, so they came up with the closest approximation, positioning the tip of the tongue onto the gum ridge and replacing "th" with a "d" or an "n" sound, saying "dose" instead of "those" or "dem" instead of "them." If the inaccuracy of a phonetic sound changes the meaning of the word, it can potentially change the story, and listeners will have difficulty following along. When you have access to an entire library of the phonetic sounds of a language, you have a greater ability to thoroughly express an idea.

These sounds can be easily accessed by anyone regardless of how they identify or where they hail from. It's just a matter of giving yourself options and going for it. One articulation exercise I use to activate the blade of the tongue for accuracy of this sound is to rapidly repeat the following words:

The lips, the teeth, the tip of the tongue . . .

Say it three times in succession. Not as easy as it seems, folks!

One regionalism from the South is the "pin"/"pen" inversion. Again, it's not a Black or white thing. It's geographical. Changing that specific pronunciation does not in any way erase your cultural identity; it simply changes the meaning of the word. If you are saying the word "pin" but the word you are actually trying to say is "pen," you are confusing your listener, unless they happen to share the exact same dialect.

If regionalisms cause confusion in the listener, it's helpful to be able to articulate certain words in a different way. Making that alteration to make your message available to a broader range of people who don't share your dialect is in no way a betrayal of your roots. It is simply a matter of allowing yourself to be understood.

The trick is to balance a sense of identity with a desire for clarity, which, after all, is foundational to telling the story of who you are.

The daily drill that follows is an effective way to replace your old habitual speech pattern with a new one. Notice that the second word of each numbered line is a more open sound (see "Vowel, Diphthong, and Consonant Sounds" on pages 141–42). The practice phrases will also help you feel the physical differences in the two sounds while speaking at conversational speed. I have inserted a word in between to make the distinction easier:

1. Pin-pet-pen
Are you adjusting the safety pin while writing with a pen?

2. Sinned-set-sent
He sinned when he sent the gem.

3. Tin-septet-ten
Hold the tin over the heads of the ten men.

4. Bin-bet-Ben
Where's the garbage bin, Ben?

5. Gin-jet-gentle
Please don't give gin to that gentle gentleman.

Over a relatively short period of time, you'll find these regionalisms begin to soften but you'll also be able to welcome them back when you choose.

Rat-a-Tat-Tat

Whether you come from Boston, Philadelphia, New York, or any other densely populated area in the North and Northeast, chances are you have exaggerated articulation. This is not necessarily a bad thing. It occurred when there was wave after wave of different groups of immigrants—Italians, Irish, Puerto Ricans—all unconsciously feeling the need to assert themselves and hold on to the status quo in the fear that their particular culture would be replaced.

The result was strong "stop plosives"—an effect that's created when a sound formed by the articulators of the mouth suddenly stops and then explodes: "puh," "buh," "tuh," "duh," "kuh," and "guh." It's a rather harsh, defensive sound, as if you're spitting out pellets, as if to say, "Don't mess with me." But you can simply soften these stop plosives by holding a mirror up and looking at the way you are expressing yourself.

You'll notice at first that the manner in which you speak may be tight and percussive, and you are visibly overexaggerating the facial muscles to form a sound. But when you consciously relax and release the facial muscles and the tongue, that particular *ism* melts away. It's a subtle shift, but the impact is huge. The lips become less rounded, the tongue becomes more limber, and the sound flows more freely and becomes more melodic.

Invisible Scars

Candace (whose name I have changed to protect her privacy) is an aspiring actress who reached out to me after she saw me on an episode of a VH1 television show. Born and raised in southern New Jersey, not far from Philadelphia, Candace shared that she knew the way she spoke would not only limit her as an actress but also limit her in life. Our work together led her to consider becoming a spokesperson for an underserved community. It took a few sessions and effective work to gain her trust and learn exactly which community she was referring to.

Candace had been a sex worker, servicing all kinds of powerful businessmen, athletes, and even a few gangsters. She'd moved to Los Angeles to get away from that world, but vestiges of the lifestyle were still very much a part of how she perceived herself and ultimately the way she spoke. Gorgeous and flawlessly coiffed, Candace could have stepped off a Paris fashion runway.

She was desperate to leave her past behind her. She wanted to reinvent herself and start afresh, so I gave her the tools of expression she needed to polish her authentic voice.

Candace had a sibilant "s," which happens to be typical of many of my clients from large northern cities. She made a distracting hissy sound whenever she pronounced the consonant, because too much air was escaping over the blade of her tongue. I am not entirely sure why that issue is so common among city dwellers, as I'm not an anthropologist, but my guess is that it's the influence of Eastern European immigrants who came in large numbers in the early part of the last century. Among some Slavic languages, this "s" sound requires the expulsion of substantial breath over the blade of the tongue.

To modify this common vocal distraction, I have my clients put their forefinger on their throat, to feel the difference between a voiced consonant (for example, a "z") and a voiceless one (for example, an "s"), where all that should be coming through is air. Then I share that it's the upward position of the tip of the tongue that's needed to execute this sound most efficiently and not the blade.

As Candace was doing this, out of nowhere she suddenly blurted out a fact about herself: "I used to be a boy!"

I burst into tears when Candace revealed she was transgender, a fact about her I would never have guessed.

"Why are *you* crying?" she asked.

"Because I'm so honored you shared that with me!"

It was a whole new day and understanding about this woman. Candace told me all about her journey—how she went to Bangkok, Thailand, for gender-affirming surgery and nearly bled to death there. She showed me the scar where her Adam's apple used to be, which she had been touching with her forefinger as she was doing the vocal/vibration exercise. She'd covered it up meticulously with makeup, perhaps the only barely visible evidence that she'd ever undergone surgery. She's sacrificed so much to become the articulate, poised woman she is today. It almost cost her life.

This was a few years before the Caitlyn Jenner headlines, but certainly during the era of powerful, beautiful, and intelligent actresses of color like Laverne Cox and Janet Mock, who were forging ahead as transgender trailblazers.

"As I get closer to my voice, I feel the need to tell the truth," she said.

"Well, why don't you?" I asked.

"Because I used to be a lady of the evening," she explained.

"What of it?" I said.

She explained that the wealthy and powerful men she'd been seeing would be enraged by what they might see as a deception. Discovering that she was a transgender woman would make them question their own sexuality—a sensitive subject for many people, but especially for the alpha males who made up her former clientele.

"I could be killed!" she said.

I understood her hesitation. But the more I got to know Candace, the more I felt she would be a powerful advocate for the transgender community, and I've been gently nudging her in that direction ever since. She was brave enough to go through the painful and risky transformation to become who she was meant to be, so I knew she could do this, too.

It's taken years for me to convince this beautiful woman to share her journey with the world. But her newly acquired tools of expression have finally given her the confidence and courage to "come out." She recently called me to say, "I'm ready."

The pendulum has swung in favor of more openness about sexual and gender identity, and Candace's fear is subsiding. Today she goes on auditions, booking dozens of television commercials and indie films. A writer is even creating a part just for her. As Candace becomes more empowered, she is slowly emerging as the face of the trans movement in Hollywood, and I am proud to have played a part in the genesis of her newfound role in life.

Candace had come to me for "regional dialect reduction," and as she found her true speaking voice, I discovered there was so much more to her story than her region.

And so did she.

~~~~~~

Speak It!

Adjusting your *isms* starts with the voice. Depending on your region, you are placing your voice in different parts of the mouth. In the case of Fran Drescher, for example, her voice has a nasal quality that is distinctive of a Queens girl—her voice is largely placed in her nasal region. We want voice placement to start from the middle of the mouth and move forward, incorporating equal amounts of head and chest resonance.

Look in the mirror to watch yourself as you are speaking. Is your jaw tight or released? Are you visibly tightening the muscles in your face to make a sound? Try relaxing your face, jaw, and tongue to soften your articulation.

Find a vocal role model, and study how they speak in YouTube videos or on news shows. Choose someone with whom you can identify or who has already arrived at your destination. Do not mimic the person—simply listen and identify what makes the voice so compelling.

Repeat, repeat, repeat challenging groups of words and phrases until the alternate pronunciation feels natural ("pin"/"pen," "tin"/"ten").

Visualize the origin of your voice and where it's going. Is it for an audience of one or one hundred? The voice is visceral; we can't see it, but we hear it and feel it. Use the power of vibrant imagery to spark your imagination and ignite the space between you and your listener.

If you find that you're too overscheduled to fit in a daily practice of vocal and articulation exercises, read aloud. People don't do this often enough. It forces you to slow down, listen, and become more aware of phonetic sounds and how they are made.

Record a voice memo on your phone, and play it back. Hearing yourself in that way will make you acutely aware of vocal distractions and help you correct them.

Love not just where you are from, but all the many places you will go!

The Sibilant "S"

As we explore regional and contemporary speech in-fractions, let's not forget the ever-present and oh-so-distracting sibilant "s." Let's be clear that this is not a lisp; it's just too much breath escaping while this voice-less sound is being made. The voiceless sound "s" is a fricative, meaning that breath is released through a very narrow opening of the articulators; in this case, the tip of the tongue and the upper front teeth. This narrow open-ing, in theory, should result in a thin, quick release of breath. Well, not so simple! The issue is with the place-ment of the tip of the tongue for this sound.

Most people make this sound with the tip of the tongue (#10 on the chart on page 185) relaxed behind the lower front teeth (#2 on the chart), resulting in a huge splash of air over the blade of the tongue (#11). Remember, the goal is to swiftly release the breath for this voiceless sound through a narrow opening. When you actually raise the tip of your tongue (#10) toward but not touching the up-per front teeth (#2), you can more efficiently control the quality and amount of air you are releasing. The result is a thin, quick release of breath for the consonant "s," and then you are able to proceed gingerly to the following sounds of the word or phrase.

Read the following sentences aloud to practice the fric-ative consonant sound "s." Remember to quickly release a thin column of air over the tip of the tongue that is point-ing upward toward the back of the upper teeth to make the sound:

I saw Susie sitting in a shoeshine shop. Where she sits she shines, and where she shines she sits.

This exercise works on both "s" and "sh" and is a fun alternative to the classic "She sold seashells . . ."!

Silly Sally swiftly shooed seven silly sheep. The seven silly sheep Silly Sally shooed shilly-shallied south.

Another exercise to practice is "s" when it's combined with other consonant sounds:

1. *Six silly sisters sitting sadly sawing six silk sacks.*

2. *Six socks sit in a sink soaking in soap suds.*

3. *He thrusts his fists against the posts and still insists he sees the ghosts.*

4. *Denise sees the fleece, Denise sees the fleas. At least Denise could sneeze, and feed and freeze the fleas.*

5. *A skunk sat on a stump and thunk the stump stunk, but the stump thunk the skunk stunk.*

PART V

Communication

Actors and broadcasters have an advantage when it comes to communicating because they are professional storytellers: they use their voices for a living. However, they honed their skills for years before achieving success, and I assure you that you can become a successful communicator as well.

It's a matter of figuring out your intention, mapping out your message, and understanding that communication is something that takes place between a speaker and a listener. At a granular level, it's also understanding how words, phrases, sentences, and paragraphs all work and flow together to tell a story. Your narrative is everything. All the work we've done thus far on your instrument is about delivering your story with power.

You might be ever so relaxed, be breathing deeply, and have a well-produced voice with crisp articulation, but if you are not able to communicate an idea effectively, your efforts will fall flat. If you are ever in a position where you need to tell a story—be it giving a speech or simply selling yourself in a job interview—do your homework to solidify the bigger idea behind it.

9.

Powers of Persuasion

....

TAKE COMMUNICATION TO
THE NEXT LEVEL

In making a speech one must study three points:
first, the means of producing persuasion; second,
the language; third, the proper arrangement
of the various parts of the speech.

—ARISTOTLE

The new girl in school, eight-year-old Rebekah Radice, employed her usual tactics whenever the family relocated to a new town: she took a desk in the front row of her homeroom, eager to get to know her new teacher and classmates.

Rebekah was especially excited this time around because she'd just been given a snazzy set of brightly colored pencils, which she proudly arranged next to her notebook. But what Rebekah, the fresh-faced and modestly dressed daughter of a Christian radio host, did not realize was that things were done a bit differently in this neighborhood. This was the eighties, when typical affluent middle school girls in California wore bright lip gloss, stretchy neon tops, and big, teased-out hair. The teacher took one look at Rebekah, rolled her eyes, and said, "We don't use those here."

"Use what?" Rebekah asked.

"Colored pencils. Put those away, go to the office, and get yourself a regular No. 2 pencil. And when you come back, take a seat at the back of the class. The front row is reserved for more mature kids."

That was the kind of personal story I told Rebekah she needed to integrate into her presentations as a social media marketing guru. A former radio host, Rebekah had already built a highly successful business helping other entrepreneurs market their services and products online. She regularly spoke to rooms full of people across the nation. But she was beginning to realize that in order to take her speaking career to the next level and fully connect with her audience, she needed to give more of herself. Even though she was addressing large groups of people, she needed to get personal and somehow develop the sense of a one-on-one rapport with her listeners, no matter how many were in the room. It's why, when we first met, I took the time to get to know her. I wanted to understand what was really driving Rebekah along her chosen path.

"I am dedicated to taking my seat at the front," she told me. "That's why I am so passionate about serving entrepreneurs. Too often, small business owners believe they can't speak up and get noticed for what they do. I want to empower them to use online marketing to give them a voice and express who they are to the world."

Hello! There it was—the missing piece. As soon as Rebekah said those words out loud, something inside her clicked. Her whole mission in life was to help others use digital platforms to be seen and heard, but until now she hadn't allowed this for herself as a speaker. She realized that full and powerful communication involves much more than giving information. It's not just reading words off a page or note cards. It's a feeling for the story that brings in the listener and gives them a sense of who you are at your core.

That's not to say that you necessarily need to share your whole life story. At a business seminar, that would be TMI! But when you can seamlessly and effortlessly weave personal details, observations, and experiences into the information you are imparting, it becomes more of a conversation. Your audience isn't just sitting there passively receiving a barrage of information. They are engaged, coming along with you on the journey. As audience members, they may not be saying anything back, at least not verbally. But they are actively listening.

That's what Rebekah accomplished when she began to integrate curated pieces of backstory into her messaging. Although she generally did well in a room full of professionals, sharing technical information and methodologies, she felt like more of a trainer than an inspirational speaker. She wasn't achieving the very thing she was trying to teach her audience to do—tell their own story in a way that seemed natural and comfortable.

"I had some self-limiting beliefs that I hadn't done enough, didn't know enough, and was somehow not the right person to be speaking in front of an audience of thousands versus hundreds," Rebekah told me.

Working through those false assumptions was critical in helping Rebekah reach the next level as a communicator. If she did not believe in herself as an aspirational figure, how could she bring self-confidence to her listeners? She had to model the qualities she wanted to inspire in her audience.

"Sharing my own struggles, that sense of not belonging, and how I got to this place was key to my audience being able to see themselves reaching the end goal of all that they are trying to achieve," explained Rebekah.

That shift had a profound impact on her speaking career. It wasn't long after we began our work together that Rebekah commanded the attention of an auditorium full of international dignitaries as a keynote speaker at a NATO international summit in Brussels!

Making herself relatable was the gift she gave those powerful men and women. This group has access to experts at the highest level, and it was Rebekah they traveled across the globe to hear. As she studied the faces of these generals and legislators, she could see how powerfully she broke through, helping them grasp the significance of social media as a communication tool that, leveraged the right way, could create a new and improved world order. The international leaders in this conference hall urgently needed to hear Rebekah's information—and, boy, did they ever, many of them scribbling down notes and nodding their heads as Rebekah made each point.

Rebekah's audiences have since swelled from hundreds to thousands, and she is in demand as a speaker and expert across industries, even addressing the largest social media marketing conference in the world as a keynote speaker. She is also a regular guest on network news shows.

"I now get that not sharing those stories about myself was doing a disservice to my audience," Rebekah revealed to me. "I just had to get out of my own way and accept that those experiences of struggle—navigating new places, dealing with the mean girls, feeling the trepidation of starting a new business—all make me more relatable, no matter who the listener, because we are all human."

Exactly!

Symphony of Speech

Like many of my clients at her accomplished level, including top executives and great actors preparing for a role, Rebekah was already a polished speaker, with a certain fluidity and quality to her voice that could land a point. She had a well-honed instrument that was free of distraction and capable of hitting the right notes. But great speech is so much more than that. Rebekah wanted to master that next level of communication, powering her words with a combination of art and science that could transport her listeners. But it doesn't just happen by accident. Communication that can move a crowd is as well-crafted, intentional, and practiced as any great actor's monologue on the stage.

I liken this level of communication to a symphony, where it's not just about how well you play your instrument but how you seamlessly connect all the elements of the music—from the opening sonata to the second movement's adagio, building to a crescendo of emotion, then closing with a rousing allegro or rondo—whatever your chosen arrangement! Just as sublime music is well rehearsed, great speech happens by design.

Of course, no two artists are going to communicate a message in the same way. It's the communicators' job to decide if they are going to play a solo, be part of the orchestra in the wind or brass section, or take the baton from the first movement to the finale. The point is to decide before you start to play. Are you playing a solo, or are you using your instrument as part of a collaboration? Is it your desire to bring joy, tears, laughter, or all of the above, and in what order? What is your objective? There are so many options to choose from in this wonderful cacophony of human discourse.

The trick is to define your narrative. Your ability to move the audience requires a sense of intention, story, structure, and phrasing. And let's not forget everyone else in the concert hall, the audience itself. Communication is much more powerful when you're aware of your audience's experience with your performance and, essentially, invite them to be a part of it.

The Other Side of the Conversation

With every great speech there is an unspoken exchange between the speaker and the listener—a kind of giving and receiving—that makes the time they have spent in the room together that much more impactful and memorable. The message lands in the way it was intended, and it sticks. As Maya Angelou said, "I've learned that people will forget what you said, people will forget what you did, but people will never forget how you made them feel."

All the work we have done paring away the vocal distractions, powering your voice with breath and resonance, and building a narrative helps facilitate not just your side of the conversation, but your listener's as well. Sadly, we rarely have two-sided conversations in this country. No one is listening or taking in the other viewpoint. No one is taking a breath. We are all so exhausted from our own diatribes that we can't even hear other people anymore. But can you imagine the benefits to our relationships and careers if we rediscovered this lost art, matching our vocal skills to our authentic personality, being truly heard and understood because we invited others to do the same?

Building Blocks

If you're overwhelmed and wondering how you are ever going to master all these moving parts, fret not. We can start small. I'm not even asking you for a whole sentence. Right now, let's just focus on the phrasing, because that is where powerful communication begins and ends.

NFL player Marcus Cromartie, whom you met in chapter 7, wasn't just dealing with the challenge of his regional dialect getting in the way of the story. The written word completely threw him. In school, when his English teacher would call on him to read a book passage, he would fight the urge to hide under his desk. Of course, Marcus could read silently to himself. In fact, he was an avid reader. But when he spoke the words out loud, his eyes could not keep up with what was on the page. This was a problem for the aspiring sports anchor and talk show host. If he froze or stumbled over the words on a teleprompter, his career would be over before it started.

I had Marcus go home and record himself reading James Baldwin's classic novel *Go Tell It on the Mountain*, which is about an intelligent teenage boy living in Harlem in the thirties. I wanted him to read the thoughts of an African American man who was a poet and political, whose social commentary would deeply resonate with Marcus. He was unfamiliar with Baldwin's work, but he ate it up, feeling the poetry of the writer's language down to his marrow. I knew he would want to do full justice to this powerful telling of the African American experience. There is one passage in particular that evocatively describes the rain beating down on the flimsy habitat of his characters, rhythmically building up a sense of the storm. Baldwin's long, complex sentences are rich with vivid descriptions. I knew this exercise would be tough for Marcus, and I was right. His reading was halting and flat. His eyes and brain were not registering all the words, which he would often flub, either mispronouncing them or dropping syllables. "I sound like a fifth grader!" he lamented as we played back his recording in my studio the next day.

At first, I thought he might be dyslexic. Then I remembered that I had similar struggles in my first year at Juilliard. No one had taught me to read the way we speak, in groups of words rather than individual words. No one had explained to me that you don't just read a whole paragraph of words straight through, without a break. The same is true of sentences, particularly longer ones made up of more than one clause. We speak in thoughts; we only read in sentences. When I speak of communicating verbally, I'm referring to turning those sentences into well-phrased thoughts. When you group words together in a phrase, it buys you a bit of time to ready your eyes for the next group of words. It's tantamount to playing the individual notes of a song as opposed to a measure of a song.

"I'm gonna go" is one phrase; "I'm gonna go to the store" consists of two phrases that create the complete thought.

It didn't take long for Marcus to get it. Once he started phrasing the thoughts and finding the musicality of the language, it all came together. It was such an "aha" moment for him that, by our next session together, his ability to read aloud without so much as a stutter or a stumble was nothing short of miraculous. But Marcus wanted to keep going. Like the disciplined athlete he was, he wanted to practice, knowing that with repetition comes consistency. He felt himself slowing down in his effort to pronounce each word correctly.

"Denise, I'm so focused on the words, I feel like it's lessening my personality," he told me one day. "I'm losing my pizzazz."

Moment to Moment

At times Marcus's speech did indeed sound monotone because he was so concerned with getting it right. He needed to find the balance between accurate notes and phrasing and his own effervescent personality.

"It will come," I told him. "When you read, you have to allow your imagination to be in the present moment."

I shared how, when I read for audiobook publishers, if I had been thinking about what I had just read I would almost certainly screw up the next phrase. Looking back and wishing I had stressed a different syllable or pronounced a certain word differently would create a domino effect. I would have to take a break, clear my head, and start all over again. But when you're recording three hundred pages of text, that ends up taking a lot of time, so you soon learn how to move on to the next phrase, and the next.

"Don't look back and tell yourself you should have said something a certain way," I told him. "That past moment is dead and gone. And don't get ahead of yourself, either. Let this current moment inform the next. Use what you have at your disposal. Just be okay with what you did, and you won't stumble." Professional actors refer to this as "moment-to-moment acting."

Marcus continues to work at it, and I can hear the confidence growing in his voice each time we meet. He wants to read thirty pages of a book in one sitting (we've moved on to Baldwin's *If Beale Street Could Talk*), and he's loving hearing himself: the vibration of sounds, the clear, concise articulation, the shaping of each thought powered by breath and matching emotion.

This man walks into the room like he knows his stuff and you can't take it from him. He is brilliant, humble, with a work ethic that is not to be believed. He rated himself a "1 out of 10" communicator when we began our work together, and now he gives himself a 5—although I would argue he's closer to an 8 as he chops away at old habits, adjusting his speech to his audience while keeping his sparkling personality.

"Denise, I just want to wow a room with stories," he told me.

Soon he'll be conducting his own symphonies. Marcus has his instrument; he's fine-tuning and hitting all the notes of his full vocal range, and now he knows how to build his message phrase by phrase, thought by thought (or measure by measure, movement by movement). Marcus is mastering rhythm, with pauses and emphasis precisely placed to land just the right verbal punch. It's feeling more natural to him as he puts together all the elements of voice and speech in support of storytelling. He now understands that each phrase he speaks contains an operative, or stressed, word and that connecting these phrases creates a fluid thought.

When to Stress

The primarily stressed nouns are spoken with more emphasis because they contain the details of the actual story, along with the verbs, which contain the action. Adjectives and adverbs receive the secondary stress because they describe the nouns and verbs.

Example: *The **children** were **laughing** and **screaming** as they **stumbled** off the **roller coaster**.*

Remember, we read in sentences, but we speak in thoughts. Each thought contains two to three phrases that are made up of stressed (operative) words. The unstressed words are also important because of the role they play making the stressed words stand out. It's just a question of emphasis placement.

We will delve into more detail about these key words later in this book.

Bridge Building

The next step is developing an intentional delivery. Ideas are like islands, and intentional communication is the bridge to your listener. Building that bridge successfully is another process that requires self-awareness and an understanding of your own personal backstory, deliberation in crafting the message, and a connection to your audience.

Philanthropist and social justice advocate Kaci Patterson made herself into that bridge, using her gifts of speech and her knowledge of various cultures to enlighten and connect the vastly different worlds in which she operates.

The California native, who consults with various nonprofit, philanthropic, and government institutions and who cofounded her own grassroots social activism fund, BLACC (Building Leaders and Cultivating Change), came to me when she found herself getting invited to speak on panels, deliver remarks, and be interviewed on camera.

"I decided I need more polish, so I'm investing in myself," the young change agent told me. "I'm often the only African American person or woman in the room, and people of affluence and influence look to me to speak on a Black perspective and provide insights into the community they are funding."

It's her mission in life to "champion community-driven social change," working with those who sign the checks to make sure their dollars go to the community and social justice programs that need it most. Given that there are few people of color working within the family foundations and philanthropic institutions, Kaci found herself trying to explain social justice and racial equity issues to well-meaning white people who often had blind spots about their own tendencies to stereotype, navigating their own discomfort with race by using terms like "vulnerable" or "marginalized" communities.

Kaci's experience and authority are unmatched. There are few people in her line of work who know about both the funding side of philanthropy and the nuts and bolts of designing, operating, and managing nonprofit initiatives from concept to implementation. She's not sequestered in some ivory tower hobnobbing with billionaires and organizing fundraisers. Kaci goes into the communities and sees what individuals are battling every day, whether that's economic disadvantage, racial profiling, lack of political representation, or other forms of systemic oppression.

A Navy brat from San Diego, Kaci began her career in the non-profit sector while studying broadcast journalism at Pepperdine University, an experience that she describes as "my first exposure to the 1 percent." It was during her year studying abroad, when she noticed she was the only Black person out of sixty-five students at orientation, that her interests started to shift. Something didn't seem right in a world where African American and Latinx kids weren't getting the same kinds of exposure and opportunity as white kids. Without even realizing she was already beginning to advocate for equal opportunity, Kaci started speaking with Black and Latinx parents at local high schools and college freshmen orientation events, encouraging them to send their children abroad for study.

"I didn't choose philanthropy," she told me. "Philanthropy chose me."

On Edge

Kaci soon developed an all-consuming passion to push the world forward by advancing social justice and expanding educational, economic, and political opportunity for people of color. But that laser-sharp focus on doing good and bridging the socioeconomic divide sometimes came with a vocal edge. The unconscious bias that is the subtext of so much of the conversation exasperated her, and you could hear it.

"Denise, I find myself code-switching all the time, and I want to be able to find the right words for a delivery my audience will understand."

Kaci had been biting her tongue a lot prior to our session together because of the work she was doing with mostly white donors. In one conversation, she recalled how a group of funders talked with righteous indignation about the devastating impact of racism, made financial commitments to support organizations fighting for social change, and then expressed negative and somewhat contradictory views about these nonprofits, doubting their capacity to know their own needs and their responsibility in managing funds.

Kaci had to do some on-the-spot educating: reminding people in the room that the organizations largely led by people of color to serve people of color were the ones best positioned to understand their work and operational needs. For too long, these community programs had to make do with scant resources because philanthropists rarely invested in them. These social justice nonprofits were constantly being held back by negative perceptions.

"They were on the right side of right, but even though they were committed to funding these programs, they were still stereotyping and didn't even realize it," Kaci shared. "I had to correct their language and assumptions along the way without insulting them, and it took a lot of time to get through."

I could hear frustration in Kaci's voice. Whenever she was at her most honest, her voice would drop. (Her biggest truths were parenthetical.) Halfway through our first conversation, she was telling me something, and I said, "Okay, stop! I need to put my glasses on so that I can understand what you are saying because you're trailing off so much at the end of each thought. I need to be able to read your lips."

Walking the Line

The more truthful and authentic Kaci was being, the more her voice went into the back of her throat. It wasn't that there was anything wrong with her instrument per se. It was a subtle issue for this poised speaker. But it was the thing that was preventing Kaci from truly fulfilling her purpose. Kaci was code-switching so much between her white listeners and communities of color that, she told me, "I feel like an imposter in both worlds."

Instead of building a bridge, she was walking the line. Instead of sharing what she really felt only with those she knew and trusted, she needed to share her full voice and full message equally on both sides of the bridge because everything that she had to say mattered. She was uniquely positioned to bring about positive change and cooperation, allowing her audiences to "walk across [her] bridge to the other side" of understanding.

"Being a woman of color who has lived many of the experiences the nonprofit community is actively battling today, but also a woman of privilege with multiple degrees who owns her own home, I sit in both worlds," she explained. "Of the concentric circles of the elite and the underserved, I occupy the space where all three of us connect."

To make the most of this gift, Kaci needed to trust not just herself, but her listeners. Instead of self-censoring, constantly worrying if something she said was going to cause offense, she had to get comfortable with her own unique backstory, integrating it into her narrative for both sides of the bridge. Initially, she was uncomfortable about being center stage. Like Rebekah, she didn't fully grasp why her own feelings and experiences were relevant to the overall message.

"Let's talk about your work with concrete objectives and actions so that it becomes the star, not you," I told her. "Then we can weave in the personal backstory to play a supporting role and make you more relatable to any group you are addressing."

Together, we started crafting her story. It had to be universal and serve both groups equally, and it could not be watered down for the donors or beefed up for the nonprofits. Rather, it had to be an authentic call to action coming from a place of love and understanding.

This process brought forth a lot of emotion. At one point, Kaci began to cry.

"Denise, why am I so scared to put my voice out there? This petrifies me!"

"If not you, then who?" I replied.

I told her that, for the longest time, I was afraid to come out about my health diagnosis. But I realized I had a platform that could help others who suffered in the shadows by putting a face and a voice to the issue.

"There's no need to be afraid, Kaci. You're the expert on this subject and a force to be reckoned with."

She needed to give herself permission to keep it real. For the first time, I got her to speak freely and frankly about her passion.

"Yes, I *am* frustrated that it's taken this long for philanthropy to catch up with the needs of the real world. I want donors to see themselves as copilots of change and leaders of color as the main drivers. I want funders to get in the car and go on the journey of social justice, trusting those leaders through the ebbs and flows of change, as well as the setbacks and breakthroughs. Giving shouldn't be from a place that's so remote. I want them to talk to people and get to know them, supporting and amplifying their leadership while building deeper relationships. They need to ask simple questions to find common ground, even if it's something as innocuous as 'Do you like ketchup with your french fries?' And I want them to walk the walk and put their trust where their money is."

An Adjustment of Tone

It was a riveting speech. But the tone was still a little acerbic, and I feared it would be off-putting to her audience.

"Kaci, my dear, you are going to catch more flies with honey than vinegar. The content of what you are saying is powerful, but you need to adjust your tone to say it more invitingly. These folks are products of their times, so be firm but also be patient with the old guard and their unconscious bias. When you hold up the mirror for people to look at themselves, you have to do it honestly and gingerly, especially if you want them to loosen their purse strings. By all means, bring them into the new paradigm of philanthropy, because it's long overdue. But do so with more compassion in your voice."

Kaci heard me. She is smart and full of kindness—the type of person most of us strive to be. Her gratitude and empathy were always there, but she was so busy rolling up her sleeves and working at the grassroots level to get it done that she'd buried that part of her personality. Once we uncovered it, Kaci was able to bring forth the necessary warmth in her voice by simply adding "without judgment or disdain" to her objective of finding a common ground between donors and the communities they serve. It required a slight shift in her perspective and quite a bit of practice. As she became more comfortable with how she shared her truth, so did her listeners.

In the past year, as social justice issues continued to be at the forefront of the national conversation, Kaci has been invited to speak at numerous high-profile conferences, including a panel with a *New York Times*–bestselling author and other leading figures in the world of progressive philanthropy.

"I've reached the point where I'm able to be transparent and trust in the receptivity of my audience," Kaci told me recently. "Instead of dreading and overthinking the communication, it feels like I've found my ministry. I'm excited to see how far I can take it."

She's come a long way, but Kaci is the first to admit she's a work in progress. The next magic ingredient we are adding to her now-formidable communication skills is wit. As I've gotten to know her better, I've realized that, privately, Kaci possesses a wicked sense of humor. As she gets more comfortable with being her authentic self, the funny will come. As we all know, every great speech requires just the right amount of wit.

Testing the Waters

Most people have filters. We don't share our whole, authentic selves with others until we get to know them well, and even then, it can be hard to let our guard down. But there are ways to slowly invite listeners in, giving them a glimpse of our true selves and infusing our communication with the kind of authenticity that leaves a lasting impression.

Start by selecting a story about yourself that few people know, something from your childhood perhaps, to give your audience a glimpse of your inner light. For instance, I always ask people I'm meeting for the first time, either at a party or an informal business gathering, where they went to high school. That period in one's life is invariably filled with angst, triumphs, and everything in between. It has been an ideal conversation starter for me, particularly because I went to a performing arts high school and I'm usually surrounded by math, science, and business people. If the room happens to be filled with other artists, all the better. I typically share how finding my artistic voice and village raised my confidence and ultimately raised all my grades. I had no idea that I was gifted in math until I discovered my love for drama. Anyone can relate to my story because, at the end of the day, we all just want to find where we fit in, particularly during our high school years.

Test your story out on close friends and family first—an intimate circle where you feel safe. Pay attention to their reaction and your comfort level in sharing. Hone the details as necessary.

Next, take that anecdote to a social situation, a dinner party perhaps, with people who don't know you quite as well. As people engage you in conversation, find the opportunity to share by bringing up the subject that relates to your narrative. Note their reactions as you tell it. It's likely they will find many elements of your story to relate to because it has come from the heart. We all want to connect with others at a human level.

Now that a piece of the true you has been road-tested, bring out more of your backstory to share with others. Explore a few more personal anecdotes for your expanding repertoire. The more you open up, the easier and more natural it will feel.

The Corner Office

Once you are comfortable with your own backstory and can convey it with intention, you need to step outside yourself. Having compassion for your listeners is a huge piece of the persuasion puzzle. Great communication is about understanding what their needs are, what exactly they need to know to come around to your way of thinking, and how they need to feel to be just as impassioned about your cause as you are. Maybe you're good at extemporizing without a planned narrative or script, but the odds are you're not as compelling a speaker as you think you are when you rely solely on freestyling or thinking out loud.

That's what Darryl Goss learned about himself soon after he was promoted to the position of president and chief operating officer (COO) of a major US corporation.

Darryl was a seasoned executive in health sciences and technology with a wealth of experience and knowledge that propelled him from one level to the next in his corporate career. He could speak the language of programmers, lab technicians, and accountants—anyone with a highly technical, analytical brain. Darryl had an MBA from the University of Chicago, and he'd gone through an international management program at Oxford University. As someone who "grinds it out to show my value," his effectiveness as a leader got him noticed, and he was soon promoted to the executive vice president level.

But his new role at Inform Diagnostics—a Texas-based pathology lab that works with hospitals and clinics across the country—put him into the business leadership stratosphere. At the top of the corporate pyramid, clear and compelling communication is everything.

"It's the difference between heading a $100 million division and running a $3 billion company," Darryl explained to me. "It's a big leap."

Instead of dealing with divisions of staff who shared his expertise, Darryl suddenly found himself having to address multiple business units, shareholders, the media, and board members. Among the company's nine hundred employees were about seventy-five doctors, as well as lab technicians and sales, marketing, and finance people. To become the kind of leader he was destined to be, Darryl needed to become much more inclusive in the way he reached out to diverse members of his vast team. He could no longer assume that everyone shared the same set of expectations or ways of thinking.

"I was more used to showing and doing than telling, but it gets to the point where you don't have the opportunity to demonstrate what you mean. You have to articulate."

Early on in his new position, Darryl's communication style came up short at a meeting with one of the divisions. He was bringing a roomful of people, including a few on a teleconference call, up to speed on how the business was doing, and he jumped right into the business at hand.

"I got right down to business because that's what I was used to, but when I looked around the conference table, all I saw were blank stares," Darryl told me.

Darryl needed to get that introduction just right, captivating his listeners' attention and setting the tone, because that's what a great leader does. Darryl had failed to familiarize his audience with the situation on which they were being briefed. He rushed ahead with a slew of facts before they fully understood why they were there. He was so used to speaking and engaging with people who were as familiar with a specialized subject as he was that he inadvertently excluded half his audience.

Underlying every strong presentation is an objective. Speakers must ask themselves, "What do I want to achieve, and what action am I going to take to get it?" Knowing the exact Who, What, When, Where, and Why (the five W's) of any situation makes talking about a subject more tangible and immediate for your audience. I encouraged Darryl to start with a concise goal, such as "Not only do I want to inform my board members of a pretty grim quarter, but I want to share encouraging data on how we can completely turn it around." This simple one-liner has all five W's.

Strengthening Darryl's statement were verbs such as "inform" and "share" along with the adjective "encouraging"—key actions and descriptions that helped him become more specific about the issues he wanted to address. He knew that his job depended on it. Darryl's board needed better profit margins by the next quarter, and as COO, he needed to trim the fat.

Once he nailed his powerful opening, I worked with Darryl to define, refine, and adapt his narrative according to his intention for his audience, crafting the message with action verbs. Choosing verbs such as "to inform," "to motivate," or "to inspire" will give a speech intention, immediacy, and power. Every movement of a speech has its own tempo. Selecting a different verb for each part of your speech prevents you from staying on the same vocal note; it gives you the ability to change it up! The point is to grab and hold everyone's attention, and this technique will ensure that you do.

Beginning, Middle, and End

I always say, no matter how simple the presentation, you need a beginning, middle, and end. All forms of communication require an essential story arc: exposition, rising action, climax, falling action, and conclusion.

1. Exposition is setting up the story, including the introduction of characters, setting, and main conflicts. Prep your audience with the tools they need to understand what will happen in your presentation.

2. The rising action builds the story. This is where you begin to weave together the elements of your narrative to explain the situation you are in or, in Darryl's case, what is happening within the company structure.

3. The climax is the height of the story. You have reached the peak of your presentation. Now you can take the story in another direction and show how all the story elements brought you to this point.

4. Falling action, where the story begins to wind down, can add reflection and further understanding of what has transpired thus far.

5. The conclusion, or resolution, is the solution to the problem that emerges as you reach the bottom of your

story. It summarizes and closes any loose ends. This element resolves the conflict and reflects on the steps taken to arrive at that point.

Life and Death

The stakes of effective communication were high for Darryl. Sitting at the helm of an organization that conducts life and death lab tests for thousands of patients each day, Darryl needed to get everyone in the organization on board not just with the accuracy and scope of the work that was done, but with how information and test results were passed along to the individual patients whose lives could be forever changed by the news. Beyond routine blood work, much of the work involved testing biopsies for cancer.

But Darryl's monotone delivery was not moving the dial when he veered away from his text and spoke extemporaneously. I explained that we communicate thoughts to build upon an idea. Each thought is the springboard for the next one, and no two thoughts are the same. Imagine that your thoughts are small islands and that the breath is the bridge that connects them. Some thoughts are larger than others and require more breath. Each thought is unique, and the voice must reflect its uniqueness by a variation in tone, phrasing, and inflection. We've spoken about these elements of communication as they relate to the voice. Now let's apply the concepts to the actual communication of an idea.

Darryl needed to let his thoughts land emphatically, with vocal power and variation on each new thought, finding the natural rhythm and emphasis, as Marcus did when he discovered the art of phrasing. Darryl's other challenge was to phrase his words in groups without relying so heavily on punctuation. He got a little too much into his own head, anticipating each word and comma. He needed to move from thought to thought with relative ease.

Of course, when you think about all that goes into communication, it can seem overwhelming at first. Darryl began dreading speaking in front of more than one or two people. But when you've done the work, you also have to trust that you've got this. It was a question of allowing himself to be more in the moment, so that he could express himself with feeling. That's why, beyond all the facts he had to communicate to his staff, Darryl needed to remind himself of his whole purpose. To that end, I decided to dig a little deeper.

"Darryl, tell me why you are in the diagnostics business?" I asked him. "Is it something that you just fell into, or do you have a sense of mission?"

Darryl had previously worked at IBM, but during a mid-career sabbatical he had a conversation with a friend about the country's broken health-care system. They talked at length about how digital technology was an opportunity to put the patient back into the center of the experience, but that the industry wasn't keeping up with this digital transformation because it lacked expertise, which Darryl had. That conversation moved him to go back into the corporate world and use his technical and leadership skills to make change from the inside. He wanted to be a part of the solution.

"I want everyone on my teams to feel the same sense of urgency and passion as I do," Darryl shared with me. "We're talking about cancer patients, or potential cancer patients, and we've all been touched by that. If I can get the answer to you one or two days earlier, that's one or two days you're not on your knees praying and worrying. That's education and information on what you can do next to save your own life, or the life of a loved one."

As he spoke, I was transfixed. I finally heard the passion he needed to bring his employees along on the journey with him. I pointed out to him how much more compelling his voice and speech would be if he translated the conviction he shared in his private conversations into his presentations.

"Darryl, that's it!" I told him. "You're remembering why you care so much. That's the missing ingredient!"

To help translate his conviction, Darryl now takes a moment to remind himself that this job is his calling, so that subtle emotion flows naturally through his speech about logistics, hard data, and potential layoffs. Board members have been visibly moved by his most recent presentations. They have a visceral connection to Darryl and a better understanding of his priorities. He can see in their eyes and by the way they nod their heads that his words are resonating. While they may not have shared his sense of urgency about certain tasks in the past, they were slowly beginning to "hear" him. And instead of just getting through presentations with a knot in his stomach, Darryl began to look forward to board meeting moments where he could share his knowledge, his passion, and his personal contribution to the fight against cancer. I'm convinced that he'd be just as comfortable sharing "his calling" as a keynote speaker at a charity event as he now is in the boardroom.

Defining his narrative, understanding the basic elements of effective communication, taking a breath before each new thought, employing vocal variety, grouping words to create phrases, and stressing verbs and nouns to emphasize critical elements of the story had liberated him. All the moving parts of his message worked together, and that gave him confidence.

Darryl also figured out which part of the symphony he wanted to play. Between the trio of leaders—CFO, COO, and CEO—he was the percussionist, beating the drum and moving everyone forward through his polished and accomplished communication. In fact, his voice became so strong, and his message so powerful, that he deservedly moved up to the position of CEO. Within the music of voice and speech, he'd found his rhythm, and it was catching!

Speak It!

Taking your voice and speech to that next level of powerful communication is often a matter of making a few effective adjustments to your tone. You may articulate the words to perfection, delivering thoughtful content that can certainly be understood on an intellectual level. But for your words to land with impact, the listener must receive the same bravado you had when you were rehearsing in the shower. How do you make a lasting impact on an audience? How do you elevate a speech to truly connect with your listeners? By setting an intention before you speak, bearing in mind the arc of your story, and practicing.

1. Use a short intention phrase with a powerful action verb to describe how you want to impact your audience. For example: I want to empower my audience to use their voices for social change by sharing my own narrative with them.
2. Remember the arc of your story: exposition, rising action, climax, falling action, and conclusion. Your intention phrase, particularly the verb, is at the core of your story and will give you the added power and vocal gravitas needed to impact your audience.
3. Practice your speech out loud, imagining the faces of your audience in all parts of the room. Find out if you will be delivering your speech behind a podium with a fixed mic or if you will be gracing the stage freely with a handheld mic. Either way, you should practice in a space that allows you to move freely but without excessive gestures. Also, find a prop, like a bottle of water, to simulate holding a handheld mic. It is imperative that your mouth remain close to the handheld mic at all times; you must never shift your head away from the mic.

10

All the World's a Stage

....

MAKE YOUR VOICE YOUR PLATFORM

Our lives begin to end the day we become
silent about things that matter.

—MARTIN LUTHER KING JR.

Blockbuster director James Cameron was considering Halle Berry for an unusual part in his new installment of *Avatar*, and he brought her in for an audition—her first in twenty years. He'd created a whole new subculture of the "Na'vi" world—people who had an alternative way of worshipping loosely based on voodoo and fire. Halle would play the matriarch and leader of this tribe, whom he described as "pure evil."

Halle, who really wanted this part, did what few actors do with a director of Cameron's stature in Hollywood. She disagreed with him.

"I don't believe people are inherently evil," she told him. "People are what they are based on their experience—the hurts and pains, what they did or didn't get as children . . ."

"Well, I see her as the bad guy, plain and simple," he responded. "But you show me what you think this woman is and bring it back to me in a week."

I'd been working with Halle's husband at the time, French actor Olivier Martinez, to help him acquire a General American accent so that he could avail himself for more work opportunities in the US. Olivier had kindly recommended me as someone who could help Halle dive in and develop a voice for this otherworldly character. It just so happened that my studio on Sunset Boulevard was a five-minute walk down the hill from Halle's home. We were neighbors!

"Well, Denise, I've just created more work for myself," she told me cheerfully as she stepped into my office and filled me in on the backstory of this role.

The Girl Next Door

I felt an instant kinship with Halle, as if I'd known her my whole life. You know how you just click with certain people, as if they are long-lost members of your tribe? I've had the privilege of working with several stars over the years, and usually the most one can hope for is a level of courteous professionalism. But there have been some notable exceptions, and Halle was one of them. We were able to keep it real and personal with one another from the get-go.

Once you see past Halle's obvious beauty, you realize how down-to-earth she is. She's a regular girl from Ohio who just happens to be extraordinarily intelligent and talented—facts about her that tend to get overlooked in an industry so hung up on looks. She doesn't have an entitled bone in her body. Like all the greats I've worked with—Mahershala Ali, Ellen Burstyn, Taraji P. Henson, Rachel Weisz—Halle prepares endlessly. She roots out all she can about her characters to make them authentic, relatable, and fundamentally human. Her one desire is to make the audience care as much as she does. She puts in the work, and then some, because of the deep and abiding respect she has for great storytelling.

"Everything I do and say as the character has to resonate with the truth of who they are," Halle told me. "I can't act, think, move, or be as they really are if I don't know *who* they really are."

The challenge for the *Avatar* role was that we had to make up a backstory because this voodoo matriarch was a work of pure fantasy. We didn't even have a script to work off. To ground the character in some kind of reality, we started researching the original voodoo cultures of West Africa and Haiti. We discovered a rich history of the religion, which was not, nor has it ever been, satanic, despite Judeo-Christian perceptions about the culture.

We developed the character's internal rhythms, voice, speech, and communication patterns through that discovery process. Even though she would be speaking a made-up language, we studied the Afro-French *patois* of these cultures to get the cadence and accent just right. Then we examined as many matriarchal societies as we could find on the internet. We dug through the layers to get to the humanity of this individual and understand why she was behaving in ways perceived as evil. Halle wrote an entire monologue, fleshing out the character she was given, describing how she became the head priestess of the "Ash People" who lived underneath a volcano that erupted. Halle created the persona of an angry, bereaved maternal figure who would do anything to protect her people but, in the practice of her supernatural powers, got carried away and lost her compass.

Voodoo Queen

Halle created the text and the subtext for her character in vivid detail. She was to have wild eyes and long dreadlocked hair, caked in volcanic ash. To figure out the physicality of this woman—the earthy way she moved—we watched videos of West African dance. We practiced some of those dances in my studio, listening and singing to the music while creating our own version of a voodoo dance, rotating our hips down low to the floor. It was serious business, though I admit I once landed butt-first, and we laughed hysterically like childhood best friends at a sleepover.

The intention was to give Halle's voice a sense of gravity. She tended to speak in a softer, higher register until we worked together. But the earthbound soul of this steely character gave a whole new depth and power to her voice. Now she was ready to show James Cameron the history and humanity of this voodoo priestess. It was all there in her voice and carriage. Anyone watching her audition would be able to see why her character felt she had to fight the world the way she did. Halle brought all her talent, perception, and passion to this character's voice, embodying an idea and changing the perception through the power of communication.

"These characters have the most layers, which is why actors love playing the 'bad guy,'" Halle later told me. "Finding the humanity in the worst-seeming people and breathing life into them is what we were put on this earth to do."

Halle did not get the part.

"Your star brand is too great for this role," she was told. "But rest assured, we have something else in mind for you."

I felt it was condescending Hollywood-speak for "You're too expensive . . . too pretty . . . too whatever . . ." But Halle didn't mind. She'd developed new layers and dimension to her voice and speech that she would always have, because she incorporated them into her daily life. She had an expanded vocal repertoire that no one could take away from her. The work we did together would stay with her, serving her both professionally and personally for the rest of her life.

"My voice work applies more to my real life than my acting life," Halle explained. "When a character is done, it's done, but the voice stays with me."

So why am I telling you this? How does the experience of a glamorous Oscar winner relate to your own life and communication needs? Because you can absolutely aspire to storytelling at this level. And you should.

We may not land a part on the big screen, or even the little screen for that matter. We may only find ourselves in front of audiences of a handful of people at most. But as Shakespeare said, we are all players on a stage. Breathing that kind of vocal life into a story makes your listener care about what you have to say. Great communication—animating words through voice, tone, cadence, phrasing, inflection, and even physical movement— connects us as humans, helping us understand one another at the deepest levels. And studying how the great actors do it can teach us volumes about how to harness the powers of voice and speech in our own daily lives.

Set in Her Power

As Halle discovered, the impact of this work can be the most profound far beyond the movie set. Her development of the powerful priestess character has led to an expansion of vocal range that's come in handy of late. Now she can speak from her base, and that lower register "sets me in my power when I want people to know I mean business."

The actress goes there whenever she needs to, drawing on her expanded vocal repertoire in her personal relationships, when dealing with studio executives, or with two young children who need to know when she's serious about setting certain boundaries.

"Anyone who hears that voice realizes I am not in a place to be messed with."

Halle's experience demonstrates the real-life possibilities of exploring and honing your vocal skills for every area of life. And that's the whole point of this book. By now, I have given you the tools you need to unleash the full power of your voice—your gift—to persuade, inspire, influence, and generally deepen the connections you have with individuals within your world, as well as in settings that may be less familiar or comfortable. The only difference between you and these great actors is that they've known about this set of tools all along because voice and speech are integral parts of their craft. There's no reason to think that you can't reach the same level of mastery, provided you also do the work to hone your voice and speech skills.

By paying attention to every small detail and nuance of their characters, actors like Halle can transport us into worlds that we would not have otherwise known, at a deep and emotional level. That in turn produces more empathy, which is not a bad thing to have in these divisive times. I am floored and inspired by the care and attention that our greatest actors give to the words on the page. They know that the little things we do in the act of communication can be profound.

Their choices are not arbitrary. Every great performance, speech, interview, or conversation starts with research. Knowing the backstory of a situation or a person is powerful. I'm not necessarily talking about a *60 Minutes* level of research, but your chances of making an impact increase exponentially when you have specific facts about people and places and a sociopolitical context in which to put them.

Actors also delve deeply into their character's relationships with other characters and places, whether they are mentioned or not. Recalling and embodying a personal connection to an individual, a place, or a situation helps deepen the connection to what you are saying, no matter how technical or clinical the narrative.

As we learned with Darryl in chapter 9, having an objective and actions is crucial for being definitive and staying on point. For example, imagine you're the keynote speaker for your sorority's annual fundraiser. You want to inspire your sorors to get out of their comfort zones and live a healthier, more fulfilling life. You are going to achieve this by being an example of what you're preaching, sharing how your life has changed significantly since you took a leap of faith to live outside the norms. You are going to give your listeners small simple steps for getting started, then present testimonials from similar women for whom a lifestyle change has worked. Your presentation will be well mapped out, leaving nothing to chance and giving you some much-needed confidence.

At the end of the day, confidence is the bottom line. The tools and anecdotes I am presenting in this book are for the sole purpose of making every speaker, in every situation, more confident. Hollywood's most elite talent grapple with some of the same insecurities that we do. The unfortunate difference is that they are under constant microscopic scrutiny, so being unprepared is not an option for them.

Stage Fright

In 2003, when Tony and Academy Award–winning actor Ellen Burstyn played Lucy Marsden in *Oldest Living Confederate Widow Tells All* at the Old Globe Theater in San Diego—a one-woman play based on the ninety-nine-year oral history of a woman who married a fifty-year-old Civil War veteran when she was only fifteen—she had to dig deep. Ellen had to dive into the archives of history to find the authentic voices of multiple characters whose realities would have been far different from her own, from a Confederate boy soldier to a former African American female slave to her own character at different ages. A mutual friend introduced us, and I was proud to be able to help this accomplished actress get the various dialects of the Deep South just right because authenticity was key in the telling of such a sensitive story.

I confess I was completely starstruck and nervous on my drive to meet her. I am usually calm and confident with my skill set and my ability to convey it. But this was Ellen Burstyn! She was the Meryl Streep of my generation, an icon, and she was calling *me* for help with not just one but several dialects. Seeking a boost to my confidence, I called my mother as I drove to the job location.

"Mom, I'm on my way to work with Ellen Burstyn, and I'm really nervous," I told her.

Her immediate response was "Who is Ellen Burstyn, baby?"

"I guess she's a woman, just like you and me," I replied, laughing.

My mother genuinely had no idea who she was. That did the trick, because Mom was basically telling me it wasn't that big of a deal. I just had to do my job well, with my usual level of professionalism, then go home.

It was even more reassuring when Ellen shared with me how nervous she was before our meeting. She wanted to serve these voices but didn't really know where to begin, particularly with the African American men she'd be portraying. She approached the story with utmost respect, paying attention to the minutest of details that would affect speech—how an old woman with false teeth living in a nursing home might sound versus her teenage-bride self, for example. Working on that play was a revelatory experience for both of us. It was two American women of different generations, backgrounds, and races coming together in a process of discovery about our painful and complex history.

We began our work with a detailed exploration of dialect samples specific to the region and period. Then we quickly moved to learning the phonetic changes, rhythmic differences, and vocal nuances of each character. As the work deepened, our trepidation and insecurities fell away. She was focused, energized, and inspired, as was I. I showed up on "the" Ellen Burstyn's doorstep with the tools to hone her craft, and she graciously accepted them. The confidence level of us both boosted exponentially.

Full-Bodied Commitment

Great actors suffer from stage fright just as much as the rest of us, and that's okay. Our trepidation simply means we care deeply about our message and how it will be received. But the Hollywood A-listers I teach have learned how to manage that fear, overcoming their nerves by throwing themselves into the work. They are all in. They research, they train, and they dive into their own past experiences to find that connection to their characters on the most fundamental, human level. It's no different from the way you might do your own extensive research into a subject to prepare for an important speech. Knowing your subject thoroughly instills the necessary confidence.

They also put their whole body into it. They know there's more to communication than the spoken word. They match posture, stance, and visual cues with the voice and words. And they do so with such a masterful subtlety that we, their audience, don't even notice all the work that goes into the messaging. Nor should we. As Hamlet told his players, "Nor do not saw the air too much with your hand, thus, but use all gently . . ."

Embodying Your Words

Just like Ellen Burstyn or Mahershala Ali, as you infuse life into your voice and speech you must also synchronize your physical language to the words. It will be subtle, of course, but your imagination and your ability to convey a narrative must affect your entire body from head to toe, even if it's imperceptible to your listening audience. Allowing visual images and the sounds of speech to resonate deeply in your mind and body will organically elicit a visceral physical response. You must see nouns, verbs, and adjectives in your mind's eye. I'm clearly not suggesting that you act them out; just see them. I guarantee that when you see and embody a story, your listening audience will as well.

Mahershala Ali lives and breathes this subtle brilliance of the actor's craft. I would give him a suggestion about posture, and he would come back the next day transformed. When he lifted the crown of his head a little higher, away from his shoulders, and straightened his spine as his character sat in the back of the Cadillac in the movie *Green Book*, it helped him develop a certain vocal timbre. Mahershala carefully considered whether his *True Detective* character was a cigarette smoker in the seventies, and how a disease like Parkinson's or Alzheimer's might impact his vocal instrument in his character's declining years. He thinks so deeply about the many complex characters he plays that he feels a spiritual connection to them.

"It's almost as if some part of you has to be translucent," he told me in one of our many conversations between takes. "Tuning in to the frequency of a character, you have to be able to disappear into people and their experiences, which makes you porous and vulnerable."

It's an act of courage. Being onstage was never about the joy of adulation for Mahershala, who, when he first embarked on his career at age twenty, had to manage stage fright and anxiety before stepping out in front of an audience.

"I always felt like I was going out into a huge arena alone," the actor shared. But he was compelled to make himself go out there anyway. "I realized that if I could jump off a cliff and fly in a scene, I could also be proud of what I accomplished that day. Had I not faced those little bricks of fear, they would've become walls."

Beyond facing his fears, he held on to the higher thought of what he was doing in service of the story. "I couldn't allow my anxiety to get in the way of having a resonant experience with the audience. That first moment of feeling connected with a community through words, moving people to tears, and changing their awareness let me in on the power of my voice."

That power can translate to other platforms besides a Broadway stage. That connection with community can be yours. Don't let your own anxiety get in the way of those transformational moments you can have with your listeners. Know that you have done the work, and recognize how far you have come.

~~~~~~~~~~~~~~~
~~~~~~~~~~~~~~~~~~~~~

Press Record, Again

It's time to rerecord the passage from "Cicely's Dream" that you read aloud at the beginning of this book. You've taken a journey with me, and here's the payoff. Be consistent and read the exact same words again. But this time, do it with the knowledge you've acquired over these ten chapters. Allow the story to star. Set the following objectives for yourself before recording: relaxation, breath, articulation, phrasing, vocal variety, and inflection. You can apply these essential technical factors more successfully when they are supported by your ability to visualize the images, the characters, and the action of the story. So, really see them, breathe, and enjoy! Your goal is to serve the story with an effortless vulnerability.

Cicely climbed the low fence between the garden and the cornfield, and started down one of the long rows leading directly away from the house. Old Needham was a good ploughman, and straight as an arrow ran the furrow between the rows of corn, until it vanished in the distant perspective. The peas were planted beside alternate hills of corn, the cornstalks serving as supports for the climbing pea-vines. The vines nearest the house had been picked more or less clear of the long green pods, and Cicely walked down the row for a quarter of a mile, to where the peas were more plentiful. And as she walked, she thought of her dream of the night before.

She had dreamed a beautiful dream. The fact that it was a beautiful dream, a delightful dream, her memory retained very vividly. She was troubled because she could not remember just what her dream had been about. Of one other fact she was certain, that in her dream she had found something, and that her happiness had been bound up with the thing she had found. As she walked down the corn-row she ran over in her mind the various things with which she had always associated happiness. Had she found a gold ring? No, it was not a gold ring—of that she felt sure. Was it a soft, curly plume for her hat? She had seen town people with them, and had indulged in day-dreams on the subject; but it was not a feather. Was it a bright-colored silk dress? No; as much as she had always wanted one, it was not a silk dress. For an instant, in a dream, she had tasted some great and novel happiness, and when she awoke it was dashed from her lips, and she could not even enjoy the memory of it, except in a vague, indefinite, and tantalizing way.

Now play both recordings, starting with the original. What has changed? Be mindful of the relaxation, breath, voice, articulation, and communication techniques. Were you able to achieve your goals? What was lacking? Above all, hear and appreciate the difference between then and now. Maybe you still have some work to do to fully master your voice and speech, but you are well on your way!

Vocal with a Cause

Increasingly, I am hearing from nonactors—professional people and ordinary citizens who wish to build their communication muscles to express themselves on behalf of a cause. These people are incredibly diverse, whether it's Kaci, the lovely young community activist and philanthropist from West Hills, California, or the Orthodox Jewish business owner who reached out to me because he wanted to run for office and represent his local district in southern Florida. The young, the marginalized, and the underserved are also finding their voices as circumstances thrust them onto the national and global stage. The students who survived the Parkland school shooting in Florida are perfect examples of this movement.

This development thrills me because I want to be remembered most for giving disenfranchised people the courage and tools to use their words, their thoughts, their voice, and their stories in ways they never thought possible. My dream is to dismantle fear, shame, and insecurity while helping build platforms so that *all* voices can be heard. I want my vocal coaching gifts to reach beyond Hollywood to that young child struggling with gender identity, to the young Black girl who never felt accepted because she thought her skin was too dark or too light, and to that small child inside all of us who is just yearning to say out loud and proud whatever is in his or her heart.

Whether you are a megastar in Hollywood, or a megastar in your own mind, it is important to remember that the real star is the story. We are simply facilitators, at best, for great material, either your own or someone else's. Getting out of your way and allowing the tools of compelling storytelling to guide you is the key to a confident and compelling performance. It's worth it. There's tremendous value in putting your story, or star, out there into the universe. We live in an era in which, through social media and the prevalence of so many burning issues of equality and social justice, many of us are feeling as if we need to speak out for the first time in our lives. If you follow the prescriptions I have been giving you throughout this book, I promise that your voice will soar above the rest.

A Voice That Carries

That's precisely what lawyer Terri Austin is hoping will happen as she takes her first steps into a more public role. The Columbia University graduate, who also has a degree in journalism, teaches advocacy communications to graduate students. In her thirty years of practice, she has felt perfectly comfortable in the role of litigator in front of judges and juries. But it's quite another thing to perform in the much larger room of television, with listeners numbering in the millions. Terri hopes to transition to a new career as a legal analyst and came to me to prepare.

A highly accomplished professional, Terri already possessed an engaging communication style. But she wanted to do her part to change society for the better, offering up her voice as a woman of considerable expertise on the law, combined with compassion and insights on different sides of the issues. To help her achieve her dreams, we needed to up her game.

"As an older Black woman, I have a perspective on current events and how people are being treated that we haven't heard enough of in the media," Terri told me. She is less interested in divisive politics than in bringing a more "nuanced" opinion to the small screen—one that brings people together through enlightenment and engagement.

"We are headed in the wrong direction in so many ways: suicide, depression, gun violence. We're separating ourselves along racial, religious, and gender lines and seeing each other through the lenses of hatred and intolerance. We have become so polarized I just want to do what I can to change minds and bring more people together."

That meant Terri had to get comfortable within the conversation. News outlets like CNN would be a different kind of platform from the one she was used to. When you appear on television as a legal analyst, you must expect that people with opposing views will try to shout over you. To be fully heard, Terri needed to be ready.

Together, we covered the full range of voice and public speaking. Her voice was a little high in pitch, to the point where she sounded ten years younger than she actually was. Although Terri was undoubtedly a legal expert, she didn't have the vocal gravitas to match. We've talked before about how common this is among women who are more cerebral. Terri needed to work on more chest resonance, which immediately makes the voice sound more commanding. When she connected her voice to her breath and diligently worked on the "m," "n," and "ng" exercises I described in chapter 5 for nasal resonance, it opened up space in the front of her face, her head, the back of her throat, and her chest cavity, for an equal distribution of powerful vocal reverberation, resulting in more vocal power and authority.

Once we completed those exercises, we did a mock interview. This was particularly challenging for Terri because she was used to having full control of the classroom. Now she had to think about pacing. In television interviews, she wouldn't have the opportunity to pause for emphasis or to give herself enough time to search for the right words. If she did, someone else would surely jump in, and she would lose the opportunity to make her point. There's a fine art to debate, where you let the other person finish without allowing them to overtake. It was not Terri's style to "go into verbal battle." When others went low, she wanted to stay high, saying what she needed to say without looking defensive or getting flustered.

Knowing when to interject or pause, handing off the conversation with aural cues, takes just as much craft as a talented actor puts into a role. Mahershala describes the pause in a conversation as a place for your own signature. "There's value in just breathing and holding space," he told me. "The moments you have to connect emotionally with your own presence without the assistance of dialogue are an opportunity to put language to silence."

Good speech is not just about talking *at* people. It's about learning the art of communication and truly engaging with your listeners. Now that you possess all the essential tools for great voice and speech, it's time to take it to that next level by paying attention to subtleties and looking for opportunities to make your message more nuanced. That includes observing what is going on with the people around you. Being aware of others and meeting them halfway are essential to making a meaningful connection with other humans—and that, after all, is what these exercises are all about. It takes a degree of humility and empathy to be able to communicate effectively and clearly.

Give and Take

At the end of the day, *you* are the gift. But to give, you also must be able to receive. It all goes back to the breath. When we breathe in, we take in the energy of the person we are speaking with. We are constantly breathing and listening, respecting the space in between when they have spoken and when we speak. Listening is the active gesture of taking in someone's thoughts, feelings, and opinions. Breathing in and receiving, taking in their thoughts and responding accordingly, gives your listener permission to breathe.

Doing so takes the kind of confidence that builds when you really know your stuff. Terri typically puts about five hours of work into a four-minute segment. To make Terri's life a little easier, I shared with her the "rule of threes"—the three main points you want to get across for effective messaging. But that still requires a lot of planning and research. As Mark Twain quipped, "It usually takes more than three weeks to prepare a good impromptu speech."

Next, we tackled body language. When you are on television, physical movement needs to support your words, not distract from them. If you are pacing or gesticulating, it can be distracting. There are several ways to use your body effectively when you are speaking, including extending your hands and opening up your palms to plead a case or build trust with your audience, or using a particular hand gesture or subtle facial expression to support a stressed word or important phrase. However, try not to repeatedly stab the air in front of you with a pointed index finger, for example, as certain political candidates tend to do, detracting from their message by angrily overemphasizing every other word. Again, match the action to the word and the word to the action. Cleaning up the extraneous gestures will only serve to make your speech more powerful, whether you are appearing on television or conversing in everyday life. Take your cue from how the best actors and broadcasters do it, and apply it to your own stage, regardless of the size.

Developing your communication skills to this level is an act of service. We all reach a point in our lives and careers when we feel the need to give back. Maybe you've already made your mark in your profession and aspire to do more than just write a check. Or maybe you suddenly find yourself in the spotlight as a young student who has experienced gun violence and wants to speak out. There comes a time in life when you've got to put your voice into action. We must speak our truth. That's what people are doing more and more as they take to the streets of Minneapolis, Portland, Hong Kong, and Paris in protest. People are in dire need of inspiration and encouragement. Why not now? Why not you? As Madeleine Albright once said, "It took me quite a long time to develop a voice, and now that I have it, I am not going to be silent."

But first you must invest in yourself and put in the work. Take all that I have shared throughout this book and practice, practice, practice. That's the other thing about Halle, Mahershala, and thespians at their level that people don't see: their work ethic!

Into the Ring

Soon after she finished playing the mysterious assassin Sofia in *John Wick: Chapter 3*, Halle reached out to me. She wanted to prepare for the role of a lifetime as a mixed martial arts (MMA) fighter in a movie she is not only starring in but directing. Her character is a woman from Newark, New Jersey, who was sexually abused as a child and fought back, became an MMA champion fighter, and is attempting to make one of life's great comebacks.

She has two strikes against her when she's born to a mother who is just fifteen and is then subjected to a string of men brought into their home as her mother struggles to get by. Knowing nothing else, Halle's character also makes poor choices in relationships. After achieving success in her MMA career, she suffers a humiliating defeat. The movie follows her as she rises from the lowest ebb in her life, cleaning toilets as a domestic on Manhattan's Upper East Side until someone recognizes her and sets her on the path to reclaim her stature back in the ring.

Halle's challenge was to find the softer side of this character's voice amid all the harshness of her life. She didn't want her to become two-dimensional, and she didn't hire me just to develop an authentic Newark dialect. Halle's marginalized character has been hurt, but she also wants to be loved. She's fighting at every turn, going from zero to sixty in a heartbeat, but she has these open, transparent moments that let the audience in. Halle wanted to create a real woman who finds strength in her vulnerability. Translating that into voice required the same exquisite attention to detail that she applies to all her roles, getting not just the dialect right but also the cadence, rhythm, and colloquialisms.

Nothing was accidental. Even the grunt—*aaaawwwwhhh!*—on the exhale as she leans into a punch, like Serena Williams driving a tennis ball into her opponent's court, was carefully thought through. We considered the appropriateness of the most seemingly insignificant of words. For example, we discovered a true Newark girl would say "aright" as a kind of throwaway line, but "okay" would be more of a question, an asking for affirmation.

At fifty-two, Halle was already in the best physical shape of her life, having learned jujitsu and done many of her own stunts for *John Wick*. But she took none of that for granted. She just kept on working. Three times a week for six weeks, Halle showed up at my studio at 9 a.m. sharp, after having been up and working out with her trainer since 6. We worked for an hour, then she boxed from 11 until 3. She didn't have a smidgeon of fat on her. All that muscle powered her voice and gave an added dexterity to her vocal instrument. Physically and vocally, Halle embodied strength. Of course, I won't tell you what happens at the end of the movie. But I will say that the character wins simply by entering the ring. She prepared, she showed up, and she fought with all she had.

And that is what I am asking you to do. If you invest even a fraction of the discipline and effort that Halle has been putting into preparing for this role, you will become a vocal powerhouse. In other words, don't stop now! I urge you to keep on reading, repeatedly delving into the more granular Voice and Speech Workout I have created for you at the end of the book. Recognize how far you have come, then keep going!

I want you to go forth into life's arena and be heard for the eloquent speaker you have become. As Ralph Waldo Emerson said, "Speech is power: speech is to persuade, to convert, to compel. It is to bring another out of his bad sense into your good sense."

Great speech combined with great voice is also empowerment.

So, no more sitting on the sidelines! Get up and strut on life's stage, using your vocal power to project all the way to the back row. Speak it! Tell your truth! Now, more than ever, the world needs to hear from you.

~~~~~~

Speak It!

For an example of communication at its most powerful, look no further than President Barack Obama's farewell speech, delivered on January 10, 2017. President Obama clearly intended to galvanize the audience: his speech is a call to action. His words are meant to be a reminder that the work is far from over and that everyone must help to keep the momentum going. If you listen to the president's entire speech, you will hear the story arc, his impeccable use of exposition, rising action, climax, falling action, and conclusion. I am going to utilize the exposition portion of his speech to illustrate how a powerful beginning can be an essential setup for a great crescendo and a rousing finish.

My fellow Americans:

Michelle and I have been so touched by all the well-wishes that we've received over the past few weeks. But tonight—tonight it's my turn to say thanks. Whether we have seen eye-to-eye or rarely agreed at all, my conversations with you, the American people—in living rooms and in schools; at farms, on factory floors; at diners and on distant military outposts—those conversations are what have kept me honest, and kept me inspired, and kept me going. And every day, I have learned from you. You made me a better President, and you made me a better man.

So I first came to Chicago when I was in my early 20s. And I was still trying to figure out who I was, still searching for a purpose in my life. And it was a neighborhood not far from here where I began working with church groups in the shadows of closed steel mills. It was on these streets where I witnessed the power of faith, and the quiet dignity of working people in the face of struggle and loss.

Now, this is where I learned that change only happens when ordinary people get involved, and they get engaged, and they come together to demand it.

After eight years as your President, I still believe that. And it's not just my belief. It's the beating heart of our American idea—our bold experiment in self-government. It's the conviction that we are all created equal, endowed by our Creator with certain unalienable rights, among them life, liberty, and the pursuit of happiness. It's the insistence that these rights, while self-evident, have never been self-executing; that we, the people, through the instrument of our democracy, can form a more perfect union.

Step 1: The president begins with a heartfelt expression of gratitude. He is allowing himself to be vulnerable and completely transparent during an obviously emotional farewell. He reminds the audience that it is they who have the power to affect change in society and to even affect change in the president of the United States. President Obama is meeting the audience where they are. He knows their disillusionment and turns it around to action.

Step 2: He continues with a personal narrative that reflects back on his humble beginnings, where he discovered the power of everyday Americans working together for a common good. Placing himself in the narrative gives the audience a sense of "if he can do it, I can do it, too." He's not above the audience as the commander in chief. Rather, he is right there with them with his sleeves rolled up, ready to get to work. "We're in this together!"

Step 3: He then brings the audience back to the current situation and begins to instill hope into a seemingly bleak situation. This speech is carefully crafted to restore faith in a discouraged audience by appealing to the basic common decency in all Americans.

Step 4: Putting it all together in the delivery: "So I first came to Chicago / when I was in my early 20s. / And I was still trying to figure out who I was, / still searching for a purpose in my life."

We read sentences, but we speak thoughts. This single thought is composed of four phrases, seamlessly strung together like a pearl necklace. There are also precious gems like diamonds and rubies in the necklace; they are nouns and verbs: came, Chicago, twenties, figure, was, searching, purpose, life. These words are more brilliant, more important. The diamond nouns reveal the story, and the ruby verbs convey the story's action. Think of these operative words as precious gems strategically placed throughout the pearls of a necklace, or throughout the phrases of your thoughts. These operative words should be stressed in a way that differentiates them from the rest of the words, giving you vocal variety, vocal modulation, and cadence. These stressed words also give your audience a clearer understanding of the story. Do not punch the words. Instead, slightly lift them from the statement, coloring them with emotional authenticity.

Now polish these diamonds, rubies, and pearls by doing the following:

Allow your voice to vary from phrase to phrase, going slightly higher in pitch on one phrase and lower on another. A phrase is a small group of words within the thought. We actually speak in phrases as opposed to individual words. Look at how I've phrased or grouped President Obama's thought in step 4.

Before every thought, breathe in through the mouth and release the voice, images, and emotions on the breath. Never feel as though you can't take the time to breathe before each thought, because the breath fuels your story. Breathing is just as essential for your audience. Once you take the time to consciously breathe, you are giving your listeners permission to breathe and receive your narrative along with you. It's quite reciprocal.

At the end of every thought, make your vocal inflection go downward, unless you're asking a question. This gives you built-in power, conviction, and authority. And who doesn't want that?

Got it? Good! Now stay with me. We will delve much more into the nitty-gritty of these voice and speech essentials in the Voice and Speech Workout that follows.

~~~~~~

Your Voice and Speech Workout Bonus

I have decided to close out this book with something more useful than an epilogue: a four-week speech workout! Having shared the triumphant anecdotes of my students and clients and even my own personal voice and speech journey, it's time for me to give you more detailed speech rules and drills to complete the tips and exercises I have already shared. You are now ready.

When I was a student at Juilliard, I had several teachers who enlightened me and helped take my talent to new heights. However, one teacher in particular went above and beyond the norms and pedagogical style of the day. Tim Monich, who is now my mentor and friend, had a passion for speech that was infectious. Although humble and affable, he taught speech like a titan. Tim left the Juilliard faculty in the eighties to become one of the most sought-after dialect coaches in the world. In 2000, he ushered me into the film industry as his replacement for a blockbuster movie when he was called away to coach an even larger one. It was the perfect teacher/student relationship. Certainly, my opera training had developed my ear, making it even more of a winning situation. My current approach to the work and my style of teaching are much like Tim's: take the work seriously, but don't take yourself too seriously in the work.

Tim encouraged me to take what I learned at Juilliard forty years ago and update the classical approach with a more contemporary flair, and that's what I have done here. This twenty-first-century makeover, stripped of anachronisms, gives these sounds more relevance for users of all backgrounds. The list that follows is your GPS, or navigational system, for the sounds of speech; it shows you where they live and how they are formed in your mouth. It will give you an acute awareness of where the sounds are placed, as well as the articulators needed to form each one.

Your Friendly User's Guide

You've probably noticed by now that I often repeat myself. That's because these principles, definitions, and concepts *require* repetition. We often don't get the meaning of a principle until we have a larger context in which to put it. As you master more of these sounds, it's helpful to go back and revisit the lists contained in this workout. When you do, your "aha" moment will come. You just have to keep practicing these sounds of speech until it clicks, and then some. Time and again I've seen the light switch on in my students days or weeks into this practice.

But first, here are the definitions you need to know. You've heard some of this before, at times with a slightly different spin.

VOWEL SOUNDS are made with a pure, uninterrupted, or un-impeded release of voice. All vowels and diphthong sounds are voiced as opposed to voiceless. A voiced sound occurs as a result of vibration of the vocal folds; a voiceless sound is the release of pure breath without vibration of the vocal folds. FRONT VOWELS vibrate in the front of the mouth. MID VOWELS vibrate in the middle of the mouth. BACK VOWELS vibrate in the back of the mouth.

The lips smile slightly for front vowels, and the smile diminishes as the vowel sounds become more open. Mid vowels are neutral and require no lip involvement at all. The lips are rounded for back vowel sounds, and the rounding diminishes as the vowel sounds become more open. The tip of the tongue is relaxed behind the lower front teeth for all vowel sounds, and the quality of the sound is determined by the arch and height of the tongue position in the mouth. The higher the tongue arch in the mouth, the more closed the vowel sound. As the tongue lowers, the sound becomes more open.

Drill each vowel sound from the most closed to the most open, using the single signature word provided. Then practice with the words, phrases, and sentences that follow it.

DIPHTHONG SOUNDS are a combination of two vowels blended so closely together that they are perceived as a single sound. The second sound of the diphthong pair is weaker than the first. You can distinguish a diphthong sound by seeing, hearing, or feeling the articulatory movement from the first sound to the second.

CONSONANT SOUNDS are made with a stop, or impeded interruption to the flow of breath or voice. Most voiced consonant sounds have a voiceless partner. These pairs are known as "cognates": two sounds formed in the same place of articulation, one voiced and the other voiceless.

Consonant sounds are grouped into six categories.

STOP PLOSIVES: The sound or breath is stopped and abruptly released.

FRICATIVES: The sound or breath is made through a narrow opening in the articulators, resulting in audible friction.

AFFRICATES: A combination of a stop plosive sound and a fricative sound, blended so closely that they become a single phonetic sound.

LATERAL: The tip of the tongue is placed on the gum ridge, and the sound is released over the sides of the tongue.

GLIDES: The articulation for these sounds begins in one place and swiftly glides to the vowel or diphthong sound that follows.

NASALS: The sound is emitted through the nose.

Begin your daily speech workout with the relaxation, breath, and vocal warm-up exercises that you learned in the previous chapters. Do your warm-up for at least 5–7 minutes, lying on the floor or seated. Say the words, phrases, and sentences of each phonetic group. The sound of each vowel, diphthong, and consonant is indicated by a signature word at the beginning of each section. The sound should remain consistent when saying each of the practice words, phrases, and sentences. As with any daily routine, start slowly for 3–5 minutes a day after the warm-up, and gradually increase your time as you begin to add more information to your daily regimen. Your total daily routine (including warm-up) by week 4 and thereafter should not exceed 25–30 minutes. Feel free to modify the times as needed once you feel secure. Finally, the goal here is accuracy, not speed. So, by all means, take your time and enjoy the ride!

Your Workout Schedule

WEEK ONE: Vowels (3–5 minutes per day)

Monday: front vowels
Tuesday: front vowels
Wednesday: mid vowels
Thursday: back vowels
Friday: back vowels

WEEK TWO: Vowels (5–7 minutes per day)

Monday: front vowels
Tuesday: front vowels and mid vowels
Wednesday: mid vowels
Thursday: mid vowels and back vowels
Friday: back vowels

WEEK THREE: Vowels and Diphthongs (7–9 minutes per day)

Monday: front, mid, and back vowels
Tuesday: long and short diphthongs
Wednesday: long and short diphthongs
Thursday: diphthongs of "r"
Friday: long and short diphthongs and diphthongs of "r"

WEEK FOUR: Vowels, Diphthongs, and Consonants (10–15 minutes per day)

Monday: front and mid vowels and stop plosives
Tuesday: back vowels and fricatives
Wednesday: long and short diphthongs, fricatives, and affricates
Thursday: diphthongs of "r," lateral "l," nasals, and glides
Friday: all vowels, diphthongs, stop plosives, fricatives, affricates, lateral "l," nasals, and glides

Now let's get serious, but by all means, let's also have fun. Like Anastasia, whom you met in chapter 6, you will add to these lists and adapt them to meet your specific needs. In the pages that follow, I will address vowels, diphthongs, and consonant sounds in words, phrases, and sentences for you to practice more in depth.

Front Vowels

The front vowel sound "Lee"

LONG: This front vowel sound is long when it's the last sound of a word, such as "see," and when it's followed by a voiced consonant sound in the stressed syllable of a word, such as "seem." The tip of the tongue is relaxed behind the lower front teeth, and the front of the tongue is arched high in the mouth. The lips are slightly smiling.

Word List
Agree, agreed, beam, fields, flea, keen, key, knee, kneel, me, mean, pea, see, seen, she, tree, trees, we, weed

Phrase List
A need to kneel
The team beamed
Agreed to flee
Fields of weeds
Sheila and Neil

Sentence List
The green team agreed to be lean mean machines of the league.
As seen on TV, we achieved the need to succeed by being mean.

Dean appeased the bees with ease.

Appeal to Eve to ease the steel beams.

Feel free to spree; it's on me.

SHORT: This front vowel sound is short when it's followed by a voiceless consonant sound in the stressed syllable of a word, such as "leaf," and in the unstressed suffix of a word, such as "leaky."

Word List
Beach, beef, cheat, discreet, eat, grease, grief, leaf, meek, neat, peace, people, seat, sheets, sleep, teeth, thief, week

Phrase List
Eat the beef

Greet the Greeks

Seek peace

The thief is weak

The people speak

Sentence List
Eating beef is a relief for the chief.

There was a meet and greet for the Greeks in Greece.

People seek peace in Topeka.

Denise and Keith teach speech.

The discreet sleek sheik has a unique physique.

The front vowel sound "will"

This front vowel sound is always short. It is found in stressed syllables of words such as "willow" and in the prefixes of most words, such as "remind." The lips are slightly smiling, the sound resonates over the front of the tongue, and there is still considerable tongue arch. The tip of the tongue is relaxed behind the lower front teeth.

Word List

British, critic, Dixon, fix, glib, him, it, kick, lilt, mix, nickel, open, pit, Richard, strip, tick, Winston

Phrase List

The British critic
Phil is fit
Pick a wish
Tickle the kitten
Bring in the bins

Sentence List

The British critic is vigilant in Bristol.

Fixing widgets is big in Indiana.

Tickle Minnie and giggle with Mickey.

Bring Rick into the gym with Phil and Jill.

Sitting still in the middle of the busy city.

The front vowel sound "let"

This front vowel sound is always short and is found in the stressed syllables of words such as "letter." The lips are less smiling than for "Lee" or "will"; the sound resonates over the front of the tongue, and there is still considerable tongue arch. The tip of the tongue is relaxed behind the lower front teeth.

Word List

Bet, cherry, debt, effort, February, get, headache, jet, leather, men, pen, Wednesday

Phrase List

Ben is ten
The jet is set
A headache never gets better on a ledge

Leather gives you cred

Trendy Wednesdays

Sentence List

Ed is ending the trend to head to South Bend at the end of
the semester.

It's an effort to bend when your legs extend.

Get Ken to send Emma cherries in February.

Betty ended economic debt in Encino.

Send an extra pen to use again and again.

The front vowel sound "pat"

This front vowel sound is always short and is found in the stressed
syllables of words such as "pattern." It is the most open front
vowel, and there is no smiling of the lips or tongue arch. It resonates over the front of the tongue with the tip of the tongue
relaxed behind the lower front teeth.

Word List

Apple, back, category, Dad, factory, happy, Jared, lamp, map,
staff

Phrase List

Apple Jacks

Back on the map

A happy dad

A blast from the past

Staff shenanigans

Sentence List

Pass Ann an apple to put in Harry's bag.

We had a blast doing fancy dances at the Hampshire.

Dr. Sam is the go-to man with a gentle hand.

Actually, Harry had to be dragged out of the lavish establishment.

Sandy's dramatic fashions are so last year.

Mid Vowels

The mid vowel sound "stir"

LONG: This mid vowel of "r" is long in the stressed syllable when it's the last sound of the word, such as "stir," and when it's followed by a voiced consonant sound, such as "stern." The tip of the tongue is relaxed behind the lower front teeth, and the middle of the tongue is arched halfway in the mouth. The lips are neutral.

Word List
Adjourn, dirge, earn, emerge, firm, girdle, heard, kernel, learn, nerd, purge, stern, turn, world

Phrase List
Bernie emerged
A stern word
The girl twirled
I heard Herb
The sermon was adjourned

Sentence List
Merle gave a stern word to the girl.

Bernie turned on Third.

Pearl stirred the curd.

She has an urge to serve on Thursday.

Early birds prefer worms.

SHORT: This mid vowel sound is short when followed by a voice-less consonant sound in the stressed syllable of a word, such as "earth," and in the unstressed syllable of a word, such as "mother."

Word List
Alert, batter, chatter, curtsy, dirt, disaster, earth, Easter, fisher, flirt, gesture, Heather, hurt, inner, interpret, jerk, joker, killer, leader, meter, neither, ogre, pertain, purple, skirt, surrender, teacher, work

Phrase List
Dirty thirty
Flirt in a purple skirt
Rehearse at work
Burt's dirty shirt
A search for turf
Surprise the ogre
The greater gesture
A picture of perfection
A batter with butter
October, November, and December

Sentence List
Kurt worshipped with a nurse.

Burt has the worst shirt in the circus.

Don't divert the search in Perth.

Eartha curtsied, then worked with a purpose.

Be alert when you rehearse with Gertie.

The disaster was after a major tremor.

Easter is neither in the summer nor the winter.

A glimmer of a gesture is better than a whisper.

Heather's mother is my sister's teacher.

It was a picture-perfect adventure with my brother and sister.

The mid vowel sound "the"

This vowel is always short. It is a weak vowel sound in unstressed words such as "the" and "a" and in the unstressed syllables of words such as "again." It's a neutral sound. The lips are neither smiling nor rounded, the sound resonates over the middle of the tongue, and there is no tongue arch. The tip of the tongue is relaxed behind the lower front teeth.

Word List
Again, balloon, Dakota, facetious, galore, Jamaica, massage, Napoleon, potato, Ramona, support, Tacoma, Valencia

Phrase List
Jamaica and Aruba
Again and again and again
Attention Alicia
Concerned about an aroma
A potato and asparagus atrocity

Sentence List
Ramona arrived ashore in Jamaica in amazingly appealing apparel.
Vanilla is considered a botanical.
The balloon careened around the ravine.
Alicia's support was appreciated.
It was an anonymous collision in the Tacoma arena.

The mid vowel sound "cup"

This vowel sound is the most open of the three mid vowel sounds and is always short. It is found in the stressed syllables of words such as "cut." This neutral sound requires no smiling or rounding of the lips. It resonates over the middle of the tongue, and there is no tongue arch. The tip of the tongue is relaxed behind the lower front teeth.

Word List

Another, butter, cut, Dutch, fudge, grudge, hunt, juggle, love, mother, oven, puppy, rough, tough, up, wonderful

Phrase List

Love another

Rough cut

Up tuck

Wonderful fudge

Tough stutter

Sentence List

The other glove was rough.

We hunted for Mother's fudge fresh from the oven.

They smuggled Dutch butter for their mother.

Another stutter will be covered.

Learning to juggle was a wonderful struggle.

Back Vowels

The back vowel sound "who"

LONG: This back vowel sound is long in the stressed syllable when it's the last sound of a word, such as "zoo," and when it's followed by a voiced consonant sound, such as "room." The tip of the tongue is relaxed behind the lower front teeth, and the back of the tongue is arched high in the mouth. The lips are rounded.

Word List

Brood, cruise, dues, ensue, grew, infuse, Jude, lewd, move, noon, ooze, Pooh, rude, two, voodoo, who, woo

Phrase List

Noon snooze
Two dues
Voodoo brood
Lewd dude
Who knew

Sentence List

The crew removed Mr. Moody at noon.
Jude brooded over the rude move.
I knew the two who flew.
Pooh chewed as the honey oozed.
Move the shoes before you snooze.

SHORT: This back vowel sound is short when it's followed by a voiceless consonant sound in the stressed syllable of a word, such as "root."

Word List

Brutus, Cooper, duet, futile, gruesome, hoot, Jupiter, lute, moot, noose, pooch, suit, tooth, Yukon

Phrase List

Moose tooth
Loose pooch
A flute juke
Refute Brutus
Tutti-frutti

Sentence List

From Yukon to Butte we had a hoot.
The moose and pooch were duped.
Bruce wore a droopy zoot suit.

Ruth was aloof as she drank vermouth.

Rufus played an uncouth spoof on a guy from Duluth.

Get fruit juice for your youth group.

The back vowel sound "would"

This back vowel sound is always short and is found in the stressed syllables of words such as "good." The lips are slightly rounded, the sound resonates over the back of the tongue, and there is minimal tongue arch. The tip of the tongue is relaxed behind the lower front teeth.

Word List

Book, bully, cookie, could, foot, full, good, hood, look, pull, push, put, should, stood, wood

Phrase List

Should've could've

Good druid

Neighborhood bully

Good book

Misunderstood adulthood

Sentence List

The bully took the cookies.

Look where the redwood stood.

Good crooks read books.

Push the rook and you should win.

The druid stood at the brook.

The back vowel sound "obey"

This back vowel sound is always short and is found in the unstressed syllable at the beginning of a word, such as "overt."

The lips are slightly rounded, the sound resonates over the back of the tongue, and there is minimal tongue arch. In General American Speech, it is often substituted by the weak mid vowel sound as in the word "the." The tip of the tongue is relaxed behind the lower front teeth.

Word List
Bohemian, Croatia, donation, grotesque, hotel, location, momentum, November, oasis, phonetic, poetic, romantic, stoic, vocation

Phrase List
A Bohemian oasis
A robust Othello
Somalian donations
The grotesque hotel
The poetic Olympian

Sentence List
Olivia's Croatian hotel was like a Bohemian oasis.
Othello received an ovation in Romania.
A robust ogre is grotesque.
The Osakan Olympian is of nobility.
The Ohio motel location is gaining momentum.

The back vowel sound "all"

LONG: This back vowel sound is long in the stressed syllable when it's the last sound of a word, such as "jaw," and when it's followed by a voiced consonant sound, such as "call." The tip of the tongue is relaxed behind the lower front teeth, and there is no back-of-tongue arch. The jaw is released and open, and the lips are slightly rounded into an oval shape.

Word List
All, ball, call, draw, gall, hall, jaw, law, mall, pauper, raw, straw, tall, wall

Phrase List
Saul called
Drawing straws
Fall squall
Tall Paul
Applause for Claude

Sentence List
The hall in the mall will lead you to the stall.
A loll in the jaw will create a drawl.
Install the laws by nightfall.
Rainfall draws the small squalls.
Paul bought a shawl in Senegal.

SHORT: This back vowel sound is short when it's followed by a voiceless consonant sound in the stressed syllable of the word, such as "caught."

Word List
Alter, Boston, coffee, Dawson, distraught, fought, halt, talk, vault, walk

Phrase List
Gawking hawk
Shot block
Halting talks
Chalky coffee
Unlocked vault

Sentence List

We caught the hawk in the vault.

Dawson gawked as he awkwardly fought the author.

The sauce was bought for naught.

I had an awesome talk with my daughter in the crosswalk.

Don't talk or walk when you're distraught.

The back vowel sound "fathers"

LONG: This back vowel sound is long when it's the last sound of a word, such as "Gaga," and when followed by a voiced consonant sound in the stressed syllable of a word, such as "calm." The tip of the tongue is relaxed behind the lower front teeth, the back of the tongue is completely low in the mouth, and the jaw is the most open of all the vowel sounds. There is no lip rounding.

Word List

Ahhhh, aria, bomb, calm, Don, fond, gone, Holly, jog, log, Mom, nod, palm, rob, Slavic, Tom

Phrase List

Long gone

Blond mom

Yonder lawn

Proton photon

Sentence List

John jogged at dawn for the marathon.

The long aria made me yawn.

Mom is gone to the Amazon.

Tom is fond of logs of palm.

The mastodon was gone in the phenomenon.

SHORT: This back vowel sound is short when it's followed by a voiceless consonant sound in the stressed syllable of a word, such as "taco."

Word List
Box, cot, dropped, flop, gotten, hock, jockey, knot, lock, mop, ox, Picasso, rock, shot, stopped

Phrase List
Hot shot
Pop lock
Dropped mop
Not hot
Pot shot

Sentence List
The hockey shot won the pot.
The ox trotted until he stopped.
I dropped my taco on the rocks.
The top robot does not stop.
I got apricots at Camelot.

Diphthongs

A diphthong sound is a combination of two vowel sounds in which the second element or sound of the diphthong is weaker than the first. Because of the weak quality of the second element, it can often be imperceptible and mistaken for a pure or single vowel sound. The sure way to identify a diphthong sound is by seeing, hearing, and feeling the shape of the sound move from one position to another. There are ten diphthong sounds. The five so-called long diphthong sounds can be long or short depending on the sound that follows. The five diphthongs of "r" are always short.

Long and Short Diphthongs

The diphthong "pay"

LONG: This diphthong is long when it's the last sound of a word, such as "day," and when followed by a voiced consonant sound in the stressed syllable of a word, such as "daze."

Word List
Arcade, bay, day, delayed, graze, haze, invade, James, maid, name, phase, play, raid, shade, trade, way

Phrase List
Pay day
Play date
Say okay
Gray haze
Made clay

Sentence List
It's a gray, hazy day at the shady bay.
James laid in the clay with no delay.
I played at the arcade on the parkway.
They made the trade to win the game.
Raise the cow to graze on hay.

SHORT: This diphthong is short when it's followed by a voice-less consonant sound in the stressed syllable of a word, such as "date."

Word List
Bait, date, fate, great, hate, Jason, Kate, late, mate, nape, plate, rate, shape, trait, vapor, wafer

Phrase List
Late date

Great shape

Eight plates

Fate dictates

Freight weight

Sentence List
Kate was late to decorate.

Don't imitate the bad traits that you hate.

Jason dictates the rate for the freight.

Concentrate to navigate the state.

The plate was great and quite ornate.

The diphthong "my"

LONG: This diphthong is long when it's the last sound of a word, such as "tie," and when it's followed by a voiced consonant sound in the stressed syllable of a word, such as "tide."

Word List
Buy, died, eye, find, guide, hide, kind, lie, mind, nine, pile, ride, sigh, tie, wide

Phrase List
Mind's eye

High tide

Kind guide

Shy guy

Dry sky

Sentence List

The guide helped me find Mount Sinai.

Buy the fried swai [fish].

Multiply by nine and pi.

Try to be kind or tell a lie.

Don't sigh or whine; just use your mind.

SHORT: This diphthong is short when followed by a voiceless consonant sound in the stressed syllable of a word, such as "tight."

Word List

Bite, dice, fight, height, ice, kite, light, mighty, ninety, pipe, sight, tight, wipe, write

Phrase List

Mighty fighter

Tight pipe

White ice

Quite all right

Right height

Sentence List

The kite is too light to survive the mighty wind.

The height of the sprite was frightening.

The knight was right to fight his plight.

It's not polite to bite.

The satellite is out of sight.

The diphthong "boy"

LONG: This diphthong is long when it's the last sound of a word, such as "enjoy," and when followed by a voiced consonant sound in the stressed syllable of a word, such as "join."

Word List

Boy, destroy, enjoy, noise, oil, poised, Roy, spoil, Troy

Phrase List

Joyful noise

Troy's toys

Spoiled boys

Oily soil

Enjoy corduroy

Sentence List

I toil in the soil.

Don't spoil Roy with toys.

They deployed the noisy employees.

Enjoy the turmoil in Illinois.

Troy is poised in his corduroys.

SHORT: This diphthong is short when followed by a voiceless consonant sound in the stressed syllable of a word, such as "joint."

Word List

Appointment, boisterous, Detroit, joint, oyster, points

Phrase List

Exploited Detroit

Adroit oyster

Jointed cloister

Boisterous appointment

Moist voice

Sentence List

The oyster joints are easy to exploit.

Detroit is a boisterous city.

Too much moisture makes joints ache.

My appointments are adroit.

The point is to stay buoyant.

The diphthong "go"

LONG: This diphthong is long when it's the last sound of a word, such as "grow," and when followed by a voiced consonant sound in the stressed syllable of a word, such as "grown."

Word List

Bowl, cold, dough, fold, go, hold, know, low, mole, old, pole, rose, sew, told

Phrase List

Low blow

Old mold

Cold coal

Dough bowl

Rose gold

Sentence List

I rolled the dough to enfold the marigold.

You know a cold will make you blow your nose.

The mole burrows low to grow its holes.

The old crow goes to Chicago.

The snow glistens and glows.

SHORT: This diphthong is short when it's followed by a voiceless consonant sound in the stressed syllable of a word, such as "growth."

Word List

Boat, coat, dope, elope, float, goat, hope, mope, note, oats, pope, rope, soap, tote

Phrase List
Boat rope
Goat's throat
Soap on a rope
Hopeful pope
Moat float

Sentence List
Tote the note that you wrote.
The pope's quote gave hope.
Moping is not coping.
The goat eats oats as he pulls his rope.
Elope on the boat.

The diphthong "now"

LONG: This diphthong is long when it's the last sound of a word, such as "allow," and when it's followed by a voiced consonant sound in the stressed syllable of a word, such as "loud."

Word List
Around, cow, down, found, ground, hound, loud, mound, noun, ounce, pound, town, vows

Phrase List
Cow sound
Brown hound
Ground down
Loud vows
Around town

Sentence List
The cow pounded through the town.
The plow ground through the mound.

The crown weighed a pound and an ounce.

I found the sound too loud.

The hound ate a mound of puppy chow.

SHORT: This diphthong is short when it's followed by a voiceless consonant sound in the stressed syllable of a word, such as "louse."

Word List
Count, devout, douse, fountain, gout, mountain, pounce, shout, south

Phrase List
About to shout
A mountain house
Counting accounts
A bout of gout
Count the scouts

Sentence List
The mountain goat pounced.

The devout shout.

The count's fountain faces south.

A mouse is in the house.

A spouse will douse love.

Short Diphthongs of "R"

The diphthong "here's"
This diphthong is always short in words, such as "clear."

Word List
Appear, beer, career, cashmere, deer, endear, fear, hear, Lear, near, pier, revere, sincere

Phrase List
Mere tears
A fearful deer
Revered cashmere
Sincere career
A veering pier

Sentence List
The deer fears the pier.

It's the time of year for cashmere.

Lear is enduring and sincere.

I hear the auctioneer.

A revered career as an engineer.

The diphthong "their"
This diphthong is always short in words, such as "hair."

Word List
Air, bear, care, compare, dare, fare, hair, share, spare, square, where

Phrase List
Bare hair
Care Bear

Share fare
A spare airfare
Spare pear

Sentence List
I don't care where the hair is.

The bear took the stairs.

Don't compare your affairs.

Share where you dare.

Clair and Blaire say their prayers.

The diphthong "poor"

This diphthong is always short in words, such as "cure."

Word List
Assure, contour, cure, insure, lure, mature, obscure, premature, secure, sure, tour

Phrase List
Your tour
Demure couture
Impure cure
Procure maturity
Alluring brochure

Sentence List
Insecurities are immature.

The entrepreneur was assured.

The lure of the tour was obscure.

The assurance of insurance is alluring.

Procure the brochure.

The diphthong "ore"

This diphthong is always short in words, such as "four."

Word List

Bore, core, door, four, gore, lore, more, or, pour, roar, store, torn, whore, worn

Phrase List

Store floor
George forswore
Worn door
Boring encore
More gore

Sentence List

The folklore was worn and boring.

The door of the store is on the ground floor.

The carnivore ate the boar.

More albacore are born.

The corps of the war were torn.

The diphthong "car"

This diphthong is always short in words, such as "start."

Word List

Are, bar, car, far, heart, jar, Mars, par, radar, star, tar

Phrase List

Bizarre memoir
Star guitarist
Jaguar car
Far radar
Departed star

Sentence List

Art comes from the heart.

The car was stuck in the tar.

Mars is charted with radar.

The bar is in a bazaar in Myanmar.

The star was seen from afar.

Consonants

There are six categories or groups of consonant sounds. I prefer to study the twenty-five consonant sounds in these groups, because once the definitions are understood, it becomes infinitely easier to produce the sounds with accuracy. It always helps to know the "how" and "why." Unlike vowel sounds, which are always voiced, consonant sounds can be either voiced or voiceless. Place your forefinger in the middle of your throat, and release an "s" sound over the tip of your tongue. You feel no vibration, right? This is a voiceless consonant. Now release a "z" sound. You should feel vibration. This is a voiced consonant. We are not only going to address consonant sounds in the six categories, but also by whether they are voiced or voiceless. As you've seen with certain vowel sounds, the voiced or voiceless consonant sounds that follow the vowel play a huge part in the length of a syllable and in the overall rhythm of speech. Finally, consonant sounds can appear in three positions in a word: in the initial position, the medial position, and the final position. Why didn't they teach us this in grade school? Oh well, it's never too late!

Stop Plosives

The breath or voice is stopped and then rapidly released or erupted.

Voiceless "p," "t," and "k"

Word List—Initial, Medial, and Final Positions

....

P: The "p" sound is made with both lips touching.

INITIAL—pea, pit, pen, panoramic, purple, puppy, Paul, palm

MEDIAL—peeping, Tippy, temper, dapper, slurpy, trouper, topple

FINAL—deep, rip, step, stamp, burp, cup, soup, cop

....

T: The "t" sound is made with the tip of the tongue touching the gum ridge.

INITIAL—team, Tim, ten, Tanner, turn, tongue, tooth, took, tall, Tom

MEDIAL—meeting, committee, better, chatter, dirty, stutter, shooter, putting, daughter, hotter

FINAL—feet, bit, get, fact, Burt, cut, root, foot, fault, hot

....

K: The "k" sound is made with the back of the tongue touching the hard palate.

INITIAL—keep, kid, kettle, Kansas, curse, cut, cool, could, call, calm

MEDIAL—seeking, picking, Becker, anchor, lurking, lucky, hooker, walking, mocking

FINAL—Greek, sick, check, bank, work, tuck, shook, talk, dock

....

Voiced "b," "d," and "g"

Word List—Initial, Medial, and Final Positions

....

B: The "b" sound is made with both lips touching.

INITIAL—beef, bitter, better, basket, burly, bump, boot, book, ball, balm

MEDIAL—Sheba, dribble, Debbie, gamble, auburn, ebony, abrupt, rubric, subdued, cobalt, LeBron

FINAL—hajib, ad-lib, ebb, cab, superb, tub, tube, kabob

....

D: The "d" sound is made with the tip of the tongue touching the gum ridge.

INITIAL—deed, did, dead, dad, dirt, duck, do, daughter, Don

MEDIAL—indeed, riddle, bedding, Daddy, girdle, sudden, Judy, woody, audit, oddest

FINAL—seed, build, led, add, curd, dud, brood, could, laud, blond

....

G: The "g" sound is made with the back of the tongue touching the hard palate.

INITIAL—greed, grid, get, gasoline, girl, gut, goose, good, gall, gone

MEDIAL—eager, giggle, forget, aghast, yogurt, seagull, kangaroo, sugar, jogging

FINAL—league, king, beg, brag, iceberg, plug, catalog

....

Fricatives

The five voiceless fricatives and six voiced fricatives are released through a narrow opening in the mouth, resulting in friction.

Voiceless fricatives "f," "th," "s," "sh," and "h"

Word List—Initial, Medial, and Final Positions

F: The "f" sound is made with the lower lip close to but not touching the upper teeth.

INITIAL—flea, fill, fret, fat, fern, fudge, food, foot, falter, father

MEDIAL—leafy, sniffle, Geffen, taffy, Murphy, muffin, goofy, awful, offer

FINAL—grief, cliff, chef, chaff, turf, tough, aloof, cough, off

Th: The "th" sound is made with the blade of the tongue close to but not touching the upper teeth.

INITIAL—think, thin, thread, thanks, Thursday, thump, through, thought

MEDIAL—lethal, tither, healthy, panther, author

FINAL—teeth, filth, breath, wrath, girth, cometh, youth, cloth

S: The "s" sound is made with the tip of the tongue pointing toward but not touching the back of the upper teeth.

INITIAL—seat, sill, set, sat, stir, scuttle, scoot, Saul, psalm

MEDIAL—ceasing, fiscal, pencil, passive, reimbursement, cussing, ensuing, installed, unstoppable

FINAL—crease, bliss, press, grass, curse, suss, loose, looks, walrus, Wass

Sh: The "sh" sound is made with the blade of the tongue raised toward but not touching the gum ridge.

INITIAL—sheep, shrill, shell, shanty, shirk, shut, shoe, shook, shawl, shah

MEDIAL—leashing, dishes, dashing, Gershwin, rushed, mushroom, cushion, bushes

FINAL—leash, fish, fresh, lash, mesh, flush, swoosh, wash

H: The "h" sound is made with an open throat. This voiceless version of the sound only appears in the initial position of a word.

INITIAL—heed, hill, help, hat, hurt, huff, hoot, hooper, hall, hah

Voiced fricatives "v," "th," "z," "zh," "r," and "h"

Word List—Initial, Medial, and Final Positions

V: The "v" sound is made with the lower lip close to but not touching the upper teeth.

INITIAL—veal, villain, vet, vat, verb, vulgar, voodoo, vault, Von

MEDIAL—reveal, evict, invent, evacuate, Lavern, improvement, movement, Nevada

FINAL—leave, live, Kev, Irv, love, improve, evolve, improv

Th: The "th" sound is made with the blade of the tongue close to but not touching the upper teeth.

INITIAL—these, this, them, than, that

MEDIAL—either, leather, tether, gather, worthy, druthers, other, father

FINAL—breathe, seethe, teethe, bathe, loathe

Z: The "z" sound is made with the tip of the tongue pointing toward but not touching the back of the upper teeth.

INITIAL—zebra, zippy, Zelda, zap, zoo, zoom, Zorro

MEDIAL—easy, business, present, pizzazz, Thursday, puzzle, cousin, kazoo, loser, causes

FINAL—sneeze, fizz, legs, razz, burns, fuzz, choose, dogs

Zh: The "zh" sound is made with the blade of the tongue raised toward but not touching the gum ridge.

INITIAL—genre, Zsa Zsa, Jacques

MEDIAL—seizure, visually, treasury, aversion, collusion, Hoosier, camouflaging

FINAL—massage, mirage, beige, Baton Rouge, luge, collage

R: The "r" sound is made with the tip of the tongue pointing toward but not touching the gum ridge. This sound never appears in the final position; "r" at the end of a word is either the strong or weak vowel ("stir").

INITIAL—read, riddle, red, rat, rupture, room, rook, raw, Ron

MEDIAL—lyric, ferret, parrot, walrus, syrup, kangaroo, enthrall

H: The "h" sound is made with an open throat. This voiced version of the sound only appears in the medial position of a word when it's preceded and followed by a vowel sound.

MEDIAL—behest, rehearse, behavior, Ohio, manhole, behoove, mahogany, unhallowed

Affricates

The two affricates are sounds that are a combination of a stop plosive and a fricative, closely blended to create one single phonetic sound. One is voiceless, and the other is voiced.

Voiceless "ch"

Word List—Initial, Medial, and Final Positions

....

Ch: The "ch" sound is made with the blade of the tongue touching the gum ridge.

INITIAL—cheese, chin, chess, chastity, church, Chuck, choo choo, chalk, charm

MEDIAL—teaching, enchilada, fetching, matching, purchase, picture, clutching, moocher

FINAL—each, itch, wrench, attach, lurch, much, hooch, Butch, crotch

....

Voiced "j"

Word List—Initial, Medial, and Final Positions

....

J: The "j" sound is made with the blade of the tongue touching the gum ridge.

INITIAL—jeep, Jill, jet, jazz, jersey, jump, Jewish, jaw, jolly

MEDIAL—Regina, digit, abject, magic, clergy, pudgy, pajama

FINAL—siege, village, edge, badge, surge, courage, huge, hodge

....

Nasals

The three nasals are the only voiced sounds that are released through the nose.

Voiced "m," "n," and "ng"

Word List—Initial, Medial, and Final Positions

....

M: The "m" sound is made with both lips touching.

INITIAL—meat, mill, metal, mat, Murphy, Muppet, move, mall, mom

MEDIAL—Beamer, limit, hemp, lament, squirming, pumpkin, gloomy, calming

FINAL—dream, Tim, gem, jam, affirm, come, room, balm

....

N: The "n" sound is made with the tip of the tongue touching the gum ridge.

INITIAL—neat, nil, net, gnat, nerd, nut, noon, nook, naughty, nod

MEDIAL—greener, grinning, planet, canal, burner, peanut, canoe, anon

FINAL—seen, pin, again, fan, churn, sun, spoon, pawn

....

Ng: The "ng" sound is made with the back of the tongue touching the hard palate. This sound does not appear in the initial position of a word in spoken English.

MEDIAL—bringing, finger, Bengal, hanger, younger, jungle, bungalow, mongoose, longer, stronger

FINAL—billing, yelling, batting, whirling, cutting, chewing, looking, walking, wrong

....

Lateral

The lateral "l" is the only sound in spoken English that's released on both sides of the tongue. It is voiced, and the tip of the tongue remains on the gum ridge while the sound is made.

Voiced "l"

Word List—Initial, Medial, and Final Positions

....

L: The "l" sound is made with the tip of the tongue touching the gum ridge.

INITIAL—lean, little, letting, lateral, learn, love, loop, loose, llama

MEDIAL—feeling, pillow, welling, family, Hurley, bludgeon, flew, flawless, wallet

FINAL—steal, pencil, fell, pal, unfurl, cull, fool, bull, ball, doll

....

Glides

The two voiced glides in General American Speech (there is a third but it's primarily used in Classical American Stage Speech) begin in a shape of articulation and then swiftly glide to the shape of the vowel or diphthong sound that follows. They never appear in the final position of a word.

Voiced "w" and "y"

Word List—Initial and Medial Positions

....

W: The "w" sound is made with both lips coming together but not touching.

   INITIAL—weep, willow, wet, whirl, wonder, woot, wolves, wallow, wonton

   MEDIAL—queen, quill, frequent, quack, quirk

....

Y: The "y" sound is made with the tip of the tongue relaxed behind the lower front teeth and the middle of the tongue arched high toward the hard palate.

   INITIAL—yield, yip, yet, yammer, yearn, yuppie, unique, yawn, Yugoslavia

   MEDIAL—million, tortilla, papaya, lawyer, royal, Sawyer

....

Acknowledgments

To Steve Ross, the best agent on the planet, who saw the potential of this work from our first conversation. Madeleine Morel, whose keen eye for literary gold put the pieces and players of this wonderful puzzle together. Samantha Marshall, whose intuitive collaboration was more of a sisterhood. My editor, Shannon Welch, who left no stone unturned and no thought uninvested. Terry Leigh (my son) and James Feimster (my nephew), whose love and dedication remain steadfast and unconditional. Deshawnna Chiles and Rebecka Jackson, who helped care for the details of my personal and professional life throughout this process and beyond. Shawn Judge, that one friend whose name should appear in the dictionary under the word "friend," and Rodney Nugent, whose words of encouragement sustained me in the final stages of the process.

Many thanks to Taraji P. Henson for bringing me to the Hollywood table, to Mahershala Ali for convincing me that I truly belong here, and to Halle Berry for grabbing my hand and taking me to a whole new creative and professional level.

And finally, *The Power of Voice* would not be the narrative it is were it not for the fearless contributions of my amazing clients, now friends. My gratitude and love are immeasurable.

About the Author

For the past twenty years, Denise Woods has been the "voice be-hind the voice" of a stellar array of talents. She has most recently been coaching for the Netflix feature film *The Harder They Fall*, starring Idris Elba, and has worked with Elba on several projects. Denise served as the creative consultant for Halle Berry's direc-torial debut of the film *Bruised*, where she contributed to the authenticity of Berry's performance in the starring role. Denise was also the vocal coach for Mahershala Ali's Academy Award– and Golden Globe–winning performances in *Green Book* and the third season of HBO's *True Detective*. She coached Golden Globe winner Don Cheadle in the critically acclaimed Showtime series *Black Monday*, Academy Award winner Common, Golden Globe winner David Oyelowo, Academy Award–nominated actor Will Smith for the title role in the film *Ali*, and Ken Watanabe for his work in the film *The Last Samurai*.

Her dialect coaching talents can be heard in *Hidden Figures*, starring Taraji P. Henson, Octavia Spencer, and Janelle Monáe, as well as the film *Harriet*, starring Cynthia Erivo in the title role. In 2018, Denise had the honor of coaching Tyler Perry for his role as Colin Powell in the 2018 film *Vice*, and she is featured in Perry's *Acrimony*, starring Taraji P. Henson, as the only-heard Therapist.

Over the past two decades, Denise's clients have also included Jessica Chastain, Audra McDonald, Zoe Saldana, Amber Heard, Anthony Mackie, Phylicia Rashad, Ellen Burstyn, Jeanne Trip-

plehorn, Soledad O'Brien, Morris Chestnut, Queen Latifah, Taye
Diggs, Paul Rodriguez, David Alan Grier, Victoria Rowell, Kellan
Lutz, Ray Liotta, Portia de Rossi, Rachel Weisz, Mekhi Phifer,
Maggie Gyllenhaal, Jeffrey Wright, and Mike Myers.

Outside of film, Denise has trained executives for public speaking at corporations such as U.S. Borax, UPS, and Bear Stearns.
She has coached broadcast news anchors at *NBC Nightly News*,
CNBC, Bloomberg News, *The Today Show*, CNN, *Inside Edition*,
KTLA News, and the TV Guide Channel, and she has prepared
NBA and NFL athletes for on-camera commentary.

She is a graduate and former faculty member of the Juilliard
School and a longtime faculty member of California Institute of
the Arts.

Denise is committed to giving disenfranchised voices the courage and tools to use their words, thoughts, and stories in ways they
never thought possible by dismantling fear, shame, and insecurity.

When not on set, Denise, a devoted daughter and mother, enjoys quality time with friends and family at her home in Oxnard,
California.